Ornamentalism

DAVID CANNADINE

Ornamentalism
How the British Saw Their Empire

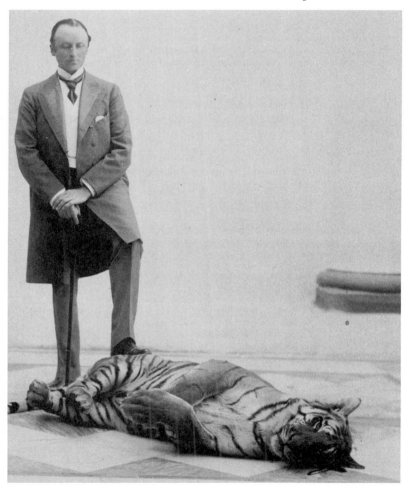

OXFORD
UNIVERSITY PRESS

OXFORD
UNIVERSITY PRESS

Oxford   New York
Athens   Auckland   Bangkok   Bogotá   Buenos Aires
Cape Town   Chennai   Dar es Salaam   Delhi   Florence   Hong Kong   Istanbul
Karachi   Kolkata   Kuala Lumpur   Madrid   Melbourne   Mexico City   Mumbai
Nairobi   Paris   São Paulo   Shanghai   Singapore   Taipei   Tokyo   Toronto   Warsaw

and associated companies in

Berlin   Ibadan

Copyright © 2001 by David Cannadine

First published in the UK by Penguin Books Ltd.

Published by Oxford University Press, Inc.
198 Madison Avenue, New York, New York 10016

Oxford is a registered trademark of Oxford University Press

Library of Congress Cataloging-in-Publication Data
Cannadine, David, 1950–
Ornamentalism: how the British saw their empire / David Cannadine.
p. cm.
Includes bibliographical references and index.
ISBN 0-19-514660-3
1. Great Britain—Colonies—History. 2. Public opinion—Great Britain—History. 3.
Social classes—Great Britain—Colonies—History. 4. Imperialism—History. I. Title.
DA16.C28 2001
941.08--dc21   2001021407

1 3 5 7 9 8 6 4 2
Printed in the United States of America
on acid-free paper

For Guy

The real challenge . . . will be to . . . integrate the local and the general
. . . Only then will we glimpse whole worlds . . . that have not been
seen before. A synoptic view, bringing metropole and colony, colonizer
and colonized, British and indigenous peoples into one frame, into a
single analytical field, will reveal not merely a catalogue of differences
and similarities, not just a series of intriguing parallels, but whole
configurations, general processes, an entire interactive system, one vast
interconnected world. — P. D. Morgan, 'Encounters between British
and "Indigenous" Peoples, *c.* 1500–*c.* 1800',
in M. J. Daunton and R. Halpern (eds.), *Empire
and Others: British Encounters with Indigenous
Peoples, 1600–1850* (London, 1999), p. 68.

A perennial theme running throughout Britain's imperial experience
has been the relationship between ideas about the ordering of society
at home and ideas about the ordering of the empire overseas. For all
the obvious difficulties involved in applying the same precepts to
societies that are likely to have been fundamentally different, generations of British people have tried to do precisely this. British models
[have] usually been projected on to the empire; less frequently what
have been taken to be the lessons of Empire have been beamed back at
Britain. — P. J. Marshall, 'Empire and Authority in the
Later Eighteenth Century', *Journal of Imperial
and Commonwealth History*, xv (1987), p. 105.

How do we describe people from a culture different from our own?
. . . It is the argument of this book that neither savagery nor race was
the important category . . . The really important category was status.
— K. O. Kupperman, *Settling with the Indians: The
Meeting of English and Indian Cultures in America,
1580–1640* (Totowa, NJ, 1980), pp. vii, 2.

Contents

List of Illustrations

frontispiece Lord Curzon, with the maharaja of Gwalior in 1899, contemplating his first tiger shot in India as viceroy.

19. Lord Curzon, viceroy of India, wearing the insignia and robes of a knight grand commander of the Order of the Star of India, *c.* 1900.

20. The begum of Bhopal, wearing the same insignia and robes as Curzon, *c.* 1890.

21. The sultan of Zanzibar at his Silver Jubilee, 1937, wearing the insignia of a knight grand cross of the Order of St Michael and St George, and accompanied by the British resident, Sir Richard Rankine, KCMG.

22. Statue of King George V unveiled in 1916, Ceylon.

23. Queen Victoria's Diamond Jubilee – Thanksgiving Service at St Paul's Cathedral, 1897.

24. Queen Victoria's Diamond Jubilee – decorations in Zanzibar.

25. Nigerian cloth commemorating the Silver Jubilee of King George V, 1935.

26. The prince of Wales in Banff on his Canadian tour, 1919, wearing an Indian headdress.

27. The prince of Wales in Accra on his African tour, 1925.

28. Vast crowds in Martin Place, Sydney, during the visit of Queen Elizabeth II and Prince Philip, 1954.

29. King George VI's coronation, 1937.

30. Nuremberg rally, 1938.

31. Sir Robert Menzies installed as lord warden of the Cinque Ports, 1966.

32. Removal of statue of Lord Curzon from Calcutta after Indian independence.

33. The end of empire, Nairobi, 1963.

34. A smashed picture of King Farouk lying on an Egyptian pavement.

35. Lord and Lady Mountbatten as the last viceroy and vicereine of India, 1947.

36. Queen Elizabeth II greeted by King Hussein on her 1984 visit to Jordan.

Preface

In post-millennial Britain, we live in post-imperial times. The captains and the kings have departed; the squadrons and the legions have come home; the plumed hats and the ceremonial swords have been put away; the Union Jack has been hauled down again and again and again; Britannia no longer rules the waves at Heaven's command; and even the royal yacht has ceased to sail the seas. The impulses towards overseas expansion and imperial domination that began in the reign of the first Elizabeth have ended – with appropriate if coincidental symmetry – in the time of the second Elizabeth. During the mere half century between Indian independence in 1947 and the return of Hong Kong to the Chinese government in 1997, the British Empire, once the earth's proudest and biggest, and for nearly three hundred years part of the seemingly immutable order of things, has passed away, and into history.[1] It is now one, not just with Nineveh and Tyre, but also with the Roman, the Islamic, the Holy Roman, the Ottoman, the Venetian, the Spanish, the Portuguese, the Dutch, the French, the German and the Russian Empires – both Tsarist and Communist. Only the United States of America remains as the last authentic western imperial power, deploying its unchallenged financial might and unrivalled military strength around the globe, even as it still prides itself on its exemplary hostility to empire, dating from the time when it was the first colony to make a revolution (and make a nation) by successfully rejecting European domination.

For most of the twentieth century, journalists, pundits and historians have naturally been concerned with trying to explain how and why this unprecedentedly vast and uniquely varied imperium came into being, how it flourished in its heyday and high noon, and (more recently) how and why it has now ended.[2] One approach, understandably favoured in Britain itself, has been to see empire primarily as the emanation of impulses originating in the metropolis. But, while it seemed easy to agree on the point of origin, there has been less unanimity about precisely what these impulses were. For some historians, following Hobson and Lenin, the motor of empire was mainly economic: the drive to safeguard overseas outlets and markets for British investment and trade. For others, the imperative was fundamentally military and strategic: the rush to conquest as a by-product of the Napoleonic Wars, and the need to protect the route to India by annexing ports and coaling stations (and their hinterlands) along the way. For yet a third group, the concerns were essentially dutiful and religious: the desire to improve the lot of disadvantaged peoples, and to bring to them the good news of the Christian Gospel. These differing and diverse versions of how and why the British Empire came into being were not only intrinsically important, they also provided, with agreeable symmetry and completeness, the no-less varied explanations as to how and why – and when – it fell: it ceased to pay; or it ceased to matter strategically; or belief in the imperial mission collapsed.[3]

These grand narratives furnished competing accounts and explanations of imperial rise and fall. But in between, and it was a very long in between, the British Empire was a formally constituted political entity, and from that perspective its history was for the most part concerned with law, governance and constitutional evolution. In the hands of such historians as Arthur Barriedale Keith and Sir Kenneth Wheare, the dominant theme of the empire story was the export of British constitutional practices and their successful establishment in newly evolving nations around the globe. Thanks largely to Lord Durham (so this argument ran), British-style responsible government was established in Canada in the 1840s, and it subsequently spread to Australia, New Zealand and South Africa, whose constitutional equality with the mother country was eventually acknowledged in the Statute of Westminster, passed in 1931.[4] Thereafter, another story of ordered evolution gradually unfolded, as the Indian Empire and then the remainder of the colonies were advanced along the same road of constitutional evolution to such a point that they achieved their own version of independence from British rule. Like the former dominions, they remained loyal to the traditions and institutions of parliamentary government, and to the idea of some form of post-imperial connection and association. Here was the preordained and triumphant ending of the empire story, not as 'decline and fall', but as merging into the 'commonwealth experience'.[5]

As the empire itself was in the process of fragmenting, these general explanations, which stressed the preponderantly British part in its creation and evolution, began to go out of fashion, and attention turned to the imperial periphery, as area studies and the history of particular regions became more popular.[6] From this very different perspective, empire was not exclusively (or even primarily) about what the British decided and did: it was about the assorted and multifarious experiences of many peoples in many parts of the world whom the British encountered, dominated, damaged and grudgingly set free. Thus approached, the history of Canada, Australia, New Zealand and South Africa was not an account of the passive part they had played as the recipients of British investment or in the evolution of empire to commonwealth; it was the story of how colonies had actively evolved into autonomous and coequal nations. In the same way, the new, post-imperial history of India presented Britain's intrusion into the affairs of the subcontinent as ephemeral and regrettable, based on a cynical policy of divide and rule, and ending with the horrors of massacre and partition. And for the nations of what had been the colonial empire, the new narratives were similar: a brief period of British subjugation, which wrought havoc with indigenous society, and which was ended only when heroically struggling nationalists eventually won back their freedom and independence.

Most recently, a variety of new approaches to the history of empire has been adopted, stimulated by work on gender and race, culture and language. Since much of it is being undertaken by literary scholars rather than by historians, it may be loosely labelled 'post-modern' or 'post-colonial', and it is telling us things about the nature and meaning of the imperial enterprise that we did not know or sufficiently appreciate before.[7] As a result, the history of native peoples in the former dominions has become an important subject, with significant contemporary political implications, as the claims of 'First Nations' (those present before the arrival of white settlers) have become increasingly vociferous. The role of women (and children) in the empire and the construction of different racial identities, both 'black' and 'white', have been brought to the centre of the imperial stage and the imperial story. And instead of concentrating on the official records of government, or the unofficial documents of business and trade, literary scholars have insisted on the need to address and analyse a wider range of imperial texts, which disclose much more about systems of power and domination, and about how what they like to call the 'hegemonic imperial project' was primarily concerned with the production of derogatory stereotypes of other, alien, subordinated societies.[8]

These many attempts to write the history of the British Empire, which might be described as being by turns conservative-metropolitan and innovative-peripheral, have each generated vast literatures, and they all have their critics as well as their defenders.[9] Those who see the British Empire primarily as the emanation of metropolitan impulses, be they economic or militaristic or moral, stand accused of being neo-imperialists, who see the periphery as passive, monolithic and inert, and who seek to perpetuate the empire in scholarship long after it has disappeared in substance. Those who stress constitutional emulation and ordered evolution are dismissed as too Whiggish and teleological: the planned and premeditated development of 'The British Empire' into 'The Commonwealth', which they celebrate and salute, is too neat, too simplistic and too complacent to bear serious academic scrutiny. Those who see empire as 'domination' and independence as 'freedom' are criticized for viewing the past in too simplified a form of 'good versus evil' and of 'us versus them', for still fighting the nationalist struggles for independence when they have already been won, and for ignoring the extent to which empire was about collaboration and consensus as well as about conflict and coercion. And those who address the empire from a post-modernist and post-colonial perspective are attacked for writing in such tortured prose that it is often difficult to understand what they are saying, for the often sketchy nature of their historical knowledge, and for constantly overrating the power and reach of the British.

All these methodologies, their strengths and weaknesses, and their many jarring inconsistencies, are to be found displayed and discussed, collected and criticized, in the *Oxford History of the British Empire*, a multi-authored work that draws on scholars and scholarship from around the world, and that has recently been published in five magnificent volumes.[10] As such, it not only serves as a summary of these different lines of historical inquiry; it also serves to remind us, by what it leaves out no less than by what it includes, of the many aspects of empire that still await sustained historical treatment. Two of them merit particular attention here. The first is that the history of the British Empire is still all too often written as if it were completely separate and distinct from the history of the British nation. Those old-style historians who stressed metropolitan impulses, be they economic, military, moral or constitutional, tended to take Britain for granted, and to have very unnuanced notions of the metropolitan economy, society and polity from whence these emanations originated. And those more recent scholars who concentrate on the imperial periphery or work with texts and discourse tend to disregard Britain – either because they want to minimize the part the imperial metropolis played in the longer history of their nation or community, or (alternatively and contradictorily) because they prefer to settle for a cardboard caricature of British omnipotence and imperial wickedness.[11]

Yet the truth of the matter is that Britain was very much a part of the empire, just as the rest of the empire was very much part of Britain. The result was precisely the sort of 'vast interconnected world', by turns both local *and* general, to which P. D. Morgan draws our attention. The first purpose of this book, then, is to approach the history of Britain and its empire in this very way, as the 'entire interactive system' that they undoubtedly formed. This, in turn, makes it possible to address a second aspect of the imperial experience that has been insufficiently studied, namely: what did the British Empire *look like*? It was, after all, in being for a long time, and it was not only a political construct but also a social entity. Yet even in the heyday of their subject, British social historians never significantly ventured overseas, while imperial social historians rarely ventured to Britain, which means that there has never been an authoritative social history of the empire.[12] And although the study of texts and representations is now very fashionable, no one has yet set out to follow the injunction of Peter Marshall, and to explore in detail how the British (both at home and overseas) envisaged and imagined this imperial society to which they belonged. The aim of this book is to break new ground by addressing both of these issues: the British Empire as social structure, and the British Empire as social perceptions. As such, it might with equal plausibility have been called *Imperialism and Social Classes*. But over half a century ago, Joseph Schumpeter, of whom more later, had already appropriated that title.[13]

In a previous work, entitled *Class in Britain*, I sketched out an interpretation of our nation's past since the eighteenth century which argued that scholars – often influenced by Karl Marx's insistence that the history of human society was more than anything else the history of class struggle – had been excessively concerned with two- and three-stage models of our social structure ('them' versus 'us', or upper-middle-lower class), and had paid insufficient attention to the traditional, enduring and commonplace notion of the layered, individualistic hierarchy, which is a more appealing and convincing way of seeing our unequal social world and of understanding many of our ancient national institutions than anything Marx ever came up with. This was, in all conscience, a large-enough subject to have taken on within the confines of one relatively brief volume; but I also wanted to make the case that these vernacular images and popular imaginings of the British social order significantly moulded, influenced and reinforced the generally held views and everyday visions of the British Empire – and vice versa. In a book chiefly devoted to social perceptions in and of the imperial metropolis (there, as here, meaning Britain as a whole), there was space only to throw out speculative suggestions about the imperial periphery (there, as here, meaning the empire beyond Britain), and it soon became clear that the subject needed separate, more sustained and more substantial treatment.

Hence this later book, which may be read as a companion to *Class in Britain*, and which certainly takes off from the arguments advanced and developed there about the imperial metropolis, but which is also meant to be read as a free-standing contribution to imperial as much as to British history. As such, it seeks to understand the British Empire in its heyday – which I take to have been from the 1850s to the 1950s, between the Indian Mutiny of 1857 and Queen Elizabeth II's coronation of 1953 – in a new and original way: as having been the vehicle for the extension of British social structures, and the setting for the projection of British social perceptions, to the ends of the world – and back again. For the imperial constructions and transoceanic visualizations that resulted were primarily (and unsurprisingly) the mirror images – sometimes reflected, sometimes refracted, sometimes distorted – of the traditional, individualistic, unequal society that it was widely believed existed in the metropolis. To the extent that there *was* a unified, coherent British imperial enterprise, there is a case for saying that it was the effort to fashion and to tie together the empire abroad in the vernacular image of the domestic, ranked social hierarchy.[14] Thus understood, the British Empire was at least as much (perhaps more?) about the replication of sameness and similarities originating from home as it was about the insistence on difference and dissimilarities originating from overseas.

This in turn means that, *pace* Edward Said and his 'Orientalist' followers, the British Empire was not exclusively (or even preponderantly) concerned with the creation of 'otherness' on the presumption that the imperial periphery was different from, and inferior to, the imperial metropolis: it was at least as much (perhaps more?) concerned with what has recently been called the 'construction of affinities' on the presumption that society on the periphery was the same as, or even on occasions superior to, society in the metropolis. Thus regarded, the British Empire was about the familiar and domestic, as well as the different and the exotic: indeed, it was in large part about the domestication of the exotic – the comprehending and the reordering of the foreign in parallel, analogous, equivalent, resemblant terms.[15] To be sure, the resulting vision of the British Empire as a layered, rural, traditional and organic society was an ignorant oversimplification of a very complex thing, as was the hierarchical vision of Britain itself from which this broader perspective was derived and developed, and which it helped to reinforce. It was never wholly convincing or universally accepted, either in the metropolis or on the periphery; but it was a powerful image that, at the zenith of empire, was embraced by many people in Britain and the colonies; and since it was also much more than an image, being in fact a social construct that gained coherence and credibility from a whole range of imperial institutions and practices, it was more important and pervasive than has generally been recognized.

Accordingly, this book is concerned with recovering the world-view and social presuppositions of those who dominated and ruled the empire, and also of those followers and supporters who went along with it in Britain and overseas, as well as with the imperial mechanisms and structures through which they dominated, ruled, supported and went along with it. This is not because I consider the victims and critics of empire to be unimportant, but because the outlook of the dominators and rulers and fellow travellers – their sense of how this empire they dominated and ruled and supported and went along with actually *worked*, and what it *looked like* – is one major element of the British imperial experience that has been relatively neglected, by historians, and by critics and admirers alike. Such a treatment of the British Empire, as the place that both reflected and reinforced commonplace perceptions of the domestic social structure, tells us things about Britain to which its historians have paid insufficient attention, and things about the empire of which the same may be said. Accordingly, this book lends support to the increasingly insistent argument that there can be no satisfactory history of Britain without empire, and no satisfactory history of empire without Britain. By stressing the interconnections between social visions of the metropolis and the periphery, and the structures and systems that unified and undergirded them, it seeks to put the history of Britain back into the history of empire, and the history of the empire back into the history of Britain.[16]

As such, this ambition derives from, reflects and contributes to the current and evolving scholarly agenda; but it also indulges autobiographical impulses and expresses a personal preference. I was born in

1950, and my interest in the British Empire began at an early age; indeed, it could scarcely have been otherwise, for empire was, albeit diminishingly, a part of the experience of growing up for the British generation to which I belong. I have recorded my own version of those experiences, and also my early, limited and faltering attempts to make sense of them geographically and historically, in an essay I wrote in 1997, which is here reprinted as the appendix. I *was* – but I also *was not* – a child of the British Empire, and those early recollections and forgettings no doubt inform (and distort?) what I have argued and written here in many ways, some of which I cannot hope to be fully aware of. I have also been reading about empire for as long as I can remember, and my first thanks must be to those many imperial actors, imperial biographers and imperial historians on whose voluminous recollections and writings this book is based, even as I must crave the indulgence of experts in particular fields who will feel (no doubt rightly) that I have oversimplified their scholarship, misunderstood their interpretations and misrepresented their views.

Although it deals with what is quintessentially a *British* subject, I should point out (and, perhaps, warn) that this is very much a *transatlantic* book, informed by experiences garnered and perspectives developed as a result of teaching and writing history in both Britain and America during the last two and a half decades. Indeed, to 'experiences garnered' and 'perspectives developed' I should probably also add 'contradictions not yet fully reconciled' since, for obvious reasons, empire is a subject that has always been treated very differently in these two countries. The United States was conceived and created on the basis of hostility to empire, and still thinks of itself as on the side of anti-colonialism; yet it is now the one authentic western empire remaining. The United Kingdom used to take pride in possessing the greatest empire the world had ever seen; but today it is, beyond question, an irreversibly diminished and post-imperial nation. Moreover, American society has generally been more preoccupied with race than with class, whereas in Britain these preoccupations have tended to be the other way round. Inevitably, these varying histories, outlooks and contemporary circumstances mean that empire in general, and the British Empire in particular, are viewed somewhat differently on opposite sides of the Atlantic; and I cannot pretend that I have fully reconciled these stimulating but nagging discrepancies in the pages that follow.

During my ten years in the United States, I learned much about the complexities and contingencies of empire from many scholars and friends in the History Department and in the Department of English and Comparative Literature at Columbia University, and about the way in which different disciplines approach the same phenomenon. It was also my good fortune to enjoy a Visiting Fellowship at the Whitney Humanities Center of Yale University, where I was encouraged to think about empire autobiographically as well as historically, and to ponder the many differences between these two modes of writing and analysis. More particularly, I am deeply indebted for help and advice to many friends and former colleagues: David Armitage, Ritu Birla, Sugata Boase, David Bromwich, Peter Brooks, Richard Bushman, Marcus Collins, Kevin Farrell, Eric Foner, Carol Gluck, Leonard Gordon, Ayesha Jalal, Paul Kennedy, the late Philip Lawson, Stephen Lee, Nomi Levy, William Roger Louis, Joseph Meisel, Farina Mir, Ken Munro, J. G. A. Pocock, Mridu Rai, Jonathan Schneer, Neil Smelser, Gayatri Spivak, Kathleen Wilson, Robin Winks and Marcia Wright. And I am additionally grateful to the editors of the *Yale Review* for originally publishing 'An Imperial Childhood?' and for kindly granting their permission for me to reprint it here.

I must also express my thanks to those friends and scholars here in Britain who have stimulated and fed my curiosity about the empire over the years since I was an undergraduate, when I first learned to think about the subject historically, many of whom have recently welcomed me back to Britain as a more active interloper into their midst: in Cambridge (which has its own view of empire), Christopher Bayly, Susan Bayly, Martin Daunton, the late Jack Gallagher, Tony Hopkins, Ronald Hyam, John Iliffe, Gareth Stedman Jones, Max Jones, John Lonsdale, Anthony Low, Ged Martin, the late Christopher Platt, Sir John Plumb, David Reynolds, Quentin Skinner, the late Eric Stokes, James Thompson and Richard Tuck; in Oxford (where empire is seen rather differently), Judith Brown, Sir John Elliott, Roy Foster, Sir Michael Howard, Alan Knight, Terence Ranger and the late Ronald

Robinson; and most recently in London (which offers yet a third range of imperial perspectives), Andrew Adonis, Brian Allen, David Bindman, Elizabeth Buettner, Pat Caplan, David Feldman, David Gilmour, Catherine Hall, Peter Hennessy, Eric Hobsbawm, Robert Holland, Sunil Khilnai, David Killingray, Roy Maclaren, Philip Mansel, Shula Marks, Peter Marshall, Andrew Porter, John Ramsden, Richard Rathbone, Francis Robinson, Lyndal Roper, Tony Stockwell, Glyn Williams and Nuala Zahedieh.

At the Institute of Historical Research, I have benefited greatly from the help, encouragement, support and forbearance of my colleagues Debra Birch, Alistair Chisholm, Harriet Jones, Derek Keene, Robert Lyons, Robin MacPherson, Jinty Nelson, Catherine Pearson and Steven Smith. I learned much about what was, in more senses than one, the darker side of empire, at the sixty-eighth Anglo-American Conference of Historians, which was held at the IHR in July 1999, on the subject of 'Race and Ethnicity'; and a more recent IHR symposium, devoted to volumes three, four and five of the *Oxford History of the British Empire*, helped me to clarify my views of that great post-imperial enterprise. Earlier versions of what follows were given as seminar papers at the IHR, at the School of Oriental and African Studies, at Sheffield Hallam University, and as the Esmee Fairbairn Lecture at the University of Lancaster, and I have been a great deal helped by the comments and suggestions (and hospitality) I received on those occasions, especially from Peter Cain and John MacKenzie.

My last debts are the largest, which must be happily and appreciatively acknowledged but which cannot possibly be repaid. My agent, Mike Shaw, has been as resourceful and reassuring as ever, and the appearance of this book owes much to his constant encouragement and never-failing enthusiasm. It has been an unalloyed pleasure to have worked with the staff of the Penguin Press: Simon Winder has been an exemplary editor, constantly urging me to make more of this enterprise than I originally intended, and always doing so with his inimitable combination of good advice and good cheer; and I am especially grateful to Cathie Arrington for work on the pictures, and to Donna Poppy for meticulous copy editing. Jeffrey Auerbach read the whole of the text at an earlier stage, and it has been immeasurably improved thanks to his wise suggestions and pertinent criticisms. Joyce Horn has corrected the proofs with characteristic care and generosity of spirit and Barbara Hird has compiled the index. But my most heartfelt thanks go, as they always do, to Linda Colley, without whose insistent wisdom, irrepressible curiosity, unflagging encouragement and resolute determination to make me visit India, this book, and a great deal more besides, would never have happened.

David Cannadine
Norfolk
1 August 2000

PART ONE

BEGINNINGS

I

Prologue

Nations, it has recently become commonplace to observe, are in part imagined communities, depending for their credibility and identity both on the legitimacy of government and the apparatus of the state, and on invented traditions, manufactured myths, and shared perceptions of the social order that are never more than crude categories and oversimplified stereotypes.[1] If this has been true (as indeed it has) of a relatively compact and contained country like Britain, then how much more true must this have been of the empire that the British conquered and peopled, administered and ruled? At its territorial zenith, shortly after the end of the First World War, it consisted of naval stations and military bases extending from Gibraltar to Hong Kong, the four great dominions of settlement, the Indian Empire that occupied an entire subcontinent, the crown colonies in Asia, Africa and the Caribbean, and the League of Nations Mandates, especially in the Middle East.[2] But, as with all such transoceanic realms, the British Empire was not only a geopolitical entity: it was also a culturally created and imaginatively constructed artifact. How, then, in the heyday of its existence, did Britons imagine and envisage their unprecedentedly vast and varied imperium, not so much geographically as sociologically? How did they try to organize and to arrange their heterogeneous imperial society, as they settled and conquered, governed and ruled it, and what did they think the resulting social order looked like?[3]

To the extent that they tried to conceive of these diverse colonies and varied populations beyond the seas as 'an entire interactive system, one vast interconnected world', most Britons followed the standard pattern of human behaviour when contemplating and comprehending the unfamiliar. Their 'inner predisposition' was to begin with what they knew – or what they thought they knew – namely, the social structure of their own home country.[4] But what sort of a starting point was this, and what were the implications and consequences of British perceptions of their domestic social order for British perceptions of their imperial social order? From Hegel to Marx, and from Engels to Said, it has been commonplace to suggest that Britons saw their own society (and, by extension, that of what became their settler dominions) as dynamic, individualistic, egalitarian, modernizing – and thus superior. By comparison with such a positive and progressive metropolitan perception, this argument continues, Britons saw society in their 'tropical' and 'oriental' colonies as enervated, hierarchical, corporatist, backward – and thus inferior.[5] But among its many flaws, this appealingly simplistic (and highly influential) contrast is based on a mistaken premise, in that it fundamentally misunderstands most Britons' perceptions of their domestic social world when their nation was at its zenith as an imperial power.

Far from seeing themselves as atomized individuals with no rooted sense of identity, or as collective classes coming into being and struggling with each other, or as equal citizens whose modernity engendered an unrivalled sense of progressive superiority, Britons generally conceived of themselves as belonging to an unequal society characterized by a seamless web of layered gradations, which were hallowed by time and precedent, which were sanctioned by tradition and religion, and which extended in a great chain of being from the monarch at the top to the humblest subject at the bottom.[6] That was how they saw themselves, and it was from that starting point that they contemplated and tried to comprehend the distant realms and diverse society of their empire. This in turn meant that for the British, their overseas realms were at least as much about sameness as they were about difference. For insofar as they regarded their empire as 'one vast interconnected world', they did not necessarily do so in disadvantaged or critical contrast to the way they perceived their own metropolitan society. Rather, they were at least as likely to envisage the social structure of their empire – as their predecessors had done before them – by analogy to what they knew of 'home', or in replication of it, or in parallel to it, or in extension of it, or (sometimes) in idealization of it, or (even, and increasingly) in nostalgia for it.[7]

This means that we need to be much more attentive to the varied – sometimes, even, contradictory – ways in which the British understood, visualized and imagined their empire hierarchically. To be sure, *one* of the ways in which they did so was in racial terms of superiority and inferiority. Like all post-Enlightenment imperial powers, only more so, Britons saw themselves as the lords of all the world and thus of humankind. They placed themselves at the top of the scale of civilization and achievement, they ranked all other races in descending order beneath them, according to their relative merits (and de-merits), and during the period 1780 to 1830 they increasingly embodied these views in imperial institutions and codes.[8] And when it came to the systematic settlement of Canada, Australia, New Zealand and South Africa, they did not hesitate to banish the indigenous peoples to the margins of the new, imperial society. By the end of the nineteenth century these notions of racial hierarchy, supremacy and stereotyping had become more fully developed, and stridently hardened, as exemplified in Cecil Rhodes's remark that 'the British are the finest race in the world, and the more of the world they inhabit, the better it will be for mankind', or in Lord Cromer's belief that the world was divided between those who were British and those who were merely 'subject races'.[9]

In short, and as Peter Marshall has observed, 'Empire reinforced a hierarchical view of the world, in which the British occupied a pre-eminent place among the colonial powers, while those subjected to colonial rule were ranged below them, in varying degrees of supposed inferiority.'[10] These facts are familiar and incontrovertible. But this mode of imperial ranking and imaging was not just based on the Enlightenment view of the intrinsic inferiority of dark-skinned peoples: it was also based on notions of metropolitan–peripheral analogy and sameness. For as the British contemplated the unprecedented numbers massed together in their new industrial cities, they tended to compare these great towns at home with the 'dark continents' overseas, and thus equate the workers in factories with coloured peoples abroad. The 'shock cities' of the 1830s and 1840s were seen as resembling 'darkest Africa' in their distant, unknown and unfathomable menaces; and during the third quarter of the nineteenth century London's newly discovered 'residuum' and 'dangerous classes' were likened – in their character and their conduct – to the 'negroes' of empire. And these domestic–imperial analogies were worked and extended in the opposite direction as well: one additional reason why 'natives' in the empire were regarded as collectively inferior was that they were seen as the overseas equivalent of the 'undeserving poor' in Britain.[11]

To some degree, then, these analogies and comparisons that Britons drew and made between domestic and overseas societies, from the eighteenth to the twentieth centuries, served to reinforce the prevailing Enlightenment notions of racial superiority and inferiority. And it is from this premise that the British Empire has been viewed by contemporaries and by historians as an enterprise that was built and maintained on the basis of the collective, institutionalized and politicized ranking of races. But, as these analogies and comparisons also suggest, this was not the only way in which Britons envisioned their empire, and its imperial society, as an essentially hierarchical organism. For there was another vantage-point from which they regarded the inhabitants of their far-flung realms, which was also built around notions of superiority and inferiority, but which frequently cut across, and sometimes overturned and undermined, the notion that the British Empire was based solely and completely on a hierarchy of race. This alternative approach was, indeed, the conventional way in which the English (and latterly the British) had regarded the inhabitants of other, alien worlds, for it was a perspective that long antedated the Enlightenment.

It has certainly been traced back to the sixteenth and seventeenth centuries, for when the English first encountered the native peoples of North America, they did not see them collectively as a race of inferior savages; on the contrary, they viewed them individually as fellow human beings. It was from this pre-Enlightenment perspective that the English concluded that North American society closely resembled their own: a carefully graded hierarchy of status, extending in a seamless web from chiefs and princes at the top to less worthy figures at the bottom. Moreover, these two essentially hierarchical societies were

1. King Kalakaua of Hawaii, *c.* 1881.

seen as coexisting, not in a relationship of (English) superiority and (North American) inferiority, but in a relationship of equivalence and similarity: princes in one society were the analogues to princes in another, and so on and so on, all the way down these two parallel social ladders. In short, when the English initially contemplated native Americans, they saw them as social equals rather than as social inferiors, and when they came to apply their conventionally hierarchical tools of observation, their prime grid of analysis was individual status rather than collective race.[12]

It is the argument of this book that these attitudes, whereby social ranking was as important as (perhaps more important than?) colour of skin in contemplating the extra-metropolitan world, remained important for the English and, latterly, for the British long after it has been generally supposed they ceased to matter. To be sure, the Enlightenment brought about a new, collective way of looking at peoples, races and colours, based on distance and separation and otherness. But it did not subvert the earlier, individualistic, analogical way of thinking, based on the observation of status similarities and the cultivation of affinities, that projected domestically originated perceptions of the social order overseas.[13] On the contrary, this essentially pre-racial way of seeing things lasted for as long as the British Empire lasted. Here is one example. In the summer of 1881 King Kalakaua of Hawaii was visiting England and, in the course of an extensive round of social engagements, he found himself the guest at a party given by Lady Spencer. Also attending were the prince of Wales, who would eventually become King Edward VII, and the German crown prince, who was his brother-in-law and the future kaiser. The prince of Wales insisted that the king should take precedence over the crown prince, and when his brother-in-law objected, he offered the following pithy and trenchant justification: 'Either the brute is a king, or he's a common or garden nigger; and if the latter, what's he doing here?'[14]

Read one way, this is, to our modern sensibilities, a deeply insensitive and offensively racist observation; read from another viewpoint, this was, by the conventions of its own time, a very *un*racist remark. The traditional, pre-Enlightenment freemasonry based on the shared recognition of high social rank – a freemasonry to which Martin Malia has suggestively given the name 'aristocratic internationalism' – both trumped and transcended the alternative and more recent freemasonry based on the unifying characteristic of shared skin colour. From *this* perspective, the hierarchical principle that underlay Britons' perceptions of their empire was not exclusively based on the collective, colour-coded ranking of social groups, but depended as much on the more venerable colour-blind ranking of individual social prestige.[15] This means there were at least two visions of empire that were essentially (and elaborately) hierarchical: one centred on colour, the other on class. So, in the *Raj Quartet*, Major Ronald Merrick, whose social background was relatively lowly, believed that 'the English were superior to all other races, especially black'. But the Cambridge-educated Guy Perron feels a greater affinity with the Indian Hari Kumar, who went to the same public school as he did, than he does with Merrick, who is very much his social inferior.[16]

The British Empire has been extensively studied as a complex *racial* hierarchy (and also as a less complex *gender* hierarchy); but it has received far less attention as an equally complex *social* hierarchy or, indeed, as a social organism, or construct, of any kind. This constant (and largely unquestioned) privileging of colour over class, of race over rank, of collectivities over individualities, in the scholarly literature has opened up many important new lines of inquiry. But it has also meant that scarcely any attention has been paid to empire as a functioning social structure and as an imagined social entity, in which, as Karen Ordahl Kupperman puts it, 'status is fundamental to all other categories'.[17] Yet throughout its history, the views expressed by the prince of Wales reflected generally held opinions about the social arrangements existing in the empire. These attitudes and perceptions were certainly still in existence in the late eighteenth and early nineteenth centuries.[18] But they were no less important between the 1850s and the 1950s, when the ideal of social hierarchy was seen as the model towards which the great dominions should approximate, when it formed the basis of the fully elaborated Raj in India, when it provided the key to the doctrine of 'indirect rule' in Africa, when it formed the template for the new nations created in the British Middle East, when it was codified and rationalized by the imperial honours system, and when it was legitimated and unified by the imperial monarchy. In all these ways, the theory and the practice of social hierarchy served to eradicate the differences, and to homogenize the heterogeneities, of empire.

Of course, even in the heyday of empire these hierarchical structures and constructs, impulses and images, imaginings and ideologies, based on status rather than race, were never wholly pervasive or persuasive. And they were often founded on serious misunderstandings (sometimes deliberate, sometimes inadvertent) of imperial society, whether in the metropolis or on the periphery. But they *were* the conventional wisdom of the official mind in the metropolis, and of their collaborators on the peripheries, and of many people in Britain and the empire who also envisaged this 'vast interconnected world' in traditional, Burkeian terms. The rest of this book will sketch out, in a necessarily abridged and schematic form, an account of the British Empire in which the concept of hierarchy as social prestige is brought more closely to the centre of things than historians have generally allowed. As such, it urges the importance of seeing and understanding the British Empire as a mechanism for the export, projection and analogization of domestic social structures and social perceptions. For most of its history, the British visualized and understood their empire *on their own terms*, and we need to know more about what they were, and about how they did so. We should never forget that the British Empire was first and foremost a class act, where individual social ordering often took precedence over collective racial othering.

2

Precursors

In governing themselves and much of the rest of the world, the English (and subsequently the British) adhered to a limited number of principles, practices and perceptions that were long-standing and deeply rooted. From the time of the Tudors, English local government was usually undertaken by those with the highest social prestige. This meant that it was in the hands of traditional authorities, the great grandees and the lesser gentry, that it was relatively inexpensive, and that it was amateur. When Wales, Scotland and Ireland were subsequently brought into a greater British realm, they too were administered through the social leaders of their respective communities, from whom power and authority descended, and who were in contact and alliance with Westminster and Whitehall. This was 'indirect rule' before its imperial time had come: the way the English, and subsequently the British, visualized themselves – and governed themselves on the basis of this visualization. England and Britain were hierarchical societies, and those at the top of the social hierarchy were also those who wielded power.[1] And when Britons turned their attention to those wider worlds that they colonized and conquered, it was with these views of how society was, and of how it should be administered, very firmly embedded in their minds.

The first British Empire consisted primarily of a western Atlantic dominion extending from Canada, via the thirteen American colonies, to the Caribbean, and reached its peak in the brief years between 1763 and 1776.[2] Out of its post-Yorktown wreckage was born its successor, which was a much more far-flung and varied realm. The Caribbean colonies were retained and augmented, and those of French and English Canada were restructured and reformed by the legislation of 1791. But as a consequence of the Revolutionary and Napoleonic Wars, the primary drive towards empire was diverted to the east: large tracts of South Asia were conquered and subdued, and new colonies were acquired from the Cape of Good Hope to Singapore. The result, it has often been argued, was an empire that would not only expand still further in Asia and in Africa during the second half of the nineteenth century, but also an empire with two very different traditions of politics and government. In what would become the great dominions of settlement, there would be a gradual but inexorable move to representative and responsible government, to nationhood and dominion status. But in the colonies of conquest, there would be authoritarian administrations, which would eventually be abruptly terminated by nationalist agitation and independence.[3]

There is much truth and insight in this picture. But, while the politics, government and constitutional evolution of these two realms of empire may have been different, their societies were believed to have more in common than is sometimes supposed. In the great dominions of settlement, there were two alternative models of the social world that the emigrants were creating. One was that, in revolt against the rigid hierarchies of Britain, and assisted by the seemingly limitless supplies of land, the new colonies would be founded on the basis of freedom, independence and equality. But the other was that, instead of rejecting the hierarchies of the imperial metropolis, the chief ambition of many settlers was to replicate them and nurture them – an ambition generally shared by the policy-makers in the metropolis itself.[4] In India and the crown colonies of conquest, there were also two discrepant views of the societies and polities thus acquired. The first was that the native regimes and hierarchies were backward, inefficient, despotic and corrupt, and had to be overthrown and reconstructed according to the more advanced model of western society and politics. The second was that they were traditional and organic, an authentic world of ordered, harmonious, time-hallowed social relations of the kind that the Industrial Revolution was threatening (or destroying) in Britain, and that therefore had to be cherished, preserved and nurtured overseas as a more wholesome version of society than could now be found in the metropolis.[5]

In other words, and notwithstanding their many differences of politics, government and constitutional evolution, the emigrant societies established in the colonies of settlement, and the indigenous societies discovered in the colonies of conquest, were both regarded from perspectives that might be anti-hierarchical (reject the British system, overthrow the native system) or, alternatively, from perspectives that might be pro-hierarchical (transplant the British system, preserve the native system). In short-term episodes of rejection and reform, when titles were scorned in the colonies, and when native rulers were deposed in India or Africa, the anti-hierarchical impulses were certainly in evidence. And in the long run they eventually won out, both in the former dominions of settlement, which came to pride themselves on being more egalitarian than the old mother country, and in the colonies of rule, which with independence became republics and abolished the structures and trappings of imperial hierarchy. But in the medium term – a period that encompasses most of its centuries-long existence – the British Empire, in both its settlement dominions and colonies of conquest, was generally built around the principles of replicating and supporting a hierarchical social structure modelled on, or likened to, and tied in with, that which it was thought existed (or had once existed) in Britain itself. These impulses and perceptions reached their fullest and widest extent in the heyday of empire, from the mid nineteenth to the mid twentieth centuries. But there were ample precedents in the earlier phases of imperial expansion and settlement, especially during the era of the Revolutionary and Napoleonic Wars, and it is worth glancing briefly at that period to set the scene for later developments.

In the British colonies on the eastern seaboard of America, these hierarchical attitudes and traditional preferences, both ethnic and social, were strongly in evidence from the beginning. There was the contemptible dismissal of indigenous non-white races, native peoples and African Americans as inferior beings, classically illustrated by the opinions of Edmund Burke. For him, 'negro slaves' were 'fierce and cruel tribes of savages, in whom the vestiges of human nature are nearly effaced by ignorance and barbarity'; and the Indians were merely 'several gangs of banditti', of 'the most cruel and atrocious kind'.[6] Now and then, in the manner of their Tudor and Stuart predecessors, the British would recognize native chiefs as superior figures in a social hierarchy that could be compared to their own (as on the occasion of the visit of four supposed Iroquois kings to London in 1710 or six Cherokee chiefs in 1730), or seek military alliances with them (as in the 1760s and 1770s). But these were the exceptions that proved the rule.[7] It was the same in the West Indies, where slavery – and the trade in human cargo from West Africa across the Atlantic – was taken for granted as part of the immutable order of things. Even its abolition was intended to reinforce, rather than overturn, a hierarchical view of society, on the presumption that although slaves should become free, they would still remain dignified and obedient at the bottom of the social order: liberty, yes; but subordination also. Thereafter, there was a general hardening of British attitudes to colonial indigenes – a view that would subsequently be replicated by British settlers in nineteenth-century Canada, Australia, New Zealand and South Africa.[8]

But on top of these marginalized and exploited native populations, many British settlers overseas sought to create a full-scale replica of the elaborately graded social hierarchy they had left behind at home. From this perspective, empire was about the replication of rank, not the rejection of it. Accordingly, in the thirteen American colonies, by the mid eighteenth century, the countryside seemed increasingly settled and ordered on the English pattern, with great estates, elegant mansions, resident gentry, and all the accoutrements of traditional society: fox hunts, coats of arms, swords and periwigs. Titles such as Esquire, Gent, Master and Honourable were used to show who was who; church pews were assigned on the basis of social position; and there were even requests to establish a colonial peerage. In such a layered, aspiring, established society, it was generally believed that everyone had 'their appointed offices, places and station'; that 'God hath ordained different degrees and orders of men'; and that there was 'a beauty of order in society, as when the different members . . . have all their appointed offices, place and situation'. Thus regarded, colonial America was indeed a very hierarchical society, a title-conscious place, with a prestige order that corresponded roughly with economic rank order. Hence, for those opposed to British government, the need to abolish titles in America after the revolution of 1776.[9]

Eventually, in the newly formed United States, these anti-hierarchical impulses won out, and the country was launched on a non-British, non-imperial trajectory of republican constitutionalism and egalitarian social perceptions. Thereafter, the British vowed that this should never happen again in their empire, which meant that elsewhere in their colonies hierarchy was nurtured and supported, and social revolution thwarted. In the late eighteenth and early nineteenth centuries 'elsewhere' meant, essentially, Ireland, Canada and India. The Act of Union of 1800 brought together Great Britain and Ireland in a new, imperial-cum-metropolitan unity. Although it was now, legally, part of the imperial metropolis, the regime established in Dublin provided the proconsular prototype for what would later evolve on the imperial periphery, in India, in the dominions of settlement, and eventually in the dependent empire. The monarch was represented by a viceroy, who resided, in appropriately royal style, in Dublin Castle, and who was invariably a high-ranking aristocrat. Among the earliest occupants of the post were the Dukes of Richmond, Bedford and Northumberland, and the Marquess Wellesley. The viceroy was the cynosure and apex of a hierarchical vision of Irish society, which was regularly proclaimed by the courtly ceremonial of state entries, audiences, investitures, levees, parades and entertainments, by the courtly retinue of chamberlains, comptrollers, heralds and pursuivants, and by the chapters and installations of the Order of St Patrick (of which the viceroy was grand master), which had been founded in 1783.[10]

These developments in Ireland, towards proconsular splendour as a reassertion of hierarchy, were also being paralleled and replicated in Canada. As it happened, French society in Quebec was pre-1789 in its seigneurial structure and veneration for monarchy, and in this regard it had much in common with the British society being established in neighbouring Ontario, where most of the immigrants were conservative refugees fleeing from the thirteen colonies, and eager to proclaim their continuing loyalty to Britain's throne and rigid social order. Moreover, in 1791 the younger Pitt planned to provide an hereditary upper house in anxious but determined response to the mistaken egalitarianism of the French (and American) Revolutions. By all these means, the principal aim was 'to avoid a replica of democratic New England', and to inculcate 'a due deference and homage for superiors' and a degree of 'subordination necessary to civilized society'.[11] And during the late eighteenth and early nineteenth centuries the full panoply of proconsular aggrandizement and mimetic monarchy was unfurled, with elaborate pageantry and ceremonial, orchestrated by such patrician governors as Lord Dorchester in Quebec, Lord Dalhousie in Canada and John Wentworth in Nova Scotia (and also, half a world away, by Lord Charles Somerset at the recently acquired Cape of Good Hope).[12] Here were precedents aplenty for later imperial developments in Australia, New Zealand and South Africa.

It was not the same – and yet in other ways it was very much the same – in South Asia, where the late-eighteenth-century British appeared as conquerors and traders rather than as settlers and immigrants. It was not the same because one of the predominant themes during the first phase of conquest and expansion was that caste-based, indigenous Indian society was ordered, traditional and layered hierarchically, and should be nurtured and appreciated in the same way that the similar society in Britain was.[13] This accounts for Burke's hostility to Warren Hastings, whom he saw as a tyrant overturning and extinguishing the time-sanctioned social order of the subcontinent – a much more sympathetic view of native peoples from that which he had taken of them on the far side of the Atlantic, where they seemed merely rootless, savage and unsettled. For Burke, as for many Britons, the social arrangements in South Asia seemed easily recognizable and comfortingly familiar. As Thomas Munro explained in 1805, 'the want due to due gradation of ranks in Society in this country is more imaginary than real, for what is effected by establishing such a gradation by property in other parts of the world is accomplished here by the distinction of casts [sic] and the manners of the people'.[14]

From these social analogies and sociological perceptions, various further consequences followed and flowed. The British became very interested in the theory and practice of caste, and in the ways in which they thought Indian society resembled their own; and many books

2. Government House, Calcutta, built by the Marquess Wellesley.

were written on the subject at this time. They also believed that the standing and status of the native princes at (as they saw it) the top of this layered hierarchy should be strengthened and supported, and that they should be treated as social equals. As Sir John Lindsay (himself the younger son of a peer) had observed, writing from Madras in 1771, 'it is by no means good policy to diminish the consequences of our friends. On the contrary, by exalting their dignity, we raise our own, and bind them to our interests'.[15] This in turn implied – and here was the similarity with the settlement colonies – that the British proconsular regime should also be of unprecedented grandeur, in its spectacle and its buildings, partly to match the pomp and circumstance of the princely states, but also to project an image of order and authority, as in the days of the Marquess Wellesley. India, he observed, 'is a country of splendour, of extravagance, of outward appearances'. As such, it must 'be ruled from a palace, not from a counting house; with the ideas of a prince, not those of a retail dealer in muslins and indigo'.[16] Thus rationalized and justified, imperial hierarchy and its ceremonial projection reached their zenith in the British Raj, initially in the early nineteenth century, and again and more lastingly in the early twentieth.

But they would also provide the models for those crown colonies that would later be acquired elsewhere in Asia and Africa, both in terms of governmental structure and social organization. Before the last quarter of the nineteenth century, Britain only teetered on the edge of Africa, and had very limited political or commercial relations – though Theophilus Shepstone is credited with pioneering a certain type of indirect rule via native Zulu chiefs in Natal in the 1840s.[17] And there were already other indications as to what future attitudes towards them might be. Sir Joshua Reynolds's portrait of Omai, a young South Sea islander who had visited London in the early 1770s and been lionized in polite society, depicted him with the flowing robes, assured standing and patrician gestures of a confident, traditional native chief. Omai was also the subject of a play by John O'Keefe, the finale of which saw him enthroned as king of Tahiti.[18] Seventy years later Sir David Wilkie's portrait of Mehemet Ali, the Egyptian pasha, was to convey very similar images: a vigorous personality and strong character, a great and powerful ruler, who sat on a throne wearing traditional

3. Omai, by Sir Joshua Reynolds.

4. Mehemet Ali, by Sir David Wilkie.

(and forbidden) Egyptian dress, and who sought independence from the Turks and recognition for his country. And two generations on, this same view was again articulated by Sir Richard Burton, whose visits to West Africa in the 1860s and 1880s meant he was fascinated by what he regarded as the 'barbaric splendours' of the Dahomean king and his court – splendours that would captivate many subsequent colonial administrators.[19]

These were essentially unifying and hierarchical views of empire, or of those societies still beyond empire. This was how the British saw their own society, and preferred it to be. So it is scarcely surprising that this was how they saw other societies too – as approximating more or less to what they knew (or thought they knew) of home. But there were also important ways in which, from within the metropolis itself, this layered vision of the empire was encouraged, unified and promoted, so as to make it more coherent and convincing. One such means was by the codification and extension of the honours system into something that was a more British, and more imperial, structure of titles and rewards. The late eighteenth and early nineteenth centuries witnessed the expansion of the (English) Order of the Garter and the (Scottish) Order of the Thistle, and the establishment of the (Irish) Order of St Patrick. The Order of the Bath, founded in 1725 to recognize military prowess at home and abroad, had initially consisted of only thirty-six knights; it was extended and remodelled in 1815, with three carefully ranked grades of honour. The Order of St Michael and St George was set up by Sir Thomas Maitland in 1818 to massage the self-esteem of the island gentry of Malta. And there were unprecedented creations of peerages, as Scottish and Irish nobles were given United Kingdom titles, and as politicians, proconsuls and military men were lavished with baronies, viscountcies, earldoms, marquessates and dukedoms.[20]

The result was the consolidation of a pan-British, pan-imperial elite that conquered and governed, unified and ordered, the empire for the first time. Nor was it coincidence that this period also witnessed a growing association between crown and empire. By definition, the British Empire 'was underpinned by the cult of monarchy'.[21] The sovereign was head of the imperial state and of imperial society;

governors ruled and viceroys governed in the monarch's name; and life in the empire, as in the metropolis, was suffused with the substance and symbolism of royalty. Before they turned against George III, the American colonies had been very loyal and royal, marking monarchs' birthdays, accessions and coronations in appropriately festive style from Massachusetts to the Carolinas.[22] And as the empire expanded again in the aftermath of Yorktown, the position of the sovereign as its political flywheel, social apex and ceremonial cynosure was further enhanced. Throughout the 1790s there were royal firework displays in the West Indies, and patriotic medals were struck with the king's head on it; there were mass petitions of loyalty from the burghers of Calcutta, Bombay and Madras; and in Nova Scotia the proconsular regime of Governor John Wentworth was embellished by the presence of the duke of Kent and the duke of Clarence. The domestic hierarchy of the British nation, and the overseas hierarchy of the British Empire, connected and converged on the person of the sovereign, who completed them and gave them their meaning, coherence and legitimacy.[23]

But however plausible it may have seemed to many Britons at home and overseas, this unified, interconnected, hierarchical picture of their empire was never more than a partial image of how things were, even at the zenith of this first great imperial impulse in the late eighteenth and early nineteenth centuries. In the American colonies, some lamented that the British social structure had not been fully replicated, and that there was no 'native aristocracy', while others insisted that the cult of freedom and independence meant the colonists were 'adverse to subordination' in any outmoded old-world hierarchy – the view that finally prevailed after 1776. In India, zealots like Bentinck, Macaulay and Dalhousie, inspired by a confident mixture of Evangelicalism and Utilitarianism, thought native rulers corrupt and native customs barbaric, and sought to supersede them with western-style law, governance and education, which would be efficient rather than ornamental.[24] And when they turned their attention elsewhere, there were those like Raffles (and Palmerston) who thought oriental rule was 'despotic' and needed overturning, and that the governing elites in Africa were 'recalcitrant' and needed reforming.[25]

Not surprisingly, then, the metropolitan efforts to complete this

British imperial hierarchy at the centre and to export it abroad, so as to forge 'an entire interactive system', were never a complete success. The American colonists eventually rejected the whole thing outright; attempts to create a peerage and orders of knighthood to tie the Canadians closer to the British did not come off; the governor of Quebec, Guy Carleton, later Lord Dorchester, opined that it was 'impossible for the dignity of the throne or peerage to be represented in the American [i.e. Canadian] forests'; and the national and imperial apotheosis of George III was scarcely replicated by his two scandal-ridden successors.[26] Moreover, although this hierarchical world-view that was extended across the British Empire was conservative in its ideology, and stressed the importance of tradition and unchangingness, it was often very innovative and inventive in its practices. The elaborate, layered social ordering of the American colonies was, at the mid eighteenth century, a relatively recent development. The caste system in South Asia was constantly evolving and mutating, and many of the ruling princes of India were upstarts rather than the representatives of an unchanging hierarchical order.[27] The honours that were given out in unprecedented numbers to Britons at home and abroad stressed chivalry and history, but many of them were novel creations. And the ceremonial surrounding proconsuls overseas and the monarch in Britain was at least as new as it was old.

Nevertheless, it bears repeating that throughout the period of the first and second British Empires, and culminating in the years from the 1790s to the 1820s, there was a powerful and unifying sense of the empire as the extension overseas, or the discovery overseas, of societies resembling that which existed, or had existed, in Britain. In the aftermath of the American Revolution, this vast, interconnected, hierarchical world was especially associated with such men as Pitt, Dundas, Wellesley and Macartney. And it provided the precedents and models for another such high-imperial cabal a century later, in the persons of Disraeli, Curzon, Milner, Lugard and Churchill, when the British Empire reached its peak as an ordered construct and 'traditional' creation.[28] To be sure, there was something of a lull in the period in between. In a *Punch* sketch of 1850, entitled 'Waiting at the Station',

Thackeray pictures some Britons emigrating to Australia, and assumes they will find an undifferentiated community that will contrast strongly with the old England, 'that Gothic society with its ranks and hierarchies, its cumbrous ceremonies, its glittering antique paraphernalia'. Perhaps they did.[29] But for the best part of another hundred years, from the Indian Mutiny of 1857 to Indian independence ninety years later, the rulers and leaders of the British Empire tried to make that hierarchical structure happen, and that hierarchical vision convince. It is time to see how and where they set about it.

PART TWO

LOCALITIES

3

Dominions

Between the mid nineteenth and the mid twentieth centuries, the four great dominions of settlement offered the most substantial scope, either for the repudiation or for the replication of the domestic British social hierarchy across the seas into the empire. Indeed, it would be more accurate to express this proposition not as 'either . . . or', but rather as 'both . . . and'. For these were not so much irreconcilable opposites, between which a stark choice had to be made, but alternative possibilities, which could in practice be embraced simultaneously. On the one hand, it is widely recognized that the dominions, especially Australia and New Zealand, developed political cultures that were democratic and liberal, out of which autonomous, post-imperial, multicultural nations would eventually evolve. But meanwhile they did so in the context of social and ceremonial cultures that were much more conservative and inegalitarian, and that thus fitted comfortably for the time being into the broader world of the British Empire, a traditional, monarchical, realm.[1] And like the thirteen American colonies before them, the dominions were hierarchical in more senses than one: there was a hierarchy of race and colour (with which we are by now very familiar); and, superimposed on top of it, a hierarchy of social status and prestige (about which we know rather less).

Following the precedent set by the colonial Americans, the four settlement dominions were established as essentially 'white men's countries', which meant the enforced disregard and sustained undermining of the 'inferior' indigenous races: the Indians and Inuit in Canada, the Maoris and Aborigines in Australasia, and the 'Hottentots' in South Africa, whose lands were taken, numbers reduced and position marginalized.[2] In Canada the native peoples had lost most of their lands east of the Great Lakes by the late 1830s, and across the southern prairies native title was extinguished in the 1870s. In Australia it was an unquestioned assumption that the British enjoyed the sole right to own and occupy the island continent, embodied in the colonists' doctrine of *terra nullius*; and by the late nineteenth century the 'white Australia' policy was fully in place. In New Zealand, after annexation in 1840, the Treaty of Waitangi ostensibly guaranteed the native chiefs' rights, powers, land and authority; but this was disregarded, as the Maori were systematically dispossessed of their land, sometimes by military force, between the 1840s and the 1860s.[3] And in British South Africa, the Xhosa were ejected from their lands in the Cape, and the Zulu from Natal, while after the Boer War, one of the principles on which the new Union was established was that of the 'abandonment of the black races'.[4]

On the basis of this rigorously enforced racial hierarchy, where chiefs and tribes were shown far less respect than would be the case elsewhere in the empire, many white British settlers were increasingly concerned to replicate the layered, ordered, hierarchical society they believed they had left behind at home. Populations in these 'new' colonies were generally sparse and scattered, and their economies were primarily agricultural; this provided substantial scope for the re-creation of metropolitan landed society overseas. For much of the second quarter of the nineteenth century, when British agriculture was generally depressed, and when the pickings from 'Old Corruption' were dwindling, sprigs of nobility and distant cousins set off for Canada, New Zealand and Australia, in the hope they might establish and enjoy the sort of genteel life there on which they could no longer count in Britain.[5] So in New South Wales, figures such as the Irby brothers, nephews of Lord Boston, and William Charles Wentworth, a distant relative of Earl Fitzwilliam, established themselves in the 'First Rank of Society'. They built country houses, became justices of the peace, founded the Australia Club in Sydney, and were much concerned with the trappings of tradition – duelling, coats of arms, genealogy and pedigrees.[6]

It was the same elsewhere in the Antipodes, where British models of gentility and hierarchy were energetically replicated and enthusiastically reproduced. In Victoria, South Australia and Tasmania, successful early settlers purchased and extended large estates in the mid-Victorian period, and the resulting new gentry elites were consolidated by intermarriage and shared ways of life. In the towns, they provided the social leadership in Melbourne, Adelaide and Hobart; and in the country, parks and mansions called Panshanger and Clarendon boasted deer and pheasant and salmon, which provided ample scope for hunting, shooting and fishing. Observers marvelled at 'well-ordered neighbourhoods', where 'the natural subordinations of society are maintained'. As Trollope noted approvingly in 1873, 'I imagine the life of a Victorian landowner is very much as was that of the English country gentleman a century or a century and a half ago'; they were, he felt sure, 'an established aristocracy with very conservative feelings'.[7] The same was true in New Zealand, where the great landowners held estates of well above 5,000 acres, engaged in conspicuous leisure and consumption, cultivated modes of paternalistic behaviour, controlled the leading recreational and cultural institutions, and constituted what one historian has described as a quasi-feudal *'ancien régime'*.[8]

Across the world in Canada, where hostility to the revolution of 1776 had been intensified by the war of 1812, the desire to replicate and defend a traditional British social structure against the egalitarian, democratic and republican ethos of the United States remained strong. Like pre-1789 Quebec, pre-1776 Upper Canada was an extremely retrograde society, controlled by a small clique known as the 'family compact', whose members were bound together by 'education, social distinction and conservative tendencies'. They dominated everything, they delighted in defending the king and the constitution, they gloried in their imperial ties and connections, and they possessed an exaggerated regard for British traditions.[9] Unlike America, they saw *their* society as layered, established and stable, and they were preoccupied with notions of rank and ideas of respectability. Indeed, the more in practice their society came to resemble that of the neighbouring United States, the more the Canadians insisted on seeing it as different, by stressing what they believed to be its defining characteristics of hierarchy and order. It was the same in nearby Newfoundland, where the second quarter of the nineteenth century witnessed the development of a vivid and vigorous colonial culture, centred on pageants, processions and ostentatious displays of 'dutiful obedience and veneration of the sovereign'.[10]

Underpinning all these mid-century settler regimes, with their traditional, transoceanic loyalties and their 'imported social hierarchies', was the view, originally pioneered by some American colonists and carried over into the nineteenth century by many people in Britain and the empire, that a mature settler society was necessarily a graded, layered society. That, in essence, was what they were seeking to establish in these new, far-distant realms: in part by the export of authentic British aristocrats overseas, who would set the social tone and the social standard; in part by the emulative creation of their own indigenous landed gentry. This was why Edward Gibbon Wakefield urged the transplanting of a complete cross-section of British society in his *Letter from Sydney* (1829), and again in *A View of the Art of Colonization* (1849). This was why the Hon. Arthur Hamilton Gordon, himself a younger son of Lord Aberdeen, urged that 'If a good number of younger sons who vegetate in England were to go out there [i.e. Canada] it might be useful as forming a sort of aristocracy which is so much wanted there.'[11] And that was why, in his novel *The Caxtons* (1849), Sir Edward Bulwer-Lytton expressed the hope that an aristocracy would develop in Australia. Far from wishing to reject the stratified society of the mother country, these pundits and politicians strenuously recommended its replication in the colonies.

Their social hopes and hierarchical predictions were in significant measure fulfilled. Some emigrants, leaving Britain, wanted to re-establish the domestic social hierarchy they regretted they were leaving behind, and set out to improve their own place within it (*vide* Dickens's Mr Micawber); others, on arrival, wanted to distance themselves from those fellow travellers whom they considered, in every sense, beneath them. Hence the verdict of Sir Henry Huntley, governor of Prince Edward Island, who claimed that 'an aristocratic instinct' prevailed among the people of all the provinces of Canada. Hence these words of Sir Roger Therry, who in the 1860s noted that 'the various observances of precedence in New South Wales, as in most colonial societies, are attended to with great, sometimes ludicrous, precision'. 'Social distinction is everywhere desired,' agreed the *Sydney Morning Herald*. All these colonial settlers – determined to replicate what they believed to be the British social order – shared what Geoffrey Bolton has called 'an Anglican and hierarchical view of society', which in its ideal form was 'one of village communities, in which an obedient and industrious tenantry enjoyed the public libraries and mechanics institutes, the ploughing matches and hospitable sporting events, organized and controlled by the landed gentry'.[12]

This 'aristocratic thread', which ran through Britain's new settler colonies, also meant a widespread eagerness for honours and hereditary distinctions: the coping stone, as Burke had long ago remarked, of any established, hierarchical society. In 1853 William Charles Wentworth proposed hereditary, titled legislative councillors in New South Wales, based on the Canadian model of 1791, and following a similar scheme put forward in South Australia four years previously. They 'would lay the foundations of an aristocracy' in the colony by encouraging and rewarding the leading local notables and would 'necessarily form one of the strongest inducements' to British aristocrats to send their relatives overseas.[13] There were also many who shared the view of Sir Charles Fitzroy that colonial orders of knighthood would 'strengthen their connections with the mother country, by holding up legitimate objects of ambition to public officers and resident gentry'. As colonial secretary, Lord Bathurst had considered the creation of a separate Order for Canada in the 1820s, and his successor, Lord Stanley, took up the idea again in 1844. At the time of Confederation, Lord Monck, then governor-general, urged the giving of titles for life to members of the new upper house and the creation of an Order of St Lawrence; and in 1881 Lord Lorne once more suggested the establishment of a Canadian order to the colonial secretary. In short, during the third quarter of the nineteenth century, the idea that 'the aristocratic element should form a wide ingredient' in colonial government and society was broadly held.[14]

Appropriately enough, these very status-conscious societies were presided over by governors who were by occupation mimetic monarchs and by standing men of high status, like Lord Elgin in Canada, and the

Fitzroy brothers in New Zealand and New South Wales, who were grandsons of the duke of Grafton. Governors were not only powerful politically: as the direct, personal representative of the sovereign, they were at the apex of the colonial social hierarchy, they legitimated and completed it, and they linked it directly and personally to the monarch and the mother country. In more senses than one, they literally ordered society. As the colonial novelist and pundit 'Sam Slick' explained, the governor was 'the fountain of honour and the distributor of patronage and rank', by determining who should (and should not) be invited to Government House.[15] And they were the centre of attention at those ceremonials when society put itself on show. Their arrivals, departures and openings of colonial legislatures were marked with uniforms, parades, processions, salutes, at which the settler community displayed itself in ordered, layered procession. And they presided over local celebrations (or observances) to mark royal birthdays, coronations, jubilees and funerals. The result, Mark Francis notes, was 'an official hierarchical society', in which orders of precedence encompassed every-one, 'from colonial viceroy almost down to a wood-chopper', just as they did in an English county, from the lord-lieutenant to the agricultu-ral labourers.[16]

During the last quarter of the nineteenth century these layered settler societies became – as their supporters in Britain and overseas had hoped – more mature, more differentiated and more elaborate. In Western Australia the speaker of the legislature from 1886 to 1903 was James Lee Steers. His father was a fox-hunting backbench British Tory, who traced his ancestry back to the eleventh century, and he himself maintained impeccable traditions of decorum and gentility strongly (and self-consciously) suggestive of his English country back-ground. In Melbourne, in 1885, J. A. Froude found to his delight a full-blown country house in the Scottish Baronial style, set in its own park, with two real English lords in it, and a son of the house who had a 'face that might have belonged to Sir Launcelot'.[17] It was the same in rural Ontario, where 'the local tradespeople and farmers deferred dutifully to the leadership of a better educated squirearchy, whose mansions, sometimes with ballrooms and chapels of their own, domi-

5. Evening reception at Government House, New South Wales, *c.* 1888.

nated the district'. And these domestic developments towards a more layered and established colonial society were reinforced by the arrival of a new generation of 'gentleman emigrants' from Britain, who were leaving behind another agricultural depression. In Manitoba, Alberta and British Columbia, Edward George Everard ffoulkes, the Hon. F. C. Lascelles and the Hon. Coutts Marjoribanks set themselves up as farmers and ranchers, with all the accoutrements of gentility: fox-hunting, garden parties, cricket and tennis, country houses and family silver and scores of servants.[18]

Froude's reassuring conclusion from visiting Australia was that there was now ample room in the colonies of settlement 'for all sorts and conditions of men', from the top of the British social hierarchy to the bottom, and the result was 'English life all over again: nothing strange, nothing exotic, nothing new or original'.[19] And as these societies became more elaborately differentiated, they also became increasingly articulated and codified. From Melbourne to Toronto, Sydney to Cape Town, gentlemen's clubs, grand hotels, railway stations, public schools, new universities, provincial legislatures and Anglican cathedrals proliferated during the last quarter of the nineteenth century, many of them constructed in Scottish Baronial or Gothic Revival style redolent of history, antiquity, hierarchy and tradition: precisely the things that Thackeray had hoped would exist but had feared did not.[20] On one side of the world this was well illustrated in the Melbourne of the 1890s: where the Victoria gentry still held sway, where social attitudes were class conscious and hierarchical, and where the young Robert Gordon Menzies (of whom more later) was growing up. And the same was true across the Pacific in Vancouver, where a highly Anglophile and self-consciously stratified society developed in the thirty years before the First World War, centring on the exclusive Vancouver Club and the *Social Register*.[21]

This stratification and Gothicization of the dominions was evident in other ways, as essential works of social reference and prestige ranking extended their coverage from the metropolis to the periphery. In 1832 John Burke had produced the fourth edition of his *Genealogical and Heraldic Dictionary of the Peerage and Baronetage of the British Empire*, which had begun with the appropriately hierarchical sentiment

6. The State Opening of Government Buildings, Ottawa, 1868.

that 'the aristocracy of the British Empire, like its other inimitable institutions, exists but as a link in the great chain which connects the community at large'. Yet for all its mention of 'the British Empire', Burke was merely following contemporary usage and referring to the 'four kingdoms' of England, Ireland, Scotland and Wales. By the late nineteenth century, however, this was all to change, as 'the British Empire' came to mean transoceanic dominions, and it was towards these that genealogists now directed their attention. Between 1891 and 1895 Sir Bernard Burke produced two large, ornate volumes, modelled on the British *Peerage* and the *Landed Gentry*, which described and codified the *Colonial Gentry*. The aim was to 'preserve in a convenient and permanent manner the records of the leading families in the Colonies' and 'to show to those at home and abroad the close bonds of kinship that unite the sister colonies to one another and the mother country'.[22]

In these spacious and expensive pages, which yielded nothing in pretence to the metropolitan *Peerage* and the *Landed Gentry*, Burke listed 535 such families. He gave details of their pedigrees, coats of arms and places of residence; and provided the dates and circumstances of their arrival in the colony. Among them were Charles Edward Herbert Orpen of the Cape of Good Hope, whose family 'claims great antiquity'; Sir James George Lee Steers of Jayes, Blackwood, Western Australia, whose ancestry could be traced 'without interruption since the conquest'; Fitzwilliam Wentworth of Vaucluse near Sydney, whose family 'is said by genealogists to have derived its designation in Saxon times'; Richmond Beetham of Christchurch, Canterbury, New Zealand, who claimed descent from King Edward the Elder; and Richard Tyrwhitt of Nantyr, West Gwillimbury, Canada, whose forebears had 'been seated for several centuries in the north of England'. Here was the ultimate reference book for the hierarchical settler society that the British dominions had become: some sprigs of British nobility, others self-established. Most of those included were self-selected, like the family of Lee Steers, 'because they felt they were entitled to be considered in some way superior in birth or breeding to the majority of their contemporaries'.[23]

It was scarcely coincidence that, from the last quarter of the nine-

7. Lord Bledisloe, governor-general of New Zealand, with his wife and staff, 1931.

teenth century, these more differentiated, elaborate and ostentatious colonial hierarchies were completed and perfected by viceregal regimes that were not only of unprecedented splendour and magnificence, but that also thereby mimicked and reflected the unprecedented splendour and magnificence of the newly refurbished British monarchy, as well as the Indian viceroyalty.[24] Canada was confederated in 1867, Australia became a federation in 1900, New Zealand was declared a dominion in 1907, and the Union of South Africa was created in 1910. These new nations were still overwhelmingly British in their social aspirations and cultural values, and they were presided over by governors-general who were more lordly, courtly and aristocratic than anything that had been seen in the empire since the 1800s.[25] The British believed that the 'colonies were not content unless a person of high rank and remarkable distinction was appointed': 'English gentlemen in the fullest sense of the word,' who stood for 'all that is august, stable and sedate in the country'. And there was clearly substantial support for this view overseas. As Sir William McMillan, a well-known Australian conservative, put it in 1902: 'Brilliant young men, belonging to the upper classes in England and, as a rule, taken from the House of Lords', were now being appointed to these posts 'because their position as the apex of our political and social system will be beyond cavil.'[26]

The result was an unprecedented efflorescence of peers as proconsuls: Devonshire and Lansdowne in Canada, Dudley and Denman in Australia, Ranfurly and Bledisloe in New Zealand, Gladstone and Clarendon in South Africa, as well as a host of lesser lords in the Australian states, such as Normanby, Brassey and Hopetoun in Victoria. Marvellously arrayed with plumed hats, ceremonial swords, ribbons and stars, and transported in ostentatious luxury in special trains, they toured their dominions, entertained grandly, made speeches and laid foundation stones. As representatives of the queen–empress and king–emperors, as members of the House of Lords, as landowners in their own right, and as the product of the traditional social order of the British countryside, they were veritable icons of hierarchy: 'high-minded Christian gentlemen' with the 'charm of a typical aristocrat of the old country'.[27] And they lived an appropriately lordly and viceregal style. 'Everything is done,' observed a visitor to Lord Carrington when he was merely governor of New South Wales, 'just as it would be in a great country house in England so that it is impossible to realize one is not in England.' And that was precisely the point. In their rank, their titles and their social lustre, these plumaged figures sent out from the imperial metropolis served to incorporate individual colonial hierarchies into the collective hierarchy of empire. As Edward Hamilton observed, 'big colonies . . . like English noblemen . . . [they] have rather snob-like tendencies'.[28]

Meanwhile, the gentlemen emigrants continued to emigrate, especially after the First World War, which witnessed the unprecedented slaughter of older and younger sons, and also the avalanche of estate sales that followed.[29] The result was that during the 1920s and 1930s a new generation of disaffected patricians, who were further alienated from the mass urban democracy of Britain, sought to re-create their leisured, landed, privileged lives in the White Highlands of Kenya, just as their predecessors had done in Australia and Canada. Men like Lords Delamere, Cranworth and Erroll, Lord Francis Scott, Sir Ferdinand Cavendish-Bentinck and Sir Jock Delves Broughton acquired large holdings of land, built great houses, installed the family paintings and silver, and treated their coloured labourers in the same way that their forebears had treated their servants back home. As Lord Delamere's biographer notes, 'the feudal system was in his bones and blood, and he believed all his life in its fundamental rightness'; and it was this system that he and others sought to perpetuate and preserve in the empire. Appropriately enough, they found their celebrant and apologist in the young Evelyn Waugh, who acclaimed their efforts 'to transplant and perpetuate a habit of life traditional to themselves which England has ceased to accommodate – the traditional life of the English squirearchy'.[30]

In 1873 Anthony Trollope had contrasted the social structure of Britain, which he thought to be traditional-hierarchical, with that of the United States, which he considered democratic-egalitarian. And from this starting point, he concluded (with relief) that 'the colonies are rather a repetition of England than an imitation of America'.[31] In this he was generally correct, and the observation continued to hold good for the next half century and more, even beyond the inter-war years. Gentlemen emigrants, combined with colonial aspirants, and topped off with proconsular regimes of signal grandeur, meant that the dominions of settlement (and settlers' Kenya) were far more traditionalist in their attitudes than were the United States of America. *They* had had their anti-royal, anti-title, anti-hierarchy revolution in 1776; the dominions desired no such rupture. They might be moving towards greater democracy and political freedom, but socially, culturally and, significantly, economically, they remained in thrall to a certain vision of the mother country: to what Geoffrey Bolton has called 'the titles, the veneration of landed estates, the hierarchical attitudes, the myth of gracious living'. They did not want to be egalitarian-American; they preferred 'imitation and deference', and were proud and happy to keep their social distinctions, their viceregal courts, and thus to remain part of traditional, Greater Britain.[32]

4

India

In social terms, the British colonies of settlement were about the export of hierarchy; India, by contrast, was much more about the analogues of hierarchy. Or, rather, it *became* increasingly about them in the second half of the nineteenth century. After the Mutiny of 1857, the Bentinck–Macaulay–Dalhousie policy (and stereotype) of overturning the corrupt, despotic, ruling regimes that they had believed India to be was largely given up. This was replaced by the alternative policy (and the alternative stereotype) that regarded the established order much more favourably, and as something that ought to be promoted and preserved. 'Traditional', 'timeless' and 'unchanging' South Asia now became an object to cherish rather than to criticize: 'once the target of reformers, India had now become the hope of reactionaries'.[1] But India was a large and complex country – an entire subcontinent populated by teeming millions embracing two powerful and competing religions. There were territories directly administered by the British, which were ruled from Calcutta (and later from New Delhi), and there were between five and six hundred autonomous princely states, which constituted roughly one third of the subcontinent. How, in the decades after the Mutiny, did the British re-envisage (and re-establish) this most resonant and romantic part of their empire, 'ordering into a single hierarchy all its subjects, Indian and British alike'?[2]

One way in which they did so was by giving more attention to the concepts and categories of caste. During the closing decades of the rule of the East India Company, the Brahmanic theory of caste had become more rigidified, and its influence spread into areas ranging from the ritual practices of South Indian temples to the honours system of Indian princes. As such, and further instrumentalized by the courts, caste penetrated deep into South Asian society, restructuring the relations of public worship, physical mobility, marriage and inheritance. The result was an immobile, status-bound, increasingly inclusive vision of the Indian social order, which in the second half of the nineteenth century became even more attractive to the British than in the years of the Company. Beginning with 'their own forms of knowledge and thinking', they came to look upon caste as 'the essential feature of the Indian social system', as the analogue to their own carefully ranked domestic status hierarchy, which seemed to make Indian society familiar. By 1901 caste was used in the Indian census as the equivalent to the social categories used in Britain.[3] Thus regarded, India seemed to the British to be an integrated and coherent hierarchy, with an 'accepted order of social precedence' that they could grasp and understand. 'Under British rule,' Susan Bayly notes, 'more of the subcontinent's peoples than ever before found themselves drawn or coerced into the schemes of ritualized social hierarchy which are now regarded as key characteristics of caste society.'[4]

Caste, and the censuses making caste 'official', gave the British an aggregative overview of Indian society as layered and traditional. But the particular, localized form that this society took was the 'village community'. In tandem with the rise of caste, the cult of the country settlement was developing during the last decades of the East India Company, and it too reached its climax during the second half of the nineteenth century, when writers such as Sir Henry Maine, Sir William Wilson Hunter and Sir Alfred Lyall, taking up and embellishing the commonplace view, praised the Indian village as 'ancient', 'organic', 'complex' and built on unwritten custom. These 'healthy agricultural communities' were the essence of 'the existing social and economic order', and as such they constituted the primordial unit of 'real', 'traditional' and 'timeless' India.[5] As a microcosm of Indian society, they were by definition hierarchical: 'in every village', Philip Mason recalls, 'there would be people who owed someone else allegiance . . . everyone you spoke to in a village fitted somewhere into this pattern'. This vision – the very image of India that Kipling and other writers evoked, celebrated and popularized – was not only intrinsically appealing to the British and a key component of their views of Indian society; its era of greatest popularity occurred at exactly the same time as the growing cult of the village in the imperial metropolis came to embody the very essence of 'Englishness'. This was not coincidence: once again, it was analogical sociology at work.[6]

It was atop this layered, Burkeian, agrarian image of Indian society that the British constructed a system of government that was simultaneously direct and indirect, authoritarian and collaborationist, but that always took for granted the reinforcement and preservation of tradition and hierarchy. The imperial presence, in the two thirds of the country directly ruled, took the form of a fixed official order. As Kipling himself once observed, mules, horses and elephants obeyed their drivers, who in turn obeyed their sergeants, who obeyed their lieutenants, who obeyed their captains, who obeyed their majors, who obeyed their colonels, who obeyed their brigadiers, who obeyed their generals, who obeyed their viceroy. And what was true of the military was no less true of civilians. They were in a parallel chain that tied together the Indian Civil Service, and that extended from the district officer of the village, to the governor of the province, and finally to the viceroy of all India. Throughout the Raj, protocol was strictly governed by the 'warrant of precedence', which in 1881 consisted of seventy-seven ranks, and which gave essential advice as to whether the government astronomer in Madras was of higher standing than the superintendent of the Royal Botanical Gardens in Calcutta. Everywhere in British India, social rank depended on official position. These were, as one of Paul Scott's characters observes, the 'rigid levels of hierarchy' for which the Raj was renowned. 'British India,' Philip Mason rightly recalls, 'was as much infected by caste as Indian India.'[7]

When it came to the implementation of justice and the collection of revenue, the Raj needed dependable allies, and they were chosen on the assumption that the preferred model of metropolitan society could be applied to India and analogized back. For just as British local government had always depended on the resident aristocracy and gentry, so their chosen partners in South Asia were the 'natural leaders': large landowners, men of 'property and rank', of 'power and importance', who 'exercised great influence' in rural society. As the British saw them, Indian landlords were to fulfil the assigned role of English notables, because they possessed traditional status and authority in the localities that made their participation in the imperial enterprise both valuable and reliable.[8] The Talukdars in the United Provinces, with their landed estates, or the Pirs of Sind, wielding religious, social and economic influence, were significant examples – the sort of people Philip Mason revealingly calls 'landowners *because that is the nearest English equivalent'*. And this was the abiding British image of South Asia until the end: gentry leaders of a caste-bound society. When governor of the United Provinces in the late 1920s, Sir Malcolm Hailey likened the zemindars to the British aristocracy and supported them on this basis, hoping that each might 'create for himself the position which was once occupied by the old-fashioned squire in English village life'.[9]

The remaining third of India consisted of the princely states, those 500-odd personal fiefdoms ruled over by rajas and maharajas, nawabs and nizams, which after 1857 were no longer reviled as alien and corrupt, but acclaimed as familiar and traditional. 'The policy of suppressing, or suffering to go to ruin, all the aristocracy and gentry of India, is a mistake,' opined Sir Charles Wood, the secretary of state for India in the aftermath of the Mutiny. During his period of office, it was put promptly into reverse, as criticism was replaced by celebration, disruption by preservation.[10] Hence Queen Victoria's proclamation of November 1858, which undertook on behalf of the imperial government to 'respect the rights, dignity and honour of native princes as our own', because they were the quintessential 'natural leaders' of South Asian society. They were to be attached directly to the British crown; there were to be no further annexations; and they were reassured that on the failure of natural heirs, the adoption of a successor would be recognized.[11] The result, as David Washbrook explains, was that 'in social terms' the British Raj was now 'happiest dealing with what it conceived to be a feudal social order . . . of inherited social hierarchy'.[12]

Put more positively, this meant the British resolved to rule one third of India indirectly through the princes, and through the 'deeply rooted hierarchical social structure' of which they were both the expression and the apogee.[13] As nominally autonomous 'native states', they administered themselves under British paramountcy, with residents from the Indian Political Service assigned to them as advisers. They were outside the government of India's tax base; their autocratic character insulated them from nationalist agitation; and they contributed substantially to the Indian Army. They were carefully ranked and ordered, they were obsessed with protocol and the number of guns they received in salute, and they delighted in 'flamboyant assertions of ritual sovereignty and extravagant contests for symbolic precedence'.[14] They seemed, then, just like the British aristocracy and gentry; and so it was scarcely surprising that in 1893 and 1900 Sir Roper Lethbridge published his two editions of *The Golden Book of India: A Genealogical and Biographical Dictionary of the Ruling Princes, Chiefs, Nobles and Other Personages, Titled or Decorated, of the Indian Empire*. Appropriately enough, the author was a Devon country gentleman, who had served in the Bengal Education Service earlier in his career and been Conservative MP for North Kensington between 1885 and 1892. He dedicated this work to 'Her Most Gracious Majesty Victoria, Queen Empress of India', and the result, according to *The Times*, was 'probably destined to take rank as the recognized *Peerage of India*'.[15]

This view of the 'basic structures of Indian society', as caste-ridden, village-living and princely-led, became the conventional British wisdom in the decades immediately after the Mutiny, and as the last quarter of the nineteenth century opened, it was more deliberately encouraged and energetically projected.[16] Here, as so often was the case with the hierarchical flowering and Gothic efflorescence of empire, Benjamin Disraeli was a crucial figure. For it was he who, as prime minister, passed the Imperial Titles Act in 1876, which declared Queen Victoria to be empress of India. This audacious appropriation consolidated and completed the British–Indian hierarchy, as the queen herself replaced the defunct Mughal emperor at the summit of the social order: she was now an eastern potentate as well as a western sovereign. As a result, and following the precedent and example of the Irish viceroyalty in Dublin, the position of her representative was ceremonially inflated and extravagantly enhanced. Thereafter, all Indian viceroys would be peers, and their courtly regimes in Calcutta and at Simla, which in turn provided the models for the governors-general of the great dominions, would far surpass anything to be seen at Buckingham Palace or Windsor Castle, where, as Lady Reading noted, things were 'simple in comparison' with all this 'show and glitter'.[17]

The first climax of what J. P. Waghorne calls this new 'culture of ornamentation' was the proclamation of the queen as empress of India by the viceroy, Lord Lytton, at the great durbar (or 'imperial assemblage') of 1877. As the son of the novelist who had Gothicized Knebworth House in Hertfordshire, Lytton was the ideal impresario for this Disraelian extravaganza. After much planning, he selected an historic site just outside Delhi, the old Mughal capital, constructed a temporary city of tents and canvas, and within a purpose-built amphitheatre, decorated with banners, coats of arms and 'bits of bunting', staged a spectacular display of pageantry, rulership and homage, which made 'manifest and compelling the sociology of India' and which was mimicked and replicated throughout the country. From one perspective, this represented the successful appropriation of the indigenous, South Asian symbolic form of the durbar, or ceremonial meeting between rulers and ruled, which articulated the traditional social order and legitimated the position of the queen–empress at the head of it. But it was also an improvised, pseudo-medieval spectacular of rank and inequality, which indicated that the British were developing in India 'a more closely defined honorific hierarchy' and increasingly projecting an image of their South Asian empire as a 'feudal order'. Appropriately enough, special emphasis was placed upon the role of the ruling princes, who were hailed and presented as the 'native aristocracy of the country', and 'whose sympathy and cordial allegiance' was regarded as 'no inconsiderable guarantee for the stability of the Indian Empire'.[18]

Thereafter, their cultivation as the most favoured (and most ornamental) side of the Raj continued apace, as the traditional rituals of princely installation, local durbars and municipal addresses, which were invariably attended by senior proconsuls and sometimes even by the viceroy himself, moved into much higher gear.[19] With their confidence (and their incomes) increased, many princes spent fortunes

8. The Procession of the Princes at the 1903 Delhi Durbar.

building new–old palaces in 'Indo-Saracenic' style, such as Lakshmi Vilas Palace in Baroda, designed by Major Charles Mant and Robert Fellowes Chisholm, and the Lallgarh Palace at Bikaner, for which Samuel Swinton Jacob was the architect. These were flamboyant confections, with turrets, domes, pavilions and towers, atavistic in their cultural resonances, and redolent of continuity, order and tradition.[20] As a viceroy with a strong sense of history and hierarchy, Lord Curzon was especially well disposed to the ruling princes, those 'colleagues and partners' who, 'amid the levelling tendencies of the age', kept 'alive the traditions and customs, sustain[ed] the virility, and save[d] from extinction, the picturesqueness of ancient and noble races'. At his durbar of 1903, for the King–Emperor Edward VII, which far surpassed Lord Lytton's in splendour and magnificence, Curzon gave the princes a much more active role than they had enjoyed in 1877. As participants, paying homage to the king–emperor in an amphitheatre specially designed in the Indo-Saracenic style by Swinton Jacob, they were no longer merely 'architectural adornments of the imperial edifice', but were regarded by the viceroy as 'pillars that help to sustain the main roof'.[21]

This was an apt metaphor, for the British were as busy in their building at this time as the Indian princes. And in the main, they did so in the same style: Indo-Saracenic which, in its exuberant asymmetries and its aura of instant antiquity, was very much the spirit and values of the Gothic Revival transported to India. Just as the maharajas' palaces were orientalized versions of Eaton Hall or Cardiff or Arundel or Windsor Castles, so the Victoria Terminus at Bombay, the High Court at Hyderabad and the University at Madras were extravagant extensions or reworkings of similar buildings in London or Toronto or Melbourne.[22] In India, as elsewhere in the empire, private palaces and public buildings, however recently constructed, projected a similar vision of imperial society as unified, venerable, time-honoured and hierarchical. Sometimes this was literally so, as in the case of the Gothic clock tower of Bombay University, which housed twenty-four statues representing the castes of western India. And this common image was not only articulated by the same architecture, but also by the same architects: by men like Henry Irwin, who designed the Viceregal Lodge

9. The maharaja of Mysore's palace at Bangalore.

10. The Viceregal Lodge at Simla.

at Simla and the Madras Law Courts, and also the Amba Vilas Palace for the fabulously rich maharaja of Mysore.[23] Here was powerful visual evidence of the shared commitment of the Raj and the princes to hierarchy and order and antiquity and tradition, as well as of the former's inclination to treat the latter as social equals.

These cumulatively conservative developments – sociological, political, ceremonial and architectural – are well illustrated in the case of the maharajas of Jaipur, Ram Singh (1851–80) and Madho Singh (1880–1922), both rich and both regarded by the British as model princes. During the last two decades of his rule, Ram Singh established a college, a school of art, a public library, a hospital (named after Lord Mayo, the assassinated viceroy) and laid out a public garden. He also built a gasworks, provided piped water in the city, invested in irrigation and road-building projects, and initiated the washing of Jaipur's buildings, which gained it the title of the Pink City. But the centrepiece of these projects was a museum called the Albert Hall, in honour of the prince of Wales, which was constructed in elaborate Indo-Saracenic style from designs by Swinton Jacob. In the next generation Madho Singh was, like his predecessor, a Hindu and a conservative who prided himself on his loyalty to the British and on his reputation as a 'progressive' ruler. In order to accommodate his many visitors, he built a European guest house and a ceremonial reception hall in the outer courtyard of his city palace, both again designed by Swinton Jacob, who was employed in Jaipur for the best part of half a century.[24]

This image of India protected and projected by the Raj – glittering and ceremonial, layered and traditional, princely and rural, Gothic and Indo-Saracenic – reached what has rightly been called its 'elaborative zenith' at the Coronation Durbar of 1911 when, at his own insistence, the King–Emperor George V appeared in person with a newly made imperial crown, thereby surpassing even Curzon's extravaganza of 1903.[25] The planning was exceptionally elaborate and, as Kenneth Rose notes, 'students of the viceregal correspondence which passed between Calcutta and London throughout 1911 might suppose that the British Raj depended less on justice and good administration than on precedence, honours and minute distinctions of dress'. So they might: for so, in many ways, it did. The king and queen duly arrived

11. King George V and Queen Mary leaving the Durbar throne
after their imperial coronation, 1911.

12. King George V and Queen Mary at the Gateway of India, 1911.

at Bombay in December, where their landing was commemorated by the Gateway of India, one of the last Indo-Saracenic creations of the Raj. They journeyed to Delhi, where a canvas city had been constructed, accommodating people in strict order of social precedence, along with pavilions, a reviewing ground and an amphitheatre; and there they resided, among princes, governors, heralds, troops and escorts, and two hundred thousand visitors. They made their formal state entry in a five-mile long procession, and they later appeared in full coronation finery to receive the homage of the princes. It was, the king recalled with rare effusiveness, 'the most beautiful and wonderful sight I ever saw'.[26]

Thus cultivated and encouraged, the nawabs and the maharajas gave generously to the imperial war effort in terms of money and men, and in 1918 they were probably at the peak of their power and prestige. The king–emperor reaffirmed the 'inviolate and inviolable' commitment of his grandmother, describing the ruling princes as those 'whose existence and security is so closely bound up with that of the British Empire'. In the same way, senior administrators, such as Sir Harcourt Butler and Sir Malcolm Hailey, acclaimed them as the embodiment of 'the sacred fires of an age-long tradition'.[27] Throughout the 1920s and 1930s the British aimed to 'call in the old world to balance the new' by utilizing them as a counterpoise to the urban nationalists of the Congress Party. They were given their own separate chamber that was inaugurated (with appropriate pomp and ceremonial) in 1921, and they were offered a major part in the federal structure proposed under the Government of India Act of 1935. They had never been so rich, they spent fortunes on palaces and jewellery, and (in more enlightened cases) on their subjects' welfare: pearls and rubies from Cartier in Paris and London, and hospitals and universities in Hyderabad. Far from being the bearers and wearers of hollow crowns, they were still regarded by the British as 'the natural leaders of Indian society'.[28]

Consider, in this regard (as Paul Scott might have said), Mysore, which the British looked on as one of the 'model states' of princely India, responsibly run on progressive lines. By the inter-war years, the maharajas of Mysore were second only to the nizams of Hyderabad in terms of wealth, with an income in excess of two million pounds a year, some of which was spent on the construction of the Lalit Mahal Palace, an extraordinary architectural fantasy just outside Mysore city, modelled on St Paul's Cathedral in London. But the maharajas were also generous to their subjects, founding and funding hospitals, schools, medical colleges and universities, and vigorously promoting the beautification of Mysore and Bangalore cities. They pioneered the provision of electricity (Bangalore was thus illuminated before Calcutta and Bombay) and promoted representative assemblies.[29] At the same time, they continued to function as the centre and cynosure of the ceremonial life of their state. Every year, during the Dasara Durbar, the city of Mysore put itself on show, with a formal gathering and homage at the Amba Vilas Palace, followed by a magnificent procession, complete with flags, arches, bands, troops, standards, palanquins and caparisoned elephants, with the maharaja and his family clad in their most gorgeous costumes, and with the British residents keeping a discreet distance. Between 1934 and 1945 these proceedings were vividly preserved in a series of murals in Amba Vilas Palace, and the rituals they recorded continued beyond the Second World War.[30]

Meanwhile, the Raj continued no less ostentatiously ornamental. As so often in India, it was the British buildings that sent out this message most clearly, especially the newly created capital of New Delhi, the construction of which George V had announced and authorized at the 1911 durbar. For, as conceived by Baker and Lutyens, it embodied the British sociology of India and its obsession with what Philip Davies calls 'hierarchy, status and rank' as accurately as, and more permanently than, the ordered and ritualized choreography of the three great durbars. The Viceroy's House was a ducal domain-cum-country house-cum-princely palace, measuring six hundred feet from end to end, and one hundred and eighty feet to the top of the dome of the Durbar Hall.[31] There were great residences for the ruling princes that mimicked Mayfair and Park Lane and Piccadilly, just as their Indo-Saracenic palaces in the countryside mimicked Whig mansions. And the houses of the British officials were clustered in 'physical and spatial forms' that reflected and reinforced the 'deferential social hierarchy' of the Raj: a bungalow for a gazetted officer being altogether superior in size and location to that of a Class I Married European Clerk. Truly, New Delhi was a city for the Raj: much liked by its greatest supporters, the civil service and the princes. Not for nothing was Lutyens married to Lord Lytton's daughter; and in synthesizing the architectural styles of east and west in a post Indo-Saracenic mode, he produced a monument to imperial hierarchy and social order that was, in Robert Byron's phrase, 'a slap in the face of the modern average man'.[32]

Of course, inter-war India was in some ways a changing place, as political reforms brought the 'Indianization' of the civil service and the beginnings of democracy, and as society became more secular and the towns more industrial. But for the British, modernized India never attained the allure of the traditional India of the maharajas and the Raj, of what Bernard S. Cohn called 'order, deference and hierarchy'. This, for the British, remained the real, unchanging, timeless India. So, when Lord Halifax paid viceregal visits to ruling princes, he yielded nothing in magnificence to Lord Curzon, travelling in a special white official train of twelve coaches that was more splendid than that of the emperor of Russia, and with a guard of honour standing stiffly to attention all along the line.[33] In the hands of such prestige-conscious viceroys as Lords Willingdon and Linlithgow, New Delhi was the setting for the grandest living on earth, with more bowing and curtseying, more precedence and protocol, than anywhere else in the empire, London included. At its peak in the 1930s Viceroy's House employed a staff of six thousand servants, and they were as carefully graded and ranked below stairs as the officialdom and princes of the Raj were above. And this ordered and ornamented regime was still mimicked (and competed with) throughout both princely and official India. The future King Edward VIII once remarked that he had never known what authentic regal pomp really meant until he had stayed with Lord Lloyd. And Lloyd was not the viceroy but merely the governor of Bombay![34]

For the British in India, and for their friends, allies and collaborators, hierarchy was indeed 'the axis around which everything turned'. The same could, of course, be said of Britain, and this was scarcely coincidence. Perhaps that was why India exercised such an appeal for so long to the romantic, Disraelian side of the British imagination. As the late nineteenth century drew on into the early twentieth, and again in the unstable inter-war years, India's was a hierarchy that became the more alluring because it seemed to represent an ordering of society – based on what Lord Lytton called 'birth, rank and hereditary influence' – that perpetuated overseas something important that was increasingly under threat in Britain. As Francis Hutchins observes, 'India seemed to offer the prospect of aristocratic security at a time when England [*sic*] itself was falling prey to democratic vulgarity.'[35] As such, this contemporary vision of 'timeless' India also represented Britain's better (but vanishing) past to itself, and seemed to hold out the prospect that this treasured yet threatened society still had a future overseas. 'The India of the Raj', Thomas Metcalf notes, 'stood forth as a model, not only for the empire, but for Britain itself.' The interests of those within metropolitan society who were dissatisfied with their own industrial-urban-democratic order were better served by what they regarded as the splendid, traditional hierarchies that still flourished east of Suez.[36]

5

Colonies

By the time the British came to annex large parts of Africa and of Asia beyond India during the last quarter of the nineteenth century, and to administer them in the years down to the Second World War, the impulses towards an integrated, hierarchical empire were everywhere at their zenith, surpassing in their range and their reach the many precedents set in the era of Pitt and Wellesley a century before. In some ways that were different, but in others that were similar, the dominions of settlement and the Indian Empire were seen as replicating and reinforcing the layered, time-hallowed social order of the metropolis. Proconsuls like Lansdowne, Dufferin and Minto moved back and forth from Canada to India, taking their plumes and their feathers with them; young Indian princes were sent to British public schools, and their parents fêted by British aristocrats; and colonial gentry in the settler dominions sent their sons to Oxford and Cambridge, and were themselves presented at court.[1] In the dominions and in India, proconsular splendour and layered societies were the conventional Burkeian wisdoms and customary conservative modes; and as the 'Scramble for Africa' (and parts of Asia) began, there were soon signs they would be followed and replicated in the new tropical empire that was rapidly being acquired.

Since the British would govern these colonies but (in the main) not settle them, the princely states of the Indian Empire provided a more immediately applicable model than the great dominions, both in terms of how these native societies were regarded, and in terms of how they should be administered. Collaboration, rather than marginalization, was to be the prevailing mode of management. Respect for traditional tribal structures and support for those rulers who headed them were early on established as the ways to appreciate and to govern this new imperium. One indication of this was in Malaya, where the Pangkor Treaty of 1874 was the first in a series negotiated by the British in the years before 1914. In each case, the sultans of the protected Malay states accepted British residents, or advisers, on the Indian pattern. These agreements confirmed the sovereignty of the Malay rulers and stressed the monarchical nature of their regimes, while obliging them to follow the advice of the British residents in all matters save religion and custom. The residents helped the sultans improve their finances and elevated their authority over lesser chiefs. These arrangements (which were extended to Brunei in 1905 to 1906) remained essentially unaltered until the Japanese invasion in 1941.[2]

In the same year that the Malay rulers accepted British residents, the British annexed Fiji, and the Hon. Arthur Hamilton Gordon was installed as governor. He negotiated a treaty with King Cakobau, which protected Fijian lands from the sort of dispossession that had taken place in Australia and New Zealand, and which codified chiefly authority and entrenched aristocracy as the established order through which the British would govern indirectly. Gordon was the younger son of the earl of Aberdeen (we have already met him urging the need to replicate the full British social order in Canada), and he had no doubt that he was dealing with people of his own social level. He learned Fijian so he could address the chiefs in their own language, and he regarded the purpose of British control as one of safeguarding the traditional social order and preserving the traditional way of life.[3] Gordon's wife was of the same opinion. She thought the native, high-ranking Fijians 'such an undoubted aristocracy'. 'Their manners,' she continued, 'are so perfectly easy and well bred . . . Nurse can't understand it at all, she looks down on them as an inferior race. I don't like to tell her that these ladies are my equals, which she is not!' Later in his career, Gordon became governor of Ceylon, where he carried out the same policies, treating the high-born members of the island's Goyigma caste as 'traditional' aristocracy, whom he vested with power as paramount chiefs. Again, he sought 'to preserve, as long as possible,

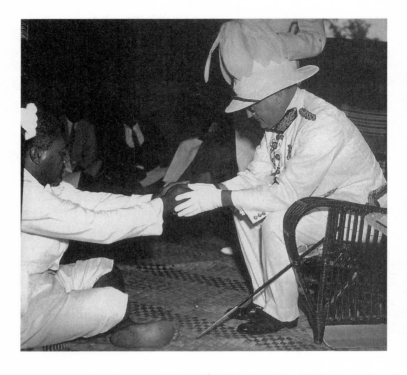

13. King Cakobau III doing homage to the governor of Fiji, 1953.

a system which enlists all natural local influences in support of authority'.[4]

As the pace of the scramble for Africa accelerated, this mode of administration, relying on indigenous hierarchies, and cultivating and supporting the native rulers at the top of them, became the obvious way for the British to govern the vast new areas of land they were suddenly acquiring – in a fit of absence of resources, if not necessarily of absence of mind. In West Africa, Sir George Goldie believed that 'the general policy of ruling through native rulers on African principles must be followed'. 'A great chief,' as Claude Macdonald, the governor of Lagos, put it in 1904, 'is a very valuable possession; his authority is an instrument of the greatest public utility, which it is most desirable to retain in full force.'[5] In the Sudan, the Anglo-Egyptian administration established after 1898 looked to the Indian princely states and the Malayan residents system for precedents, and soon began 'to support the sultans and sheikhs in their dealings with their own subjects'. In Kenya, local government through the chiefs was established between 1901 and 1912, especially among the Kikuyu. In Uganda, the chiefs and regents of Buganda continued to govern, subject to their traditional sovereign, the kabaka, and the British ruled through him and through them. And a similar system operated in southern Africa, where Bechuanaland, Basutoland and Swaziland were governed indirectly by the British through kings, chiefs and tribes.[6]

If Joseph Chamberlain had had his way during his years as colonial secretary (1895–1903), the traditional policies that had emerged in Malaya and Fiji, and that were now being replicated across British Africa, would have been put abruptly into reverse. He might now be the Unionist colleague of Salisbury and Balfour, but in some ways Chamberlain remained the radical hater of hierarchy he had been as Birmingham's mayor and a Liberal MP. Like an earlier generation of reformers in India, he wanted to intervene aggressively in the new colonies that were his responsibility, and to overthrow the indigenous rulers because they were unequal to the tasks of modernization and development that he wished to carry out.[7] But this policy was neither popular nor permanent. There was African resistance to such disruptive intervention, as with the Sierra Leone rebellion of 1897 to 1898. In an era when revelations of malpractices in the Belgian Congo were raising humanitarian consciousness, there was also public disquiet. And there was resistance to such radical interventions on the part of the Colonial Office staff. Accordingly, Chamberlain's policy was put into reverse, and the colonial secretary recognized that 'the agency of the native chiefs' was to be relied upon in future: reform would be given up, discontent would be avoided, African consent would be secured, and government would be through indigenous hierarchies. 'No pains,' Chamberlain observed of the Malayan sultans in words that became equally applicable to African chiefs, 'should be spared to safeguard the position and dignity of Native Rulers.'[8]

It was in this context that the preservation of traditional local rulers and native society became accepted after 1900 as the preferred technique of management in Britain's new colonial empire. There was nothing original about it: but Lord Lugard's implementation of 'indirect rule' in Nigeria (which owed something to the Indian princely states, and something to the residential system in Malaya) was soon acknowledged as the most important and influential example in British Africa.[9] From 1900 to 1906 he was high commissioner of Northern Nigeria, a vast area that he had to administer with a small staff and a limited budget. But he was enthralled by the splendour of the Muslim ruling chiefs, and impressed by the order and efficiency of their administrations. So he resolved 'to retain the native authority and to work through and by the native emirs', with British residents duly installed to advise them. But he always insisted that 'native chiefs have clearly defined duties and an acknowledged status, *equally* with the British officials'. Lugard later returned to Nigeria as governor-general, and between 1912 and 1918 he oversaw the extension of indirect rule to the southern and western regions of the colony. The proconsul then turned propagandist, and *The Dual Mandate*, which he published in 1922, made the case that indirect rule was, according to Margery Perham, 'the most comprehensive, coherent and renowned system of administration' in British imperial history.[10]

In the inter-war years Lugard's model, or what was thought to be his model, came to be regarded as by 'far the most significant movement

14. The king of the Asante and the governor of the Gold Coast, 1935.

now proceeding in our colonial Empire'. It was adopted widely throughout colonial Africa: the cultivation of traditional societies 'whose hierarchies could be harnessed to serve British ends'. In the early 1920s a concerted effort was made in the Northern Sudan to establish rule through tribal chiefs, Arab sheikhs whom it was thought resembled those in Northern Nigeria. And at the end of the decade Sir John Maffey, who had previously served with the Government of India's Political Department, introduced it into parts of the Southern Sudan as well.[11] In the former German colony of Tanganyika, which Britain now held as a League of Nations Mandate, Lugard's protégé, Sir Donald Cameron, superseded the German system of direct rule by 'restoring the old tribal organization' that he supposed had previously existed, and that he also hoped would act as a countervailing force to the white settlers in Kenya.[12] In the Gold Coast, indirect rule was codified and extended during the inter-war years: the king of the Asante, whose forebear had been exiled by the British in 1896, was allowed home in 1924, and in 1935 his successor was installed as head of an extensive confederation. And in Northern Rhodesia, which was taken over from the British South Africa Company in 1924, the same system was subsequently implemented by Sir James Maxwell.[13]

What did the end result look like? The colonial empire never rivalled the dizzy, caparisoned splendours of the Raj, since Malayan sultans, Nigerian emirs and African kings rarely ruled over societies that were as venerable, as settled, as ornamental or as rich as the grandest princely states seemed to be. But traditional India remained the model, which meant that this new empire of indirect rule depended on the cooperation and support of kings who were presumed to be at the apex of 'a clearly defined hierarchical society'.[14] As a result, chiefs and emirs and sultans were treated with great shows of public respect by British officials, especially on such ceremonial occasions as installations, coronations, investitures, birthdays and jubilees. In Malaya, after federation, the ruling sultans held a durbar every two years, travelling in style by yacht or train or elephant, bringing with them large retinues and participating in grand ceremonials before large crowds. Across the Indian Ocean at Budo in Uganda, the British built a public school, just before the First World War, for the education of local rulers and notables. They sited it on the Coronation Hill of the Bugandan kings, and thereafter coronation services took place in the college chapel, combining British and African ceremonial elements. At the school's golden jubilee festivities, pride of place was given to the 'four kings at high table'.[15]

As in India, indigenous royal splendour was matched by imported proconsular pomp. A British governor was the direct representative of the imperial sovereign, as well as the chief executive officer of the colony. As such, he was a potent and impressive figure, an image memorably captured and vividly conveyed in John Singer Sargent's swagger portrait of the Malayan proconsul, Sir Frank Swettenham. He might not aspire to the courtly grandeur and regal magnificence associated with the viceroys of India or the governors-general of the great dominions, but he was entitled to a salute of seventeen guns, and he lived in appropriate splendour at Government House, where protocol and precedence, bowing and curtseying, mattered a great deal, and where he was surrounded by entourages of ADCs and retinues of servants.[16] Margery Perham, who was a regular visitor to British Africa during the inter- and post-war years, and a punctilious observer of proconsular etiquette, loved all this 'pomp and imperial circumstance'. When staying in 1948 at the Palace, the official residence of the governor-general of the Sudan at Khartoum, she felt a sudden spasm of affection for 'the house, the servants, the troops, the ceremonial, the statues of Gordon and Kitchener'. Even in the 1950s British proconsuls remained impressive (sometimes, even, flamboyant) figures. Among them was Sir Edward Twining in Tanganyika: tall, fiercely royal and an ardent student (and inventor) of ceremonial, his biography was appropriately entitled *A Gust of Plumes*.[17]

These proconsuls were very grand: at the annual dinners in London of the Corona Club, founded in 1901 for high-ranking officers of the colonial service, governors and former governors occupied the top table 'in all their dazzling splendour', 'begartered and bemedalled' and 'festooned with colourful decorations'.[18] But they were also the apex of an elaborate local social hierarchy, which (as in India) reached upwards to the British monarch in London, and downwards to the smallest provincial village. It was a complex, many-layered structure, as paramount kings were directly responsible to the governor-general, and beneath them were often many levels of subordinate chiefly authority. This almost Kiplingesque sense of the imperial chain of being is well caught in a contemporary account of the Pathfinder Scouts of Northern Rhodesia, who were all members of the Bantu tribe, and who were described as 'loyal to the King, to the King's representative in Northern Rhodesia, to his Chief, and Tribal Elders, to his officers, and those under him'. It was the same in Tanganyika after Cameron had done his work: 'the peasant', hitherto isolated, was 'now linked up to his Headman, the Headman to the Sub-Chief, the Sub-Chief to the Chief, and the Chief to the District Office'. And from there, the chain of connection was clear: the district officer was linked to the governor, and he was linked to the king.[19]

Of course, there were variations across the colonies in the exact mode and extent of indirect rule, and in the nature of the local hierarchies through which this rule was exercised. But the general picture is clear. Or at least it was clear to the members of the British Colonial Service. For, however different their social backgrounds, the governors, residents and district commissioners sent out from Britain shared a similar social vision of their homeland, which they thought they had found reproduced and confirmed in Africa. Their preferred society was paternalistic, hierarchical and rural, with individual layers and gradations of status, such as survived in Britain on great landed estates, although even there it was being eroded.[20] One of the greatest colonial governors, Sir Hugh Clifford, never forgot being taken, as a child in the late 1870s, around the farms and cottages of his cousin, Lord Clifford, at Ugbrooke Park in Devon: 'It seemed to me,' he recalled, 'as though I had suddenly become part of a great family and congregation.' He thought it was 'a nearly perfect social organization', and in his years of colonial service he hoped to identify and to nurture similar social structures abroad. There was about all this what has been called a 'fundamental Burkeian conservatism' – a sense of natural rightness and rootedness of traditional structures and slowly evolving institutions, and an 'easy understanding of the position of indigenous elites by analogy with their own'.[21]

But it was not just that societies found overseas seemed to resemble society as it existed in Britain, as (in Clifford's case in Malaya) 'castle and cottage became court and *kampong*'.[22] For it seemed to the more romantic imperialists that society overseas was (like the Indian villages and princely states) actually *better* – purer, more stable, more paternal, less corrupted. As the metropolis became ever more urbanized, industrialized and democratized, and as its social fabric correspondingly decayed, these faraway societies, with their traditional hierarchies still intact, not only became more appealing, they also needed protecting from the very same forces of modernity that were destroying traditional Britain. Such were the views of Charles Temple, a resident in Northern Nigeria before the First World War, and the son of Sir Richard Temple, the governor of Bombay. He 'admired aristocracy, despised individualism, and regarded European industrial capitalism as a decadent form of society'. For him, 'the duty of colonial trusteeship lay . . . in protecting the virtues of northern aristocratic life and its communal economy from the "barbarizing" effects of European capitalism, democracy and individualism'.[23]

As in India, so in Africa: these opinions were widely shared among British politicians and administrators. From this perspective, indirect rule of dark-skinned races was about admiration rather than condescension: much more 'a recognition of indigenous genius' on the part of native peoples than it was 'a sentence of perpetual inferiority' for them, a genuine wish to hold back the corrupting forces of capitalism and exploitation, so as to let tradition thrive and hierarchy flourish. This was how the British saw things in their new, tropical empire, and it was (as usual) on the basis of how they saw things at home. Indirect rule, Margery Perham once revealingly admitted (and she was herself the product of 'an ordering of society based upon the existence of social class'), 'derives from our conservatism, with its sense of historical continuity and its aristocratic tradition'.[24] Time and again, the British viewed their dependent empire as like the Raj: the landed, layered order that they feared was being lost at home, but that they wanted to nurture and protect overseas. On the eve of independence, the indigenous elite of Ceylon was described by the young Patrick Gordon Walker as 'extremely rich landowners with local power and influence comparable to a Whig landlord's in George III's time'.[25]

15. The Banqueting Hall of Richmond Castle, Ceylon, 1916,
the country seat of chief Wijayasinghe.

Here was a classic (and by now familiar) instance of visualizing the empire by analogy to the social structure as it had once existed in Britain. Nor should this continuing cult of connection and equivalence come as any surprise. For between 1919 and 1948 the person primarily responsible for recruitment to the British Colonial Service was Sir Ralph Furse, whose vision of British society, both domestic and imperial, was unashamedly rural, hierarchical and nostalgic. He was the scion of a county family in Devon; country life, country virtues and country people were his 'ultimate realities'; he possessed 'an unswervingly aristocratic bias in social and political arrangements'; and he saw colonial administration abroad as 'a crusading service', 'forming the natural counterpart to the obligations of squires to tenants in England'.[26] In selecting the young men who would go out and administer the empire, Furse did everything he could to ensure that they shared his vision. Ruling through 'traditional' authorities was how the English had always governed themselves; it was how they had come to govern Wales, Scotland and parts of Ireland; and now it was how they came to govern their overseas empire. As such, 'Merrie Africa' reflected, matched – and even in some ways surpassed – 'Merrie England'.[27]

And it lasted until the Second World War, when, like the princely rulers of the Indian states, the emirs and chiefs and sultans once again came to Britain's aid, supporting the supreme sovereign in his time of supreme need. Consider in this regard the career of the man who, in 1948, became King Lewanika III of Barotseland. He was born in 1888, and before assuming the kingship was chief of the district of Kuta at Mankoya. During the First World War he had led the Barotse War Carriers to the East African campaign, and between 1939 and 1945 he (in the words of his *Who's Who* entry) 'encouraged the war effort by the production of rubber and funds'.[28] In the same way, during 1939 and 1940 the rulers of the Federated Malay States provided the British government with gifts totalling £1.5 million, and the rulers of the Unfederated States were scarcely less generous. And in 1943 the colonial secretary, Oliver Stanley, visited Nigeria, where the emir of Bauchi declared: 'I and my brother Emirs, and all of our people, are continually praying that God will bless and prosper the armed forces of the Allied Nations and speed the day of victory.'[29]

It was these people – the 'chiefs, landowners, sultans or sheikhs' – on whom the British felt they could rely, and with whom (as with their counterparts in India) they were most comfortable.[30] Indeed, this policy and these perceptions were still in operation in some parts of the colonial empire towards the end. During the late 1950s, when convinced that they would remain a military and imperial power in the Indian Ocean, the British sought to secure the future of their naval base in Singapore – a large, bustling, cosmopolitan town, with a huge Chinese working class of disturbingly (and increasingly) Communist sympathies. The traditional and long-pondered solution was to merge the city into a larger Federation of Malaysia, where the rural and conservative cultures of Malaya (where the sultans remained dominant), of Sarawak (where the Brookes had been 'white rajas' between 1841 and 1941) and of North Borneo (where company rule had belatedly been replaced by indirect rule) would outweigh the urban radicals of Singapore. The federation duly came into being between 1961 and 1963 – almost the last such imperial impulse, and still using the old system nearly one hundred years from the signing of the Pankgor Treaty that had effectively initiated it.[31]

6

Mandates

On the eve of the First World War, and notwithstanding the participation of France, Germany and Belgium in the 'Scramble for Africa', the British Empire was still very much the greatest and the grandest in the world. Taken together, the dominions of settlement, the Indian Empire and the tropical colonies comprised an imperium that was without rival in terms of its territorial extent, its mixture of variety and coherence, and its unifying characteristics of hierarchy and tradition. By comparison, the German and Belgian Empires might also be royal, but they were rather small; the Portuguese and Spanish Empires were also royal, but demoralized; and the French Empire might be large, but it was republican. After the First World War the final extension of the British Empire took place in the Middle East, with the dissolution of the Ottoman Empire, and the setting up of new kingdoms in the League of Nations Mandates in Jordan and Iraq. Not surprisingly, given what had happened in sub-Saharan Africa since the 1870s, these new–old kingdoms were explicitly conceived on the model of the Indian princely states. The First World War may (or may not) have made the world safe for democracy; for another generation, and in yet another part of the world, it certainly made the British Empire safe for hierarchy.

This last act of traditional-cum-imperial social engineering also needs to be set in the broader contexts of cultural attitudes and historical precedents. Before the late nineteenth century most well-born, well-read and well-travelled Britons, following the South Asian examples set by Bentinck and Dalhousie, had despised what they regarded as the despotic politics and squalid conditions of the orient. But, as with the

British in post-Mutiny India and post-Scramble Africa, their attitudes subsequently underwent a significant change. This was partly because of the more romantic image of the Arabs projected by writers such as Sir Richard Burton, which increasingly depicted them as English gentlemen 'translated into another idiom'; and partly as a consequence of their growing feelings of insecurity in what they regarded as an increasingly hostile domestic environment. When confronted by agricultural depression, mass politics in the cities, anti-landlord agitation in Ireland and attacks on the House of Lords itself, many anxious and disenchanted patricians came to admire (and to envy) the magnificent Bedouin chiefs and their remote, unspoilt deserts – where it seemed that established social order endured and traditional deference still prevailed, where the ancient values of chivalry and honour were preserved, and where there was 'a feeling of escape from the furies of modern life – disillusion, doubt, democracy'.[1]

Thus appreciatively regarded, the Arab emirs and sheikhs seemed like the Indian princes and Nigerian emirs, only more so: noble and superior leaders, the patrons and protectors of a traditional, ordered world, which had once existed in Britain, but which was now under serious threat. These opinions, which clearly had much in common with those of Harcourt Butler in India and Charles Temple in Africa, were shared by Wilfrid Scawen Blunt. A Sussex squire who hated the middle classes, mass politics, 'selfish financiers' and 'greedy Jews', he travelled extensively in the Middle East and bought an estate near Cairo; he also spoke Arabic, bred Arab horses and wore local costume.[2] They were shared by Mark Sykes, who was the heir to a baronetcy and the Sledmere Estate in Yorkshire, disliked the French and the Industrial Revolutions, admired Arab society as layered, ordered, traditional and deferential, and regarded the great sheikhs and Kurdish chiefs as fellow aristocrats with whom he might talk on equal terms. And they were held by the Hon. Aubrey Herbert, the model for John Buchan's Sandy Arbuthnot, who 'rode through the Yemen, which no white man ever did before', hated politicians, the bourgeoisie and Lloyd George, and loved 'thrones, chieftains, bandits, dangerous territories and fierce loyalty'.[3]

This growing attachment to the Arab world, by turns patrician, romantic and escapist, coincided with the gradual extension of British power into the Middle East – an extension that took for granted that these traditional rulers should be sustained and supported. When Egypt was invaded and occupied in 1882, Britain governed indirectly through the khedive (later sultan, and the direct descendant of the figure in Wilkie's painting), following the precedents and practice of the Indian princely states, and relying on their resident consul-general to ensure that order was preserved, that the national finances were restored, and that the Suez Canal was protected.[4] On the Arabian peninsular and in the Persian Gulf, the British made treaties with the sultan of Muscat, with the sheikhs of the Trucial Coast of Oman, with the ruler of Bahrain, with the sheikhs of Qatar and with the sheikh of Kuwait, which established them as the 'paramount power in much of the Arabian peninsular'. And when Britain went to war with the Ottoman Empire in 1914, it supported Sherif Hussein (the most prominent member of the Arabian nobility, the paramount chieftain in the area and the founder of the Hashemite dynasty) and his sons in their revolt against the Turks.[5] This policy was especially advocated by the Cairo-based Arab Bureau, with which Herbert and Sykes were both connected. The latter was especially influential in urging the need for Britain to create post-war Arab kingdoms, 'agrarian in nature and almost medieval in structure', where 'squires, lords and peasants might live in reconstituted amity', and all 'doing homage in their lives and thoughts to the divine eternal order of which their society on earth was but the mirror'.[6]

With the defeat of the Ottoman Empire, this romantic, hierarchical impulse became the basis of Britain's post-war policy, and two people pursued it with particular vigour, determination and success. The first was T. E. Lawrence, himself a great admirer of Sherif Hussein and his sons, and a firm believer in the traditional order in Britain no less than in the Middle East. In seeking to establish a new Arab settlement, he was sure that Britain would have the edge over France because of its layered social structure culminating in the monarchy. 'Ancient and artificial societies like this of the Sherifs and feudal chieftains of Arabia,' he explained, 'found a sense of honourable security when dealing with

16. The Emir Abdullah of Transjordan with, among others,
Lord Allenby and Colonel T. E. Lawrence, *c.* 1922.

us in such proof that the highest place in our state was not a prize for merit or ambition.'[7] In seeing himself as a king-maker, Lawrence was at one with the second influential Briton, Winston Churchill, who as colonial secretary in the Lloyd George coalition was responsible for putting these ideas into practice. In the aftermath of war, Churchill had evolved into a fully fledged social conservative, who was dismayed by the demise of the 'old world', with its 'princes and potentates', its secure ruling classes and its splendid social pageantry. He much regretted the disappearance of the Habsburgs, the Hohenzollerns and the Romanovs, and the 'collapse of settled values and ancient institutions'. And, as colonial secretary, he was convinced that in the Middle East, as elsewhere in the empire, 'British interests were best served by friendship and co-operation with the party of monarchy and tradition'.[8]

At the Cairo Conference of March 1921, Lawrence and Churchill sought to implement their social-imperial ideas by establishing new royal regimes in the League of Nations Mandates that the British had been awarded in the Middle East. For Churchill, they had two special attractions: they would mean empire on the cheap at a time when public spending was under severe strain and scrutiny; and they would establish 'the very best structure', which would be 'analogous to princely states in India'.[9] In conformity with Britain's wartime policy (the so-called 'Sherifian solution'), the intention was that these new Arab nations would be ruled by sons of Sherif Hussein. In Transjordan, Hussein's second son, Abdullah, was installed as emir, supported by an indigenous administration under British supervision, headed by a resident, and with an Arab Legion officered and supplied by the British. In neighbouring Iraq (Mesopotamia), Abdullah's younger brother, Faisal, who had been ignominiously ejected by the French from the throne of Syria, was installed from the outset as king, once public support had been effectively mobilized (by the British) in his favour, and he reigned until his death in 1933.[10] As in Jordan, British influence over the king and his country was exercised by a high commissioner, who sought to control the rural tribes by increasing the powers of their head sheikhs. This mode of indirect rule continued essentially unaltered well after the mandate expired in 1932.[11]

Although the result of less premeditated and determined policy, two

17. King Fu'ad of Egypt with the prince of Wales, 1927.

additional new kings appeared in the British-controlled Middle East. On the outbreak of war, Egypt had been formally (and belatedly) annexed by Britain, but in 1922 the country was declared independent, and the sultan was elevated to royal status as King Fu'ad. Like his fellow monarchs in Jordan and Iraq, he was advised by a British high commissioner; and imperial communications, the defence of Egypt, the protection of foreign interests and the ostensibly 'Anglo-Egyptian' Sudan remained explicitly and exclusively under British control. Under these terms, Egypt was essentially 'a princely state on the Indian pattern'.[12] Across the Red Sea, on the Arabian peninsula, the British had initially backed Sherif Hussein, and had hoped that he might become king of Arabia as his sons eventually became rulers of Jordan and Iraq.[13] But Hussein fell out with his sons and with the British, and refused to accept the settlements of the Cairo Conference. He was deprived of British support as a result and forced to abdicate in 1924. Soon after, he was driven out of Arabia by his long-standing rival, Ibn Sa'ud, who thereupon established himself as king. In 1927 Ibn Sa'ud signed a treaty that effectively recognized Britain as the paramount power in the region. Ten years later, and using the Malay treaties as a model, Britain concluded negotiations with tribal rulers in the hinterland of the port of Aden, including Sultan Saleh of Mukalla and Sultan Ja'far of Seiyun. This completed and consolidated its inter-war dominions in the Arab world.[14]

So by this time the British Middle East was organized on the basis of what Gertrude Bell called 'creating kings', resulting in regimes that stressed 'solid magnificence' and 'ordered dignity'. There were proclamations and coronations for the new kings, and durbars at which 'big sheikhs and nobles', 'magnates of the wilderness' and 'great chiefs of the desert' pledged allegiance and paid homage, and the countryside, the cabinets and the legislatures of these new royal dominions were dominated by the sheikhly landowners. And the British residents and high commissioners behaved with appropriate proconsular pomp: Lord Lloyd in Egypt, with his cocked hat, orders, ribbons and Rolls-Royce, and Sir Percy Cox in Iraq, with his white uniform and gold lace, 'his air of fine and simple dignity'.[15] The result was a large new imperial dominion based on a romantic, admiring, escapist view of Arab social structure, which closely resembled Rudolph Valentino's celebration of the Bedouin characteristics of 'nobility, dignity, manliness, gracefulness and virility' in his film *The Sheikh* (1921). Such perceptions persisted well on into the inter-war years, exemplified by the Hon. Wilfred Thesiger, nephew of Lord Chelmsford (viceroy of India, 1916–21), who was born in Abyssinia and spent the 1930s travelling in the Middle East. Like Blunt, Herbert and Sykes, he had 'a lifelong craving for barbaric splendour, for savagery and colour and the throb of drums', a 'lasting veneration for long-established customs and ritual', a 'deep-seated resentment of western innovations in other lands' and a 'distaste for the drab uniformity of the modern world'.[16]

Throughout the 1930s these 'traditionalist' views of Arab society, and especially of its leaders, remained the basis for British policy towards its mandates and territories in the Middle East – a structure of government that has been aptly described as having been 'born by the great war, out of the Indian Raj'. Like the princes of South Asia, the Hashemite rulers of Iraq and Jordan built palaces designed by British architects, employed British nannies, tutors and governesses, and sent their sons to public schools. In Iraq, Faisal ruled with Valentino-like demeanour: 'his voice seemed to breathe the perfume of frankincense and to suggest the presence of richly coloured divans, green turbans and the glitter of gold and jewels'.[17] And after his death, and the ending of the mandate, the climactic years of the monarchy were dominated by the regency of Crown Prince Abdulillah, who was devoted to such courtly pastimes as protocol and pedigree. It was the same in Jordan, where the Emir Abdullah's regime was no less regal, with his palace in Amman, his birds and his falcons, and with the British resident, Sir Alec Kilbride, in close and cordial attendance. As James Morris notes, relations between residents and monarchs genuinely seemed 'a meeting of equals'. The officials admired the Bedouin ethos and, as in the colonial service, 'most of the Britons were men of the rural gentry', who thus felt 'at ease and at home with Arab gentlemen'.[18]

During the Second World War, kingship and rural hierarchy remained the essential basis of the British perception of the Middle East, and of the imperial presence there, as they did in India and Africa. In Saudi

Arabia, Ibn Sa'ud was consistently loyal, playing up the 'Bedouin Arab conception of kingship'. When visiting him after the Yalta Conference, Winston Churchill felt 'deep admiration' for the 'warrior vigour' of this 'patriarchal king of the Arabian desert'. In Jordan, the Emir Abdullah (whom Churchill rightly described as 'one of my creations') matched the Indian princes and Malayan sultans in his 'loyal and unwavering co-operation', believing that 'with every addition to the number of enemies, his devotion to the allied cause increased, and that His Majesty's Government could depend upon him to work for the common good in all circumstances'. In Iraq, the army rebelled against the Regent Abdulillah in 1941, whereupon there was a counter-coup by the British in favour of the regent and his chief political ally, Nuri Pasha, after which they both gave long-standing support. And in Egypt, Farouk and his government led by Nahas Pasha collaborated with the British from February 1942 until the end of the war.[19] Indeed, by 1945 the British sphere in the Middle East was more extended (and more royal) than ever before, encompassing kingly regimes from Libya to Persia to Greece. The 'traditional' monarchies in Egypt, Jordan and Iraq, and the sheikhdoms in the Persian Gulf and the hinterland of Aden, were the key to it. Here was the final extension of the Churchillian enterprise begun in Cairo in 1921.[20]

Thereafter, these kingly connections and hierarchical perceptions continued in essence unaltered. As foreign secretary in the post-war Labour government, Ernest Bevin aspired to be the reformist successor to Dalhousie, Bentinck and Chamberlain. He believed British imperial policy in the Middle East had hitherto 'rested on too narrow a footing, mainly on the personalities of kings, princes or pashas', and he wanted to give Britain's relations with these Arab kingdoms 'a new and more attractive look' by working with 'the peasants' against 'the pashas' – to develop these countries politically, economically, educationally and socially.[21] But in practice very little changed. In Egypt, the British continued to rely on King Farouk, whom they thought was popular and should not be antagonized. 'The monarchy has prestige and it has continuity,' one Foreign Office mandarin observed. 'Let us give it a run.' And so they did. It was the same in Transjordan, where the mandate ended in 1946, and where the British (following the Egyptian precedent of 1922) showed their gratitude to the Emir Abdullah by creating him king. He was regarded, in sub-Churchillian terms, as belonging 'to a generation in which kings were hardy souls, capable of riding all day, fasting if need be, and feasting with zest whenever opportunity arose'. At the end of his highly theatrical coronation, he thanked the British 'for having raised them, within twenty-five years, from an unknown corner of the Ottoman Empire to the status of an independent kingdom'.[22]

It was still the same too in Iraq, where the British continued to rely on Nuri Pasha, the Regent Abdulillah, the young King Faisal II and the 'old gang' or 'old guard' of sheikhs and pashas, with whom, and despite Bevin's reformist intentions, they felt 'underlying sympathy'. It was generally believed, according to one diplomat, resorting to a familiar analogical trope, that the regent 'has a great admiration and liking for Britain and for British methods and persons. His cars, his aircraft, his clothes, his hunters, his foxhounds, even his swans, are British, and so are many of his closest friends.' He was, indeed, the very model of an English country gentleman, or perhaps, more appropriately, he resembled a young George III.[23] And it was the same in the Persian Gulf where, after Indian independence, the British residents who had advised the rulers continued their work. All that had changed was that whereas previously they had been recruited from the ICS and reported to New Delhi, they were now provided by the Foreign Office, answered to London, and received their instructions from the foreign secretary instead of the viceroy. Even in the early 1950s British advisers, both civilian and military, remained in post and in power across the Middle East, where (like Sir Michael Wright in Baghdad) they still adhered to a 'rigid style of pomp and imperial circumstance', and where the kings they had created still seemed the only dependable allies.[24]

As late as the 1950s and early 1960s the southern part of Arabia near Aden and the coastline of the Persian Gulf remained areas where traditional notions of empire and of imperial hierarchy survived and were even extended. In the Eastern and Western Aden Protectorates, indirect rule via the sultans and sheikhs had always been the British mode, and in 1959 these varied and assorted emirates were united in a

18. King Faisal II of Iraq, paying a state visit to London, 1956.

federation. Four years later they were merged in their turn with the port and colony of Aden so as to form the Federation of South Arabia. The aim was clear, and redolent of the India of the 1920s and 1930s: to use (in Prime Minister Harold Macmillan's words) 'the influence and power of the sultans' as a counterpoise to the urban world of radical, middle-class nationalism – not, this time, in regard to Calcutta (or Singapore) but to the cosmopolitan port city of Aden.[25] Further north, the Gulf sheikhdoms were still advised by a British resident in a time-warp version of indirect rule, unchanged in its essentials since the sultan of Muscat and Oman had sworn 'eternal devotion and fidelity' to Lord Curzon on his viceregal visitation in 1903. In the 1960s the sultan's descendant still lived in his palace, and the Union Jack still flew over the nearby residence of the British consul-general (as the resident was now more tactfully called). But by then the princely state of Oman was little more than a relic of the empire that had been.[26]

PART THREE

GENERALITIES

7

Honours

The settlement dominions, the Indian Empire, the crown colonies and the League of Nations Mandates were different and diverse realms – geographically, ethnically, historically, culturally, economically, politically and administratively. And there were many variations in the workings and arrangements of indirect rule, from the Persian Gulf sheikhdoms and the Indian princely states (which were relatively autonomous), via Uganda and Northern Nigeria, to the Malay states, Zanzibar and especially Egypt, Iraq and Jordan (which were at the other end of the spectrum).[1] Yet these separate, constituent parts of the British Empire were easily visualized as one general, all-encompassing whole. This was partly because large areas of the map of the world were coloured red, and that cartographical image provided a reassuring picture of coherence and uniformity. But it was also because there was a sociological image that provided a similar picture – and that was the image of hierarchy. That was how the British saw their own society, and in the main preferred it to be; and so it is scarcely surprising that that was how they saw their empire, and in the main preferred *that* to be. Hierarchy, it bears repeating, homogenized the heterogeneity of empire. Indeed, there were important ways in which, from within the metropolis, this vision of empire was encouraged and promoted, so as to make it more coherent and convincing. One such means was by the expansion and codification of the honours system.

The late nineteenth and early twentieth centuries were periods of unprecedented honorific inventiveness, far surpassing that which had taken place one hundred years before. This meant that Britain's titular hierarchy was exported to the far boundaries of empire, and that at home and overseas it reached further down the social scale, and brought more people together, than ever before. But the precedents were already in place and, as so often in imperial Britain, they merely required extension and adaptation. The Most Noble Order of the Garter was used to unify and merge different elites: in this case, foreign royalty (including by 1924 the kings of Italy, Sweden, Norway and Belgium) and British grandees (among them Lansdowne, Derby, Curzon and Devonshire).[2] The creation of the Most Illustrious Order of St Patrick had been as an instrument for the assimilation of the Irish colonial elite into the imperial metropolis, and it was presided over by the Irish viceroy. And the reformed and extended Most Honourable Order of the Bath was used to rank and classify military and civilian service to the state, as well as to honour and reward it. Since the major expansion of the Order in 1815, there had been three different levels – companion, knight commander and knight grand cross – which both differentiated those of varied distinction, and provided a ladder of advancement for the ambitious in the army, the navy and the civil service.[3] As the empire expanded from the last quarter of the nineteenth century, more honours were created and awarded, following these precedents and practices, to structure and unify this greater British world.

The beginnings of these developments may be dated from 1868, and it is not coincidence that this was when Disraeli's first administration was briefly in power. At the behest of the duke of Buckingham, who was colonial secretary, the Most Distinguished Order of St Michael and St George, which had previously been confined to residents of Malta and the Ionian Islands, was re-established and enlarged as the pre-eminent order of chivalry for those who governed, administered and had gone to settle in the British Empire.[4] Following the precedent established with the Order of the Bath, there were three ranks – companion, knight commander and knight grand cross – and as members of the colonial service rose up their professional hierarchy, they rose up this honorific hierarchy as well. Almost any competent administrators became CMG (known among recipients as standing for 'Call Me God'); governors of second-class crown colonies were advanced to KCMG ('Kindly Call Me God'); and governors of first-class colonies were promoted to GCMG ('God Calls Me God').[5] For the same reason, knighthoods were also given to lieutenant-governors of Canadian provinces, to governors of Australian states, to British residents and high commissioners in the Middle East, and to governors-general of the great dominions.

Thus reinvented, and appropriately based at the Colonial Office, and with its chapel in St Paul's Cathedral, the Order of St Michael and St George gave the British proconsular elite a degree of prestige and social recognition far beyond anything that could be obtained in the German or French Colonial Services. In an empire constructed and conceived on strict hierarchical principles, such rewards and ranking were considered essential, and as the representative of the crown, a governor or governor-general had to be equipped with a ribbon and star and title. Among proconsuls we have already met, Arthur Hamilton Gordon was made a KCMG when he became governor of Mauritius in 1871, and seven years later, shortly after he had been translated to Fiji, he was promoted to the GCMG at the relatively tender age of fifty. In the next generation Frank Swettenham rose through the order as he ascended the Malayan Civil Service: the CMG in 1886 for his work as acting resident in Perak, the KCMG in 1897 as resident-general to the Federated Malay States, and the GCMG in 1909 in his retirement, and on his appointment as chairman of a royal commission to report on the finances of Mauritius. Later still, Hugh Clifford was made CMG in 1900 on taking up the post of governor of North Borneo, KCMG in 1909 while colonial secretary in Ceylon, and GCMG in 1921 as governor of Nigeria.[6]

But in addition, and in response to the pressure that had built up from settlers in the mid-Victorian period, whose repeated requests for specifically colonial orders of chivalry had been regularly rebuffed, the Order of St Michael and St George was awarded to senior political and social figures in the colonies themselves – to dominion prime ministers such as Sir Wilfrid Laurier, Sir Robert Borden (both Canada, and GCMGs) and Sir Edward Morris (Newfoundland, and KCMG), and also to senior figures in the colonial judiciary. And it was bestowed on native rulers, such as Charles Brooke, the 'white' rajah of Sarawak, who was made a GCMG. Most recipients, however, were dark-skinned

Indian princes, Malayan sultans, Sudanese sheikhs or Nigerian emirs: an emphatic sign that they were being treated as social equals.[7] These ribbons and stars were much sought after, and local ceremonies of investiture by the governor or governor-general on behalf of the sovereign were invariably grand occasions. As Lord Elgin put it, 'in the colonies, premiers and chief justices fight for stars and ribbons like little boys for toys, and scream at us if we stop them'.[8] This was scarcely different from how things were in Britain; and that, of course, was precisely the point. For this common lust for titles brought together the British proconsular elite and the indigenous colonial elites into a unified, ranked, honorific body – 'one vast interconnected world'.

In the Indian Empire there were parallel developments, as three new orders of chivalry were set up specifically for the subcontinent, to complement the Order of St Michael and St George for the dominions and the dependent empire. The Most Exalted Order of the Star of India was established in 1861 (just after the Mutiny), and extended many times in the ensuing half century; the Most Eminent Order of the Indian Empire was inaugurated in 1878 (to coincide with Victoria's assumption of the imperial title) and was also much elaborated in subsequent decades; and the Imperial Order of the Crown of India was instituted in the same year.[9] The two senior orders were of three levels, based on the Order of St Michael and St George, while the Order of the Crown of India was for women. Taken together, their explicit purpose was to rank, reward and reconcile the British proconsular elite and the Indian princely elite, and their respective civil services. As Charles Lewis Tupper explained in 1893, the whole point of these orders was that they were 'open to Europeans and natives alike'. They would, he insisted, 'have entirely missed the mark had they been restricted on any principle of race'. 'All,' he concluded, 'should be united in the service of the Empire.' And so indeed, and in practice, they were.[10] Just as the Order of the Garter brought together British aristocrats and foreign royalty, and as the Order of St Michael and St George brought together the proconsular elite from the metropolis and the indigenous elites of the dominions and the dependent empire, so the aim of the Indian orders was to unify the British governors and the ruling princes.

On the British side, junior British officials in the Indian Civil Service might expect to obtain the CSI or the CIE, just as their counterparts in the colonial service received the CMG. This was the career reward for those who never rose high in the order of precedence: surgeon-generals, private secretaries to governors, inspector-generals of police, members of the Boards of Revenue, and so on. More senior figures, including high-court judges, residents to the ruling princes and members of the viceroy's council, were given the KCSI or the KCIE; and both Lutyens and Baker received the KCIE for their work on New Delhi.[11] The governors of Bombay, Madras and Bengal invariably received the GCIE and sometimes the GCSI as well; so did those members of the Indian Civil Service who rose to the top career governorships of the Punjab and of the North Western Provinces; so did the commander-in-chief and the secretary of state for India in London; and so, of course, did the viceroy, who (following the precedent of the Order of St Patrick) was ex officio grand master of both the great Indian orders. At the same time, the Order of the Crown of India was given to governors' ladies, to the vicereine, and to the spouses of the commander-in-chief and the secretary of state for India in London.[12]

But these awards were also given to Indians, partly to unite them with the British, partly because it was believed they cared very greatly for honour and recognition. This accepted the conclusion, and followed the recommendation, that had been put forward earlier in the century by Sir John Lindsay, who had urged that 'marks of distinction are exceedingly pleasing in this country; and could any means be fallen on to add to the apparent dignity of Indian princes from Europe, it would be exceedingly flattering to them'. Fifty years later, Charles Lewis Tupper agreed. 'There is,' he opined, 'no doubt that Indians of rank and position wish to share our honours, and think highly of them.'[13] Indeed, since the ruling princes were fiercely competitive in any matters to do with status, they vied with each other to obtain the recognition they deemed appropriate to their station. Kipling caught (and mocked) this well:

Rustrum Beg of Kolazai – slightly backward Native State –
Lusted for a CSI – so began to sanitate

Built a Gaol and Hospital – nearby built a City drain
Till his faithful subjects all thought their ruler was insane . . .

. . . Then the birthday honours came. Sad to state and sad to see
Stood against the Rajah's name nothing more than CIE.[14]

Accordingly, the two Indian orders were also given out to the ruling princes (occasionally including sultans in Malaya and in the Persian Gulf as well as Indian ruling princesses) with careful consideration to their relative rank and standing (and loyalty and cooperation): the CIE (as Beg discovered) to those of lowest status, then the CSI, then the KCIE, then the KCSI, then the GCIE, then the GCSI. Princes who were very rich and very grand, like the maharajas of Mysore, could reasonably expect to be made knights grand commander of the Order of the Star of India in every generation. As a result, many a ruling prince posed for his portrait in the mantle, star, collar and sash of the Order of the Star of India, as did the governors of Bombay, Madras and Bengal, and also the viceroy himself: another sign of ordered hierarchy and honorific equality, as the British proconsuls and Indian princes were merged together. In the same way, and along with the spouses of British proconsuls, the wives and other female relatives of the most senior Indian ruling princes were made members of the Order of the Crown of India.[15] And it was customary, in the grandest and best-run princely states, to give knighthoods in the Indian orders to the dewans who administered their princes' affairs, such as Sir Mokshagundum Visvesvaraya and Sir Mirza Ismail in Mysore, both of whom were given the KCIE.

These innovations and developments help to explain why the British honours system had become so elaborate and so imperial by the early decades of the twentieth century, as they tied together the dominions of settlement, the Indian Empire and the tropical colonies in one integrated, ordered, titular, transracial hierarchy that no other empire could rival. Thus, for those who served in both the Indian and the Colonial Empires, there were very rich and elaborate pickings indeed, as they zigzagged up the interlocking ladders of the two Indian orders

19. Lord Curzon, viceroy of India, wearing the insignia and robes of a knight grand commander of the Order of the Star of India, *c.* 1900.

20. The begum of Bhopal, wearing the same insignia as Curzon, *c.* 1890.

and the Order of St Michael and St George. Consider in this regard Sir Percy Cox, whom we have already met in the early 1920s as Britain's high commissioner in Iraq. This was the climax of a career in which he had shuttled back and forth between the Middle East and South Asia, and for which he received appropriate honours on an ascending scale: the CIE, CSI and KCIE between 1902 and 1911 for his work in the Persian Gulf; the KCSI and GCIE during the First World War when he was chief political officer of the Indian Expeditionary Force on the Western Front; the KCMG in 1920 when he was acting British minister to Persia; and the GCMG in 1922 while he was high commissioner in Iraq. No wonder he was an impressive sight when calling on King Faisal, his official uniform covered with these accumulated baubles.

But these were not the only honours that were invented and distributed in the heyday of empire. The number of knights bachelor, who did not belong to any specific order of chivalry, increased from 230 in 1885 to 700 in 1914, and many of these recipients were from the empire, often senior judges, among them the first African to be knighted, Samuel Lewis from Sierra Leone in 1896.[16] In 1896 the Royal Victorian Order was set up to reward personal service to the crown, and this was often given to proconsuls or native rulers to whom the sovereign took a particular liking, such as the Malayan Sultan Idris of Perak, who was already a GCMG, but was given the GCVO in 1913. And in 1902 Edward VII instituted the Imperial Service Order, as a sort of junior branch of the Order of St Michael and St George, which was further extended in 1912. It was restricted to the administrative and clerical branches of the imperial civil service, and total membership was limited to 750. One third were from the home civil service, another third from the Indian Civil Service (one half European, the other half Indian) and the last third from the services of the dominions, colonies and protectorates.[17]

Yet such was the expansion of empire, and such was the demand for imperial honours, that one final award was invented by George V in 1917, when he inaugurated the aptly named the Most Excellent Order of the British Empire. It consisted of five classes: not just GBE, KBE and CBE, but also OBE and MBE, plus a separate British Empire Medal. As this suggests, the novel appeal of this order was that it was open, not just to the proconsular and princely elites, but to all of the king's subjects, of both sexes, whatever their social status, and wherever in the empire they might live. Domestically, it was the order of Britain's democracy, designed to reward people from all walks and stations of life who had contributed to winning the war. Imperially, it was the order of the whole dominion, which could be given to anybody from Singapore to Sierra Leone, Johannesburg to Jaipur.[18] The result was that within two years of its inauguration, there were 22,000 members of its different levels and categories; by 1938 there were 30,000. Most of these were lowly folk with OBEs, MBEs and the BEM. But inevitably, given the name of the order, there were also British governors and native rulers, who received senior knighthoods. Sir Hugh Clifford was made a GBE in 1925, to add to the GCMG he already possessed; in the year of its foundation, the maharaja of Mysore was given the same award to complement his GCSI; and in 1937 the kabaka of Buganda was given the KBE to add to the KCMG he had received in 1925.[19] With this innovation, Britain's imperial honorific hierarchy was complete.

This system worked in a similarly extended way at the higher level of ennoblement, as some imperial knights became imperial peers – partly as a preparation or reward for services rendered overseas, partly to export a complete honorific hierarchy to the empire itself. Outstandingly successful colonial governors might hope to be ennobled at the end of their careers: one such was Sir Arthur Hamilton Gordon, who after governing Fiji, New Zealand and Ceylon, ended his days as Lord Stanmore; another was Sir Malcolm Hailey, who eventually added a barony (and the OM) to the GCIE and the GCSI he had acquired as a governor of Indian provinces. For certain positions, a peerage was considered essential: before taking up his duties as British high commissioner in Egypt, George Lloyd insisted on ennoblement because he believed (as did many others) that 'all orientals think extra highly of a Lord' (so, also, did the British).[20] Commoners who were appointed governor-general of Canada or South Africa or Australia, or viceroy of India, were almost invariably made peers so as to represent the king–emperor in fitting fashion: Curzon and Wavell in India, Gladstone and

Buxton in South Africa, and John Buchan in Canada. And many holders of these senior imperial positions were further promoted in the peerage on their return: Bledisloe (New Zealand), Byng (Canada) and Chelmsford (India) were advanced from barons to viscounts; while Buxton (South Africa), Gowrie (New Zealand), and Lytton and Curzon (both India) all eventually became earls.

Indeed, the most successful British proconsuls and imperial soldiers were knights and peers several times over, veritable walking Christmas trees of stars and collars, medals and sashes, ermine robes and coronets, who personified the honorific imperial hierarchy at its most elaborate. Here are three examples from a lengthy list of contenders.[21] Lord Dufferin was an Irish peer and landowner who was governor-general of Canada (1872–8), viceroy of India (1884–8), and in between held most of the top European embassies. In the course of his career, he accumulated knighthoods in the orders of St Patrick, the Bath, St Michael and St George, the Star of India and the Indian Empire; and he was given a British peerage and twice promoted, ending his life as the marquess of Dufferin and Ava. No less decorated for imperial service was Field Marshal the Earl Kitchener of Khartoum and of Broome, who received the GCB for pacifying the Sudan, the GCMG for his part in waging and winning the Boer War, the GCSI and GCIE as commander-in-chief in India, the OM, the St Patrick and the Garter to give him even greater lustre, as well as a barony, a viscountcy and an earldom.[22] And in a later generation Mr Freeman Freeman-Thomas was almost continuously employed between 1912 and 1936 as governor of Bombay, governor of Madras, governor-general of Canada and eventually viceroy of India. Along the way, he acquired the senior knighthoods of both the Indian orders, grand crosses of the orders of St Michael and St George and of the British Empire and, as he moved from one proconsular posting to another, was advanced in the peerage to a barony, then to a viscountcy, then to an earldom, and finally to a marquessate.[23]

But peerages, like knighthoods, were also now being given to those who lived in the empire and aspired to join its elite. (Baronetcies were a halfway house, and were sparingly awarded to rich colonials such as the Canadians Sir Allan MacNab and Sir Samuel Cunard, and the

Australians Sir Charles Nicholson and Sir Daniel Cooper; peerages, by contrast, usually assumed some form of public service.[24]) Before 1914 there were three Canadians thus ennobled: Sir John Macdonald's widow, Donald Smith (Lord Strathcona) and George Stephen (Lord Mount Stephen); there was de Villiers, the first native-born chief justice of South Africa; and there was the premier of Newfoundland, Sir Edward Morris. Thereafter peerages were given to Beaverbrook and Atholstan in 1917, and between the wars to Ashfield, Sinha, Morris, Rutherford, Forrest and Strickland. The last of these was an especially noteworthy and resonant figure, moving as he did between the aristocracies of Malta and Britain, and the governments of the periphery and the metropolis. For Gerald Strickland was a Maltese count by birth and a British imperialist by inclination, who married into the Hornyolds, an ancient gentry family in Westmorland. He began his career as a colonial official in Malta, for which he received the CMG in 1889 and the KCMG in 1897; he was then governor of the Leeward Islands, Tasmania, Western Australia and New South Wales (which brought him the GCMG in 1913); and he was subsequently both prime minister of Malta and MP for Lancaster (which brought him his peerage in 1928).[25]

Unlike Strickland, most overseas imperial notables were content with their own indigenous titles: but these 'model' princes and sovereigns of empire were amply rewarded and abundantly honoured in ways that deliberately paralleled the treatment of the most decorated British proconsuls. One of these pre-eminent accumulators was the maharaja of Jaipur, who ruled his state from 1880 to 1922, and garnered honours with inexorable and monotonous frequency: the GCSI in 1888, the GCIE in 1901, the GCVO in 1903 and the GBE in 1918. But there were many others who did almost as well. The last ruling nizam of Hyderabad succeeded in 1911, when he was promptly given the GCSI; six years later he was (like the maharaja of Mysore) a founding knight grand cross of the Order of the British Empire; and in 1946 he was awarded the Royal Victorian Chain in recognition of his seniority and his wartime support. But such appreciation was not confined to Indian princes. In the same generation the sultan of Zanzibar, who succeeded in the same year as the nizam and reigned until 1960, did even better,

21. The sultan of Zanzibar at his Silver Jubilee, 1937, wearing the insignia of a knight grand cross of the Order of St Michael and St George, and accompanied by the British resident, Sir Richard Rankine, KCMG.

receiving the GBE in 1935, the GCMG in the following year and the GCB in 1956. And in the Pacific Ocean, Queen Salote of Tonga was made a DBE in 1932, promoted to GBE in 1945, given the GCVO in 1953 and finally the GCMG in 1965. These were the honorific high-achievers: ruling sovereigns who were every bit as decorated as the British proconsular elite. Here, again, across the varied races of empire, there was convergence and equality. As James Morris notes, 'Native dignitaries from Hong Kong to the Gold Coast became knights of English orders, queerly uniting in their persons the legacies of gonfalon and seneschal with heritages of tribal stool or ancestral carapace'.[26]

As such practices and such schemes implied, the honorific system that had once been English, and had then became British, was during this period extended and developed into something that was authentically imperial, encompassing and layering the globe. In the aftermath of the First World War, which witnessed the disappearance of the elaborately graded and royal-based honours in Russia, Germany and Austria-Hungary, it was the most complex and comprehensive titular hierarchy in existence anywhere in the western world, rewarding and recognizing the greatest range of people, racially, geographically and sociologically. Throughout the empire many people at many social levels – both light *and* dark skinned – did genuinely 'yearn' for these baubles and elevations, and great attention was given to deciding who should receive precisely what. As Lord Curzon observed, there was an 'insatiable appetite of the British-speaking community all the world over for titles and precedence'.[27] For it was widely believed that 'imperial' honours were, like those families in *Burke's Colonial Gentry*, the node at which the metropolitan culture of outreach and replication converged and connected with the colonial culture of aspiration and assimilation. As such, this carefully graded system of titles and orders, ribbons and stars, helped to promote a sense of common belonging and collective participation, and it created and projected an ordered, unified, hierarchical picture of empire.[28]

Consider, in this regard, the New Year's Honours List of January 1920, which cast a wide imperial spread. Here are some names from it, drawn at random. At the top of the list, but carrying no title, were privy counsellorships for Lord Lugard, lately retired as governor-general of Nigeria, and for the acting prime ministers of Canada and Australia, Sir William White and William Watt, who had been holding the fort at home while their premiers had been away negotiating peace at Versailles. In the dominions list, the minister of railways and native affairs in New Zealand was made a KCMG, the premier of Tasmania was created a knight bachelor, and a member of the House of Assembly of the Union of South Africa was awarded the CMG. In the Indian section of the list, the maharaja of Idar was given the KCSI, a member of the Board of Revenue in Bengal was awarded the KCIE, the municipal commissioner for Bombay received the CSI, the chief collector of Customs at Rangoon obtained the CIE, and two brigadier generals in the Indian Army were allotted the CVO. In the colonial empire, the governor of Barbados was made a KCMG, the chief justice of Nigeria was created a knight bachelor, the judicial commissioner of the Federated Malay States was given the CMG, and the director of agriculture in Zanzibar was awarded the CBE. Finally, in the Middle East, the senior judicial official in the Civil Administration of Mesopotamia was given the KCMG, as was Sir Percy Cox for his work in Teheran, and the grand chamberlain to the sultan of Egypt was made an honorary KBE.[29]

These imperial honours, which had proliferated on an unprecedented scale, were an essentially Gothic enterprise, concerned as they were with costume, ceremony, heraldry, religion and monarchy – all the accoutrements of hierarchical display and imperial ostentation. They were concerned with costume because many proconsuls and potentates were portrayed in the mantles, stars, ribands and collars of the orders that they held, and because statues of viceroys and of governors-general that were placed in the imperial capitals invariably depicted them clad in the robes of the Order of the Star of India or of St Michael and St George. They were concerned with ceremony because the installations of senior knights were splendid occasions, which took place in London or Calcutta or Delhi, and special chapters of the Indian orders were also held at the three great durbars, presided over by the viceroy. They were concerned with heraldry because the banners of the knights, complete with coats of arms and mottoes, were hung in the chapels of their orders. They were concerned with religion because, with the exception of the Indian orders, all the orders of chivalry were Christian foundations. And they were concerned with monarchy because, as another authority on India observed, 'The Crown is the Fountain of Honour, and those who accept its decorations or privileges owe, and admit their liability for, something in return.'[30]

As this remark implies, the acceptance of an honour did not merely elevate someone in the social and imperial hierarchy; it also put them formally in a direct, and subordinate, relation to the monarch. For as the 'Fountain of Honour', British kings and queens were, among other things, sovereigns of all the orders of chivalry. As their day-to-day political involvement lessened in Britain, they became ever more interested in the creation, regulation, extension and distribution of these imperial honours. Victoria, Edward VII and George V were closely involved in designing and naming the new orders that were inaugurated during their reigns; George VI was most at ease at investitures, and revived the installation ceremonials associated with the Order of the Garter and the Royal Victorian Order; and all of them were preoccupied with uniforms, heraldry, precedence and genealogy, and with decisions concerning the award of British honours to foreign potentates.[31] During the inter-war years, successive sovereigns gave particular attention to deciding the location of the new chapel for the Order of the British Empire. It was eventually dedicated in St Paul's Cathedral, the 'parish church of the Empire', in 1960. It was just in time – or perhaps it was just too late?[32]

8

Monarchs

'Is the Queen of England,' inquired Lord Elgin while governor-general of Canada (1847–54), 'to be the sovereign of an Empire, growing, expanding, strengthening itself from age to age?' The answer soon became – and remained – unhesitatingly in the affirmative. From the mid nineteenth century, the political power of the British sovereign waned, while the territories of the British empire waxed. Here was a coincidence that was also an opportunity – to create a new function, purpose and justification for monarchy, at a time when it was in need of all these things, by connecting it with, and lending its historic lustre to, the recently and rapidly expanding empire. And so, thanks largely to Disraeli, the British monarchy was refurbished and reinvented as an imperial crown of unprecedented reach, importance and grandeur.[1] One indication of this was that from 1876, successive sovereigns were empresses or emperors of India as well as queens or kings of the United Kingdom of Great Britain and (Northern) Ireland. Another was that from King Edward VII onwards, all of them were additionally styled as ruler of the 'British Dominions beyond the Seas'. More substantively, this meant that from Victoria to George VI, British sovereigns unified an imperial dominion of ever greater dimensions, and ordered an imperial hierarchy of ever greater complexity.[2]

But this was not just a matter of titular elevation and stylistic innovation. For as British monarchs were themselves becoming much more imperial, so the British Empire was itself becoming much more royal. This two-way process, whereby an imperialized monarchy merged with and moulded a monarchicalized empire, was exceptionally complicated, and we still know (and care) strangely little about it.[3]

Indeed, from the generally egalitarian-cum-republican perspective of the early twenty-first century, it is easy to forget the extent to which, in its heyday, the British Empire was a *royal* empire, presided over and unified by a sovereign of global amplitude and semi-divine fullness, and suffused with the symbols and signifiers of kingship, which reinforced, legitimated, unified and completed the empire as a realm bound together by order, hierarchy, tradition and subordination. But it is already possible to sketch the outlines of the end result – the creation and projection of a transcendent vision of this right-royal realm, mimicking and mirroring in its earthly social order the divine ranks and celestial hierarchies of the heavens.[4]

One indication of this was that many places in the British Empire were named for and after British kings and queens. This was a sign both of possession and of commemoration, of acquisition and veneration, and no royal name was more widely or frequently bestowed in this way than that of Victoria. Her reign coincided with one of the greatest eras of geographical exploration and imperial expansion; and the ubiquity of her appellation across the globe and around the world merely accentuated the semi-divine status she acquired by the 1880s and 1890s, since to have so many parts of the world labelled for the queen–empress was itself a sort of geographical deification and earthly apotheosis. For her name was literally *everywhere*: there was the Victoria Nile in Uganda, the Victoria Colony in Australia and the Victoria Falls on the Zambezi; there were six Lake Victorias and two Cape Victorias; and around the world there were Victoria Range, Bay, Strait, Valley, Point, Park, Mine, Peak, Beach, Bridge, County, Cove, Downs, Land, Estate, Fjord, Gap, Harbour, Headland and Hill. By such means the queen–empress seemed to be omnipresent in her own empire; and, as James Morris has noted, this set 'such seal upon the world, in cartography as in command, as no monarch in the history of mankind had ever set before'.[5]

But in addition to being a period of unprecedented exploration and expansion, the Victorian era witnessed unprecedented urban growth. Many new towns were named, and old towns renamed, after the Gas-Lit Gloriana: in West Africa, Labuan, Guiana, Grenada, Honduras, Newfoundland, Nigeria, and on Vancouver Island. And in these cities (and many others) the pervasive sense of royalty was further enhanced with the provision of permanent images and icons of monarchy. Statues of Victoria (especially), and also of Edward VII, George V and George VI, were prominently placed in city squares and in front of government houses. From Cairo to Canberra, Wellington to Johannesburg, Vancouver to Valetta, the image of the queen–empress appeared, often in canopied magnificence. She was commemorated almost everywhere in her lifetime. It was more usual for the king–emperors to be sculpted on horseback, and only after their deaths. There were also more specific constructions, many of them very extravagant, including the Victoria Terminus in Bombay (appropriately opened in 1887), Curzon's Victoria Memorial in Calcutta (which was not completed until twenty years after the queen's death), and the Royal York Hotel in Toronto (for long known as 'the largest hotel in the Empire').[6] More mundane, and yet more ubiquitous, were the roads, streets, drives, lanes, terraces, squares, crescents, ways and avenues named King or Emperor, or Queen or Empress, or Victoria or Edward, or George or Elizabeth, or Coronation or Jubilee, which could be found in villages, towns, suburbs and cities in every colony and every dominion.

This powerful and widespread sense of the royal presence throughout the empire was not just cartographical, sculptural, architectural or cadastral. For the imperial monarchy intruded itself into the individual lives and collective consciousnesses of imperial subjects in numerous ways and at many levels. The sovereign was head of the armed forces of the empire, from whom all officers held their commissions directly. The supreme reward for military valour was the Victoria Cross, while that for civilian courage was the George Cross. Throughout the empire, coins and stamps bore the image of the queen–empress or the king–emperor. All letter-boxes were dignified by the royal cypher; the post that was collected from them was called the royal mail; and official correspondence was sent in envelopes marked *On Her* or *On His Majesty's Service*. In Christian churches throughout the empire, the monarch was prayed for each Sunday. The national anthem of the empire was neither about nation nor empire, but was the martial,

22. Statue of King George V unveiled in 1916, Ceylon.

chivalric and hierarchical exhortation that 'God Save the King'.[7] Colonial law courts, dominion parliaments, regimental headquarters and government houses were decorated with royal portraits and coats of arms. The loyal toast was drunk at the end of all formal and many informal dinners. And schoolchildren were taught the history of their empire as the history of Britain's kings and queens – though Lord Lugard discouraged schools in Nigeria from teaching about the Stuarts, since this might 'foster disrespect for authority'.[8]

These were the day-to-day convergences between empire, monarchy and hierarchy: an amalgam of names, places, buildings, images, statues, rituals and observances that made it impossible for anyone to forget or ignore the fact that they were subjects of a sovereign rather than citizens of a republic. This, in turn, explains why governors were garlanded with ribbons and stars, why governors-general were bowed and curtseyed to, and why the viceroy of India was preceded by the playing of the national anthem when he entered the state dining room in New Delhi – not so much because these proconsuls were great men in their own right (although some undoubtedly were), but because they were the representative of the monarch, and as such enjoyed regal consequence, speaking for the sovereign almost as a priest might speak for God.[9] That was, in a sense, their most important public function: to show imperial subjects overseas that while imperial monarchs might live in London, they reigned over everyone in the empire, wherever they might be, and were to receive appropriate expressions of homage and fealty in return. As Lord Elgin explained when viceroy of India in the 1890s, the prime purpose of going on large tours was 'to afford opportunities to Her Majesty's subjects in the presence of Her Majesty's representative in India for manifestations of loyalty and affection for her throne and person'.[10]

The British Empire as a royal empire was not only about maps and statues and coins and stamps and bending the knee to the sovereign's representative: it was also, as Lord Elgin's comments imply, about the creation and performance of public ceremonials that were, like the honours system, globally inclusive, elaborately graded and intrinsically royal. At the most routine level, grand receptions were held in government houses throughout the empire on the official and unofficial birthdays of the monarch, and invitations to these occasions were eagerly sought. At a higher level of ceremonial intensity, the anniversary of Queen Victoria's birthday was (from 1904) observed as Empire Day in schools in villages, towns, cities and capitals around the globe. There were processions and parades, hymns were sung, and speeches were made by scoutmasters and schoolmasters, mayors and lord mayors, governors and viceroys, in which the ordered unity of the empire was extolled, and the sovereign was presented as 'all-knowing and all-caring'.[11] In addition to this shared annual festival, dominions and colonies evolved their own special fêtes of royalty, marking particular episodes and connections, such as King's Day in the Sudan, which throughout the inter-war years was observed as a way of commemorating the stop-off by George V and Queen Mary on their journey back from their durbar in India in January 1912.[12]

From this settled and secure base of regular and routine royal observances, a whole range of public ceremonials was evolved and elaborated, invented and inaugurated, to commemorate the rites of passage of imperial British monarchs in ways that were both far-reaching and of unprecedented extravagance. Of course, there had been local recognition of coronations, weddings, jubilees and funerals for as long as there had been a monarchy, and at the time of the Napoleonic Wars these festivities had been successfully extended to the colonies. But in the late nineteenth century they were propelled on to a much higher plane of efficiency, self-consciousness and ostentation, and as the empire expanded, they were taken and carried along with it. The result was that from Victoria's Golden Jubilee to George VI's coronation, these ceremonials were observed, not just in Glasgow and Birmingham, Cambridge and Bath, Leeds and Manchester, Norwich and York, but also in Hong Kong and Rangoon, Sydney and Lagos, Nairobi and Gibraltar, Montreal and Auckland, and in countless smaller towns and villages. These were shared imperial occasions, with a common style, involving banners and flags, speeches and street parties, military processions and religious services, the unveiling of statues or the opening of memorial halls. And they all stressed history and hierarchy, unity and order, crown and empire.[13]

23. Queen Victoria's Diamond Jubilee – Thanksgiving Service at St Paul's Cathedral, 1897.

24. Queen Victoria's Diamond Jubilee – decorations in Zanzibar.

These local festivities also provided the building blocks from which national and imperial spectaculars were developed and evolved. Once again, there were precedents in the late eighteenth and early nineteenth centuries, associated with the Golden Jubilee of George III and the pageants marking the end of the Napoleonic Wars, when local observances fed into London-based celebrations that complemented, completed and raised these provincial pageants to a higher level of national significance and theatrical splendour.[14] There was also the more immediate stimulus emanating from India, where the durbars of 1877, 1903 and 1911 served to nationalize a local ceremonial idiom by bringing together princely India and British India in week-long festivals of chivalric unity, feudal hierarchy and imperial subordination.[15] But it was not only east of Suez that what Lord Lytton called 'a bit of bunting' was being made to go a longer way than ever before. For in response to these Indian extravaganzas, a similar culture of ceremonial ostentation was developed in the imperial capital. From Victoria's Golden and Diamond Jubilees, to the Silver Jubilee of George V and the coronation of George VI, every great *royal* event was also projected as an *imperial* event: marked in London by carefully orchestrated processions, with everyone in their properly assigned place. Thus was the British Empire presented as an ordered, unified hierarchy, with a semi-divine sovereign at its apex.[16]

In London, as elsewhere, the greatest of these occasions was Victoria's Diamond Jubilee in 1897, when the queen–empress processed through the crowded and decorated streets of London, escorted by fifty thousand troops drawn from all the colonies of the empire, to receive the homage and acclaim of her subjects, to attend a thanksgiving service held on the steps of St Paul's Cathedral, and to enjoy a supreme moment of earthly apotheosis. The poet laureate, Alfred Austin, wrote commemorative verse. A provincial composer named Edward Elgar produced an 'Imperial March', 'something broad, noble, chivalrous', which he later developed into the 'Pomp and Circumstance' Marches.[17] The prime minister of Canada, Wilfrid Laurier, was knighted on Jubilee morning. There was an Imperial Fête in Regent's Park, and an Imperial Ballet at Her Majesty's Theatre. Here was the empire – 'like a huge work of architecture . . . castellated against all comers,

25. Nigerian cloth commemorating the Silver Jubilee
of King George V, 1935.

turreted for effect, audaciously buttressed, and crowned at the top, as other edifices might be completed with saint or angel, by the portly figure of Victoria the Queen Empress, holding an orb and sceptre, and already bathed in the refulgent light of legend' – putting itself on parade as never before. It was, wrote G. W. Stephens of the *Daily Mail*, 'a pageant which for splendour of appearance and especially for splendour of suggestion has never been paralleled in the history of the world'.[18]

In this era of heightened ostentation, Delhi and London became the twin exemplary centres of these new–old, royal-cum-imperial extravaganzas, which pulsed outwards towards the localities of the imperial periphery, where they further strengthened and reinforced the community-based festivities from which they simultaneously drew their own inspiration and legitimacy. By these interconnected pageants and mutually reinforcing ceremonials, the British Empire put itself on display, and represented itself to itself, more frequently, more splendidly, more ostentatiously and more globally than any other realm. The unrivalled extent of its dominions meant this was already true before 1914; and after the fall of the great monarchies in the First World War, the British Empire was a uniquely royal and ritualized realm. And this was no mere ephemeral ceremonial confection: the spectacular projection of the queen–empress and king–emperor was the essence and the heart of the matter.[19] For here was a transcendent vision of the earthly realm as a global hierarchy with the sovereign at its head, which mimicked the celestial realm, which was another hierarchy with another sovereign at its head. As the *Daily Mail* put it, on Jubilee Day 1897, it was fitting that the queen should have gone to pay homage to her God at St Paul's, for in all the world, He was the only 'One Being' who was 'More Majestic Than She'.[20]

These pageants also served another, and interrelated, royal purpose: for the British monarch was King of Kings in the empire, just as he was Lord of Lords in Britain. There might be only one sovereign above him; but there were plenty of them below, those agencies and beneficiaries of indirect rule who, once placed and ranked according to their standing and degree, acknowledged the supreme authority of the queen–empress or king–emperor.[21] Accordingly, these great London ceremonials, centring on coronations, jubilees and funerals, were not just mass, spectacular parades of hierarchy extending outwards towards the periphery from the metropolis; they were also occasions when distant monarchs came to the imperial capital to pay tribute and pledge fealty. Adorned in costumes that yielded nothing in magnificence to western ceremonial dress, or clad in the sashes and stars, the collars and mantles, of the Indian orders, or the Order of St Michael and St George, or the Order of the British Empire, they made journeys to London that were widely reported in the local press and acclaimed by their subjects. For there was nothing more grand than going half a world away to do homage – a gesture of well-connected obeisance that merely increased prestige at home.

Nothing like this had happened much before Victoria's jubilees. But thereafter it became a well-rehearsed and well-repeated pattern, modelled on the homage done to the viceroy by Indian princes at the three great durbars, and providing *them* with the opportunity to pay tribute in London as well as in Delhi. These ceremonial visits were serious and elaborate enterprises: no elephants, but much trumpeting. The highly decorated maharaja of Jaipur travelled to London for King Edward VII's coronation 'with one hundred and twenty-five of his officers and attendants, a whole ship being chartered for the voyage'. Appropriately enough, the architect of these arrangements was Swinton Jacob, the maharaja's resident expert in the Indo-Saracenic style, who received the KCIE for his pains on this occasion, and who would later add to this a CVO in 1911 for his work on the Delhi Durbar.[22] The equally decorated sultan of Zanzibar, whom we have also already met, did even better, being present in London for the coronations of King George V, King George VI and Queen Elizabeth II, and as a result he received three Coronation Medals to add to the three grand crosses he already held in three British orders of knighthood.

There were many other potentates who appeared in London to pay homage to their supreme sovereign. From Malaya came Sultan Idris of Perak to the coronation of Edward VII, and his party included two leading local chiefs, his son, his son-in-law and his 'bodyguard of Indian troopers'. When he was told of the king's illness and of the postponement of the 'tremendous ceremony' that he had travelled across the world to see, the sultan went into retreat, spending two days in prayer for his sovereign's recovery.[23] From Barotseland came King Lewanika for the same coronation. He was enthusiastically welcomed by metropolitan society, he had royal carriages put at his disposal, the horses were taken out in a Dorset village where the locals pulled the king in triumph, and the visit was in all ways the climax of his career. 'When kings are seated together,' he observed, 'there is never a lack of things to discuss.' Lewanika's successor, Yeta III, achieved equal glory at the coronation of 1937, when he was received by King George VI, and an account of his visit was published by his secretary. This king had no doubt of the cosmic transcendence of the ceremonials he had witnessed: 'Nobody,' his secretary wrote, 'could think that he is really on earth when seeing the coronation procession, but that he is either dreaming or he is in paradise.'[24]

In between these ceremonial encounters, the ruling princes and subordinate royalties of India, Africa, Malaya and the Middle East made regular private visits to Windsor, Balmoral and Buckingham Palace, where they were greeted, honoured and entertained. As at coronations, they were viewed, from one perspective, as traditional feudatories in the imperial hierarchy visiting their supreme sovereign: so when in 1919 the paramount chief of Basutoland visited Britain for an audience with George V, he was refused permission to proceed to Rome, for fear that he 'might be unduly impressed by the pomp and state of reception at the Vatican, and might form the conclusion that the Pope was more important than the King'.[25] But they were also regarded as fellow sovereigns, as members of the imperial trades union of royalty that, after 1918, came to matter much more to the British crown than the (in every sense) much reduced European monarchies. Hence, in 1944 King George VI sent the already-much-decorated sultan of Zanzibar a message of congratulation on the bicentenary of his dynasty, paying tribute to 'the friendship and loyalty so generously extended to my Father and to myself throughout the thirty-three years of Your Highness's reign, and especially through two long and bitter wars'. Here, in more senses than one, was the British Empire as a royal empire – a point made, more brutally, by Sir William Slim to King

Farouk of Egypt, when, as chief of imperial general staff, he reminded him that there were 'no kings on the other side of the Iron Curtain'.[26]

In this empire of kings, there was also reciprocation from the metropolis, as British royalty, and eventually the British monarchs themselves, journeyed out to the empire. During the second and third quarters of the nineteenth century, the most ardent loyalists in Canada and Australia had urged that Queen Victoria send out her younger children to found cadet branches of the British monarchy in the colonies. These schemes (which were supported by Anthony Trollope) came to nothing.[27] But they echoed down the decades until the Second World War, as alternative arrangements were evolved for associating the monarchy with the empire in a more personal way. One solution was to export close relatives of the sovereign as governors-general of the great dominions, thereby tying them in ever closer association to the crown, and placing the most illustrious possible representative of the king–emperor at the apex of the political and social hierarchy. The first such appointment, appropriately by Disraeli, was of the marquess of Lorne (husband of Princess Louise, and thus son-in-law of Queen Victoria) as governor-general of Canada from 1878 to 1883. Here was a 'new experiment in statecraft by which the Crown was employed as an instrument to proclaim the greatness and unity of the empire'. The colonials could scarcely contain their delight.[28]

Thereafter, this experiment was several times repeated, which meant the imperial monarchy was made a real presence and vital element in the empire. The duke of Connaught, Victoria's favourite son, was governor-general of Canada from 1911 to 1916 – the first proconsul of royal blood, who gave dominion life 'a focus of great dignity and prestige'.[29] In the inter-war years, royal attention turned to South Africa, where from 1920 to 1924 the governor-general was Prince Arthur of Connaught, whose father had been governor-general of Canada; and he was followed by the earl of Athlone, who was married to Princess Alice, a granddaughter of Queen Victoria. There was also a scheme, widely canvassed at this time, to appoint George V's four sons simultaneously governors-general of all four dominions. It came to nothing, but the notion that the British Empire was a *royal* empire, which should be governed and unified by royal proconsuls, reached its apogee during the Second World War: the earl of Athlone, who had already been governor-general of South Africa, was dispatched to Canada; the king's elder brother, the duke of Windsor, was sent to govern the Bahamas; and the king's younger brother, the duke of Gloucester, was installed in 1945 as governor-general of Australia.[30]

There was one yet more immediate way in which the crown was made truly imperial, and the empire authentically royal. That was by majestic journeys to the empire, which reciprocated and paralleled the pilgrimages made by potentates from the periphery to the imperial metropolis. These were grand progresses by land and sea, lasting for many months and covering many miles, involving countless receptions, dinners, parades and speeches, and all carried on before vast, delighted and admiring crowds. The prince of Wales made the first such visit to Canada in 1860, when he toured Quebec and Ontario, and crossed over into the United States. He was followed seven years later by his younger brother, the duke of Edinburgh, who made the first royal journey to the Australian colonies. But the tone and tenor of such tours was really established when, at Disraeli's urging, the prince of Wales went to India in 1876. He held receptions and durbars in Bombay and Calcutta; he met many Indian princes and expressed his strong support for them; he held a chapter of the Order of the Star of India; and he shot tigers for recreation.[31] Thereafter, his brother, the duke of Connaught (whom we have already met as governor-general of Canada), visited India as the king's representative at the durbar of 1903 (when he was rather upstaged by Curzon); and he returned in 1921 for the opening of the new legislatures in Madras, Bombay, Calcutta and New Delhi under the Montagu–Chelmsford reforms of 1919.[32]

These royal progresses within the empire moved into even higher gear during the next two generations, as kings and queens set out to present themselves in person to their far-off subjects. This meant that the arrangements became ever more elaborate, and the tours ever more novel, thrilling and spectacular, as the royal lineaments and sovereign symbols of empire were brought vividly and vitally alive. The future George V visited the Antipodes in 1901 to inaugurate the parliament of recently federated Australia; and he first went to India in 1905. He

26. The prince of Wales in Banff on his Canadian tour, 1919,
wearing an Indian headdress.

27. The prince of Wales in Accra on his African tour, 1925.

returned there amidst unprecedented pomp in 1911 as the first reigning monarch to set foot in his overseas empire, and crowned himself as emperor.[33] Thereafter, he stayed determinedly at home, but his eldest son, the future Edward VIII, travelled to almost every part of the empire between 1919 and 1925; not just to each of the great dominions, but also to India (where there was a durbar held at the Red Fort in Delhi for the ruling princes), to much of British Africa and to the West Indies. And his younger brother was almost as well travelled, touring East Africa (1924–5) and Australia (1927) as duke of York, and Canada (1939) and South Africa (1947) as King George VI, when he became the first reigning sovereign to visit either dominion.[34]

Such majestic appearances made the faces on the stamps and coins, the celebration of Empire Day, the possession (or pursuit) of imperial honours and the invitations to Government House more real and meaningful than ever before. As such, they were the direct descendants of the great domestic progresses of Queen Elizabeth I, 'metaphysical road shows' in which the sovereign, or a near relative, symbolically marked out, took possession and beat the bounds of this greater royal realm.[35] Of course, these progresses meant slightly different things in different parts of the empire. In the old dominions, a royal visit was a visible reaffirmation of the continuing Britishness of the sovereign's overseas subjects, and of their place in that metropolitan social order. In South Asia, the monarch appeared as the successor to the Mughal emperor, gloriously ensconced at the apex of an indigenous hierarchy. And he went to the colonies, among the tribes and chiefs of Africa, to show that 'the King continues to watch over you with fatherly care'. But for all these local differences and particular meanings, there remained one overriding impression across the length and breadth of empire. As James Morris notes, 'to have met, or even to have seen, a King, a Queen or a Prince of Wales remained, for millions of the old imperial subjects, one of the great experiences of life'. 'You are the big potato,' Field Marshal Smuts once informed Queen Mary; 'the other queens are all small potatoes.'[36]

It is in this royal-imperial context that we may best understand these words of George VI after his coronation: 'I felt this morning that

28. Vast crowds in Martin Place, Sydney, during the visit of
Queen Elizabeth II and Prince Philip, 1954.

the whole Empire was in very truth gathered within the walls of Westminster Abbey.' Virtually it was, and visually it was, with its whole diverse social hierarchy unified, ranked, ordered, layered and arranged.[37] And this symbiosis between crown and empire seemed set fair to continue into the next generation. When accompanying King George VI and Queen Elizabeth on their tour of South Africa, Princess Elizabeth took the occasion of her twenty-first birthday to pledge herself to the service of the great imperial family to which she belonged. Her own coronation in 1953 was another imperial spectacle, at which another monarch reigning under British protection, the much decorated Queen Salote of Tonga, almost stole the show by refusing to make any concessions to the inclement weather. And the queen's subsequent tour 'of a still-surviving Empire and of Dominions that fervently believed in their Britishness' was a sensational success, especially in Australia, where it was brilliantly organized by Robert Menzies, the obsequiously loyal federal prime minister. 'Perhaps,' he was later to speculate, in inadvertent corroboration of Edward Hamilton's words of half a century before, 'we are snobs, and love a hierarchical society?'[38]

9

Perspectives

What, then, in its heyday from the late 1850s to the early 1950s, did the British think the empire they had conquered and settled, governed and administered, gone along with and collaborated in, *actually looked like*? To be sure, it was a global phenomenon of unrivalled spaciousness and amplitude, which in its reach and range was both local and international, particular and general, and as such it undoubtedly formed one 'entire interactive system'. It was also as much a part of the 'tangible world' as it was of the intangible imagination, and in both these tangible and imaginative guises, it represented – as Peter Marshall has very properly observed – a deliberate, sustained and selfconscious attempt by the British to order, fashion and comprehend their imperial society overseas on the basis of what they believed to be the ordering of their metropolitan society at home.[1] And it cannot be sufficiently emphasized that *that* society, from which these powerful imperial impulses and imaginings originated and emanated, was deeply conservative in its social attitudes and in its political culture. The social structure was generally believed to be layered, individualistic, traditional, hierarchical and providentially sanctioned; and for all the advances towards a broader, more democratic electoral franchise, it was in practice a nation emphatically *not* dedicated to the proposition that all men (let alone women) were created equal.[2]

Thus, the imperial metropolis: and thus, unsurprisingly, the imperial periphery. To be sure, it was made up of varied dominions and diverse realms. But there was a homogenizing convergence about their social structures, and about perceptions of them, which was seen by turns as rural-aspirational (the dominions of settlement), caste-based and princely (the Indian Empire), chiefly and traditional (the crown colonies of rule), and Bedouin and tribal (the Middle East). It was further tied together by a shared sense of Britishness, in which this sense of an ordered imperial society was graded, reinforced, generalized and proclaimed by an elaborate system of honours and titles, and by a pervasive cult of imperial royalty, which surged out from the metropolis to the periphery, and back again. And all this was brought alive, made real, and carried along from past to present to future by unrivalled and interlocking displays of regular ritual and occasional spectacle.[3] In these ways, and by these means, the British exported and projected vernacular sociological visions from the metropolis to the periphery, and they imported and analogized them from the empire back to Britain, thereby constructing comforting and familiar resemblance and equivalencies and affinities.

The result was, indeed, 'one vast interconnected world'; and the phrase that best describes this remarkable transoceanic construct of substance and sentiment is *imperialism as ornamentalism*. Drawing on precedents established during the period of the Revolutionary and Napoleonic Wars, the British created their imperial society, bound it together, comprehended it and imagined it from the middle of the nineteenth century to the middle of the twentieth in an essentially ornamental mode. For ornamentalism was hierarchy made visible, immanent and actual. And since the British conceived and understood their metropolis hierarchically, it was scarcely surprising that they conceived and understood their periphery in the same way, and that chivalry and ceremony, monarchy and majesty, were the means by which this vast world was brought together, interconnected, unified and sacralized. As such, hierarchy was the conventional vehicle of organization and perception in both the metropolis and the periphery: it provided the prevailing ideology of empire, and it underpinned the prevailing spectacle of empire.[4] Thus envisaged, the British Empire was, like the British nation and the British people, a quintessentially Burkeian enterprise of 'faith ... family ... property ... monarchy', organically evolving in its structure across the centuries, across the continents and across the seas, and with ample available plumage for showing it and for showing off.[5]

It bears repeating that one aspect of this hierarchical-cum-imperial mindset was indeed the cultivation and intensification of racial differences based on post-Enlightenment attitudes of white and western superiority and of coloured and colonial inferiority (along with the cultivation and intensification of gender differences based on attitudes of white and male superiority and white and female inferiority). When, as they sometimes did, Britons thought of the inhabitants of their empire (as they sometimes thought about the inhabitants of their metropolis) in *collective* rather than in individualistic categories, they were inclined to see them, literally, in terms of crude stereotypes of black and white, and no-less crude relationships of superiority and inferiority. So, when the House of Commons debated Britain's administration of Egypt in June 1910, even the high-minded Edward Wood, who later won fame as the first viceroy of India who would parley on equal terms with Mahatma Gandhi, spoke conventionally of 'the white man' ruling 'inferior races' of 'black people'. And when the Tory leader, Arthur Balfour, observed with characteristic scepticism that 'it is not a question of superiority or inferiority', the rest of the House did not seem to share his views.[6]

But in the broader perspective of imperial relationships, Balfour was not entirely wrong. For when, as they usually did, the British thought of the inhabitants of their empire (as they usually thought about the inhabitants of their metropolis) in *individual* terms rather than in collective categories, they were more likely to be concerned with rank than with race, and with the appreciation of status similarities based on perceptions of affinity. From one perspective, the British may indeed have seen the peoples of their empire as alien, as other, as beneath them – to be lorded over and condescended to.[7] But from another, they also saw them as similar, as analogous, as equal and sometimes even as *better* than they were themselves. 'He was,' the Viceroy Lord Willingdon observed on the death of the Indian prince (and cricketer) Ranjitsinhji, the maharaja jam saheb of Nawangar, 'an ambassador of co-operation, friendship and goodwill between the two races ... a great ruler and a great gentleman.'[8] And this view was not just socially conservative, but politically conservative too. For as Lord Lugard once explained, anticipating Sir William Slim's later remark about the lack of kings on the other side of the Iron Curtain, the whole purpose of the British Empire was 'to maintain traditional rulerships as a fortress of societal security in a changing world'. And in that enterprise, the colour of a person's skin was less significant than their position in the local social hierarchy: 'the really important category was status', and as such it was 'fundamental to all other categories'.[9]

That was certainly the case when it came to the realities of running the empire and making it work, rather than merely talking about how it was (or was not) working in terms of vague, abstract generalizations. Since most Britons came from what they believed to be a hierarchical society, it was natural for them, when doing business or negotiating power, to search for overseas collaborators from the top of the indigenous social spectrum, rather than from lower down, whom they supported, whose cooperation they needed and through whom they ruled.[10] The British chose the allies they did abroad because of the social conditioning and social perceptions they brought with them from home. Moreover, and in conformity with the historic traditions and practices of British local government, this also made financial sense. If the empire was to be run on the cheap (as with a low-taxing metropolis it had to be), there must be voluntary collaborators; and, as the history of Britain itself made plain, the best people to collaborate with were likely to be the rich, well-born and powerful. In short, these imperial peoples were no aggregated, collective mass, all regarded as inferior and potentially hostile: they were seen differentially and often individually.[11] Depending on context and circumstance, *both* white *and* dark-skinned peoples of empire were seen as superior; or, alternatively, as inferior.

This in turn helps to explain why it was that when the British contemplated and imagined their far-flung empire, and thought about and visualized those many diverse races who inhabited it, they were at least as likely to look down on whites as they were to look up to those with darker skins, to disparage those who resembled themselves, but to acclaim those who belonged to other races. It may have been true that the British overseas came from the same original racial stock as the British at home, but, for all their shared skin colour and racial kinship, the metropolitans never lost 'the basic sense of their superiority of rank and wisdom over mere colonials'. In the eighteenth century, Whig grandees and their clients looked down on returning nabobs as vulgar upstarts.[12] In the nineteenth century, Britons in Australia were dismissed for being Irish Catholic, or the descendants of convicts, or both. And in the twentieth century, visitors to Britain from the great dominions were often treated with extreme condescension, as in Noël Coward's 1938 play *Hands Across the Sea*. All of which is simply to observe that throughout its history, many metropolitan Britons saw their settlement empire, not as a great white hope, but as a sociological dumping ground for hicks and bumpkins and (even) criminals: as 'a last resort for people who have ruined themselves at home'.[13]

Thus regarded, the British Empire seemed to be full of the dross and detritus of the British metropolis: convicts and their progeny sent as far away from home as possible; poor rejects from the slums and the back streets of Birmingham and Glasgow; failed professionals in the law and the church and the military; and indebted and scandal-blighted aristocrats shipped off and out of the way. These were rootless, marginal people, unable to find or take or keep their place in the metropolitan social order, or cast out from it. They were the poor whites or the white trash of their time.[14] By contrast, the native princes, ruling chiefs, lordly emirs and exotic sheikhs seemed much more like black gold: better people, at the apex of a better world, which was ordered, traditional, settled, time-honoured, face-to-face, decent, wholesome and uncorrupt. In certain contexts and situations, the British *did* regard the dark-skinned members of their empire as more admirable, more important and more noble than white men. This is not the whole truth of things. But it is a substantial, a significant and a neglected truth. And to the extent that it is, we ourselves need to recognize that there were other ways of seeing the empire than in the oversimplified categories of black and white with which we are so preoccupied. It is time we reoriented orientalism.[15]

For we should not suppose that the only way to approach and recover the history of the British Empire is through the antagonistic, stereotypical and unequal collectivities of race (any more than we should suppose that the only ways to approach and recover the history of humankind or of production are through the antagonistic, stereotypical and unequal collectivities of men versus women or of middle-class bosses versus working-class labourers). That these were a part of imperial (as of gender and of economic) history it is no purpose of this book to deny. *But they were only a part.* For as well as collective conflicts, there was in the British Empire (as in interpersonal relationships and the productive process) much individual cooperation, based on a shared recognition of equal social status. And to the extent that such 'cultivation of affinities' transcended the boundaries and barriers of colour, they were, as Harry Liebersohn has observed, 'an antidote to racism'.[16] Indeed, it may be that hierarchical empires and societies, where inequality was the norm, were in this sense less racist than egalitarian societies, where there was (and is?) no alternative vision of the social order from that of collective, antagonistic and often racial identities. Such a conclusion – that past societies and empires, predicated on individual inequality, had ways of dealing with race that contemporary societies, dedicated to collective equality, do not – may not be comforting for us today. But that does not necessarily detract from its historical validity.[17]

Understood in this way, as a conservative, traditional, ordered phenomenon, the British Empire was not exclusively about race or colour, but was also about class and status. This in turn means that it was about antiquity and anachronism, tradition and honour, order and subordination; about glory and chivalry, horses and elephants, knights and peers, processions and ceremony, plumed hats and ermine robes; about chiefs and emirs, sultans and nawabs, viceroys and proconsuls; about thrones and crowns, dominion and hierarchy, ostentation and ornamentalism.[18] And that brings us back to Joseph Schumpeter's original insight, in *Imperialism and Social Classes*, where he argued that the creation and administration of nineteenth-century empires was the result of a shared sense of personal identity between the most atavistic social groups in Europe, seeking escape from the travails of industry, democracy and big cities, and those traditional tribes and rulers overseas whom they resembled and found most sympathetic.[19] From *this* perspective, the impulses to empire were ancient rather than modern, and there was a powerful, traditional social vision

29. King George VI's coronation, 1937.

that underlay and informed these impulses. The British Empire may (or may not) have been the highest stage of capitalism. But it was certainly the highest stage of hierarchy.[20]

This was partly because hierarchy offered a cogent and appealing vision of imperial society and also therefore of imperial purpose. For as Stephen Howe has argued, the British Empire was, in its government and its administration, characterized by 'a romantic, anti-capitalist ethos'.[21] In these endeavours, the significance of religion and duty (and the military) has long been recognized: of the Church of England and the public school (and the officers' mess).[22] But far less attention has been given to the sociological underpinnings and expressions of these sacred and secular (and military) impulses: the belief in the importance of preserving hierarchy as something that was God-given and pre-capitalist, and therefore the best of all possible worlds.[23] This was true of the imperial metropolis, where many of its ruling institutions were in their ethos and their ideology anti-capitalist and pro-hierarchy. And it was equally true in the empire: great estates and Gothic cathedrals in the dominions; ruling princes and Indo-Saracenic architecture in South Asia; native chiefs and traditional tribes in Africa and the Middle East; imperial chivalry, royal images and icons, everywhere. In all these ways, and by deliberate design rather than absence of mind, the British Empire in its heyday was very much an anti-capitalist and pro-hierarchical construction.

But it was also that the empire was not *just* as hierarchical a construction as British society in the metropolis: it was significantly *more* so, a kind of enlarged and heightened version of the metropolitan model, blooming with brighter colours, greater radiance and stronger perfume. So: viceroys and governors were treated with more fawning deference overseas than ever they received at home, where many of them missed the saluting and the curtseying they had taken for granted in their palmy proconsular days. So: district commissioners were responsible for larger areas of administration than most English country gentlemen would ever have known on their estates. So: imperial civil servants and colonial administrators lived in greater splendour and comfort overseas than they did when they returned, 'exiled from glory', to Eastbourne or Bedford.[24] So: middle-class emigrants to the dominions might hope

30. Nuremberg rally, 1938.

to establish themselves as 'somebody', as indigenous gentry, a status and a position to which they might never realistically have aspired at home. Small wonder, then, that many people who went out to the empire, as settlers or as administrators, or as proconsuls, sought to replicate Britain's social hierarchy overseas, on account of their *enhanced position within it*, rather than to overturn it.[25]

Viewed and evoked in this way, as an hierarchical construction, and as a 'traditional' enterprise, the British Empire must rank as one of modern history's most extraordinary creations, and it is only now that it is finally dead and gone that we can begin to grasp – if we are so inclined – the full extent and varied nature of its many extraordinarinesses. And among them must be counted its conservatively cultured settler dominions, its Indian Empire built around caste and village and prince and Raj, its African colonies and Middle Eastern mandates governed according to the theory of indirect rule, its honours system that was unrivalled in its inventiveness and Byzantine in its complexity, and its royal and imperial crown that intruded itself at every jubilee and on every pillar-box. Indeed, by the inter-war years, when the royal regimes and theatrical empires of Germany, Russia and Austria-Hungary had disappeared, there was nothing left like it anywhere else in the western world. The splendid anachronism of its pageantry at the time of George V's Silver Jubilee and George VI's coronation was deliberately projected as a powerful and reassuring antidote to the high-tech parades and search-light rallies in Mussolini's Italy, Stalin's Red Square and Hitler's Nuremberg.[26]

It was, then, not only the imperial metropolis, but also the imperial periphery that may be described in George Orwell's famous phrase as 'the most class-ridden country under the sun'. As such, they were mutually reinforcing: on the one hand, the empire was built around notions of an exported domestic social hierarchy; on the other, empire served to reinforce from abroad the hierarchy of home. By the late nineteenth century the substance and semblance of the British Empire as an hierarchical empire had become increasingly important in bolstering the British perception that they still belonged to what was in the metropolis a traditional, agricultural, layered society.[27] In an era of mass democracy, advanced industrialization, unprecedented urban growth and the beginnings of aristocratic decline, the elaborate layers and gradations of empire, which were underpinned by, and helped to underpin, the newly revived monarchy, served to persuade the British that they continued to inhabit an ordered society, and to persuade those plumed and plumaged proconsuls that even in the era of Lloyd George, the patricians remained at the top of the social hierarchy. In these ways, 'ideas about the ordering of Empire' continued to be closely connected to 'ideas about the ordering of Britain itself'.[28]

From these perspectives, the British Empire was about land and agriculture and the countryside, and about the ideal, divinely sanctioned social order to which this gave rise: a way of life, and a social structure, that still existed on the greater and lesser estates in Britain, but that was increasingly threatened; and a way of life that was better preserved (and being preserved) in the empire. As Sir Edwin Lutyens once noted with pleasure and recognition, going out into 'India, like Africa' made him feel 'very Tory and pre-Tory Feudal'. It was a shrewd observation – and it held good throughout the inter-war years when the presumption that even the dominions would remain preponderantly agricultural societies continued all but unquestioned.[29] Indeed, such conservative-rural sentiments were held at least down to the end of the Second World War, and in some cases even beyond. As late as 1950 the Tory Party could still proclaim itself the champion of a national and imperial community characterized by 'an infinity of gradation', which was essentially and primordially rural both at home and abroad. Historically, the Conservatives had always been 'associated with agricultural interests and the idea of empire' – interests and ideas that were both essentially hierarchical.[30]

All this was well displayed in two speeches delivered on Britain and the empire by Leopold Amery in 1943. He was well read, well educated and well travelled, a former colonial secretary in the Baldwin government of 1924 to 1929, and Churchill's secretary of state for India during the Second World War. Amery's Britain was an organic, evolving, traditional community, whose inhabitants were uninterested in mechanical forms or abstract doctrines, but preferred to trust to personal feelings and individual instincts. As such, it was a nation renowned for its exemplary monarchy, its country houses and paternal landowners, and its matchlessly beautiful countryside, in which individual distinctions and inequalities of status were blended into the seamless fabric of life. Extended from here, Amery's empire was 'the translation into outward shape, and under ever varying circumstances, of the British character and of certain social and political principles, constituting a definite British culture or way of life which, first evolved on British soil, has since been carried by our people across all the seas'. Created by the 'compromising, conservative, adaptable' national character, the British Empire was identified by its unity and continuity that blended local variations and common patriotism, by its strong love of order and authority and its hostility to systematic schemes and logical conclusions, by its belief in compromise and toleration, by its common devotion to the king–emperor, and by its respect for tradition, antiquity, 'old substance' and 'old form'.[31]

Described (and praised) in this way, the wartime British Empire, over whose liquidation Winston Churchill had no intention of presiding, was still recognizably the same traditional, royal, layered, Burkeian organism that the American colonists had so vehemently rejected back in 1776, when they had set themselves against monarchy, titles, aristocracy and hierarchy by embracing the revolutionary principle that 'all men are created equal'. It was the same traditional, royal, layered Burkeian organism that Woodrow Wilson had rejected in the aftermath of the First World War, when he had eagerly joined in dismantling the Russian, the German and the Austro-Hungarian Empires, and had sought to create a civilization that was safe, not for British imperialism, but for western democracy. And despite his patrician upbringing, Harvard education, friendship with King George VI, and delight in being 'in the same decade' as Churchill, it was the same traditional, royal, layered, Burkeian organism that Franklin Roosevelt disliked so intensely. After all, the American colonists had rejected Britain's empire of hierarchy in the late eighteenth century: why, one hundred and fifty years later, was this reactionary undertaking still around?[32] Only during the early years of the Cold War, when the British Empire appeared a potentially useful ally in the battle against communism, were these hostile American perceptions briefly reversed.

31. Sir Robert Menzies installed as lord warden of the Cinque Ports, 1966.

Throughout most of its existence, the British Empire *was* on the side, both at home and overseas, of the established order. Small wonder, then, that its zenith coincided with the heyday of spectacular ceremonials, and with the hegemony of the Conservative Party. And small wonder that its heroes all had their place in the Tory pantheon. There was Benjamin Disraeli, who initiated the Order of St Michael and St George and the Order of the Indian Empire; who dispatched Lord Lorne to be governor-general of Canada and the prince of Wales to visit India; who made Queen Victoria empress of India; and who believed that 'it is only by the amplification of titles that you can often touch and satisfy the imagination of nations'.[33] There was Lord Curzon, who adored landed estates, old buildings, the feudal order and its ceremonial expression: 'who always seemed to live in spirit on the back of a highly caparisoned elephant'; who accumulated knighthoods and peerages with an insatiable appetite for chivalric aggrandizement; and who was more at ease with Indian princes than with the worthy bourgeoisie of Derby. And there was Winston Churchill, who loved the empire for its 'glitter, pomp and iced champagne', its 'high-sounding titles', its 'tradition, form and ceremony'; who devoted his political life to 'two public causes which I think stand supreme – the maintenance of the enduring greatness of Britain and her Empire, and the historical continuity of our island life'; and whose state funeral in 1965 would be the last, defining, valedictory imperial pageant.[34]

As such, the British Empire as an hierarchical enterprise was never merely the 'one-sided creation of British imagination'. It was never just one-sided, because many colonials, like Menzies (who eventually became a companion of honour, knight of the Thistle and lord warden of the Cinque Ports, and was rumoured to hanker after a peerage), believed in it, and were delighted to belong to it, to be involved in it and to be rewarded by it.[35] And the empire was never just imagination because there were abundant materials, both at home and overseas, out of which that picture was fashioned and constructed. As a result, most Britons saw their empire as an extension of their own social world rather than in contradistinction to it. They exported social perceptions on the presumption of sameness as much as they imported social perceptions on the presumption of difference. They were as eager to make it seem familiar as they were to recognize that it was unfamiliar, to see it as a social hierarchy rather than as a racial hierarchy. Their empire existed overseas: but the British tried to make it seem like home. They saw what they were conditioned, what they wanted, and what they expected, to see.[36]

10

Limitations

This was a persuasive (and pervasive) picture of Britain and its empire, which needs to be recognized and retrieved. But it was also a partial (and partisan) picture, and that too needs to be recognized and retrieved. For in the attempt to create, unify and envision the British Empire as 'one vast interconnected world', which replicated and reinforced the domestic social order, there was – as in most fields of metropolitan control and peripheral collaboration, and as there had already been during the late eighteenth and early nineteenth centuries – a significant gulf between theory and practice, intention and accomplishment.[1] In reality, the empire was never as fully hierarchical or as convincingly homogenized as those Britons who governed it, collaborated in it and went along with it tried to make it, wished it to be or believed it to be. This in turn meant that in the imperial metropolis, there was always a view on the left (from Paine and Cobden to Morell and beyond) that the empire was a 'Tory racket': not so much an ordered, paternal, traditional organism, encompassing all levels of society, but a system of outdoor relief and exploitation for those at the top – the titled and the rich. These domestic critics tended to be urban, middle class and intellectual and, as the empire expanded and evolved, they were joined by colonials on the periphery, who tended to be from similar backgrounds and hold similar views.[2]

Even in the great dominions of settlement, and notwithstanding the best efforts of those who wished it otherwise, the British social hierarchy was neither fully nor successfully replicated. In nations with less developed and largely agricultural economies, the extremes of wealth and poverty were not as great as in Britain, which meant that society was less unequal and less layered. As Walter Bagehot explained, the 'whole series of attempts to transplant to the colonies a graduated English society' had 'always failed at the first step', with 'the base of the pyramid spread abroad and the apex tumbled in and perished'.[3] Indeed, for many settlers, the entire point of emigrating was to get away from what they perceived as the suffocating hierarchy (and hierarchical attitudes) of the mother country, and to begin a new life where equality and opportunity were more important, as this had also been true in an earlier century of their colonial American forebears. From such a perspective, the *lack* of hierarchy in the colonies – known in Australia as 'mateship' – was a measure of *success*, not failure.[4] 'The overseas British,' John Darwin notes, 'generally had little sympathy for what they regarded as an over-rigid class system at home.' And when the overseas British were Irish, who were Catholic rather than Anglican, and Home Rulers rather than imperialists, they were even less likely to accept the imperial hierarchy, preferring (as in parts of Australia) to apply their domestic grievances to colonial agitation.[5]

Hence too the real opposition among many in the settlement dominions to those failed and faded sprigs of immigrant nobility: those 'gentlemen emigrants' and aristocratic 'remittance men', trying to live in absurdly extravagant and lordly and leisured style in the meritocratic colonies, on the basis of a regular but limited income from home, and who gave themselves airs and graces that impressed none and enraged many. They too were signs and symbols of the world that most settlers had thankfully left behind, and of which they did not wish to be reminded. Hence too the disapproval of the excessively expensive proconsular paraphernalia of Government House, with its petty snobberies, its 'sham' courts, its obsession with precedence, and all the toadying and title-hunting sycophants who sought invitations to go there.[6] Hence, finally, the criticism of the office of the governor-general itself as being no more than 'a glittering and gaudy toy', and of those who held it as the 'party dumpings of Britain', the 'imported pooh-bahs', the 'untried juvenile noblemen' and the 'aristocratic fainéants' with whom the dominions were all too often fobbed off as governors-general, such as Buxton in South Africa, Bessborough in Canada, Bledisloe in New Zealand and Dudley in Australia.[7]

It was the same in India, where the hierarchical nature of the imperial embrace was less complete and less convincing than its supporters and beneficiaries claimed. In part this was because, despite their efforts and inquiries, the British were very ignorant of India and Indian society.[8] Caste was an exceptionally complex thing, which meant both more and less to South Asians than it did to the Raj. The relationship between the hierarchy of caste and the hierarchy of the princes was particularly problematic, and many Britons did not understand that they did not understand it, among them King Edward VII, who mistakenly (but revealingly) supposed that nawabs and rajas were of purer caste than Brahmans.[9] Moreover, many of the princes were regarded, not as the upholders of traditional society and values, but as idle, profligate, rapacious, degenerate, authoritarian and corrupt, and even well-disposed viceroys like Curzon felt obliged to intervene to mitigate the most severe abuses. As for the Raj itself: the British believed that its hierarchy, pageantry and splendour guaranteed its appeal to the native imagination across the length and breadth of India. At all three imperial durbars, this was offered as the justification for the scale and the cost of the proceedings; but there seems little evidence that the majority of the population were much interested in, or lastingly influenced by, these displays. By the Second World War this viceregal splendour was seen as the 'laboured continuance, apparently for reasons of prestige, of opulence that seemed unrelished'. Few Indians, Philip Woodruff recalled, 'were stirred by the pomp of Empire'.[10]

This British preoccupation with 'traditional' India – with village, caste, landowner and princely state – was not only based on mistaken perceptions and misleading analogies. It also encouraged them to ignore, or wish away, or disregard, the alternative India that was coming into being: urban, educated, modernizing, radical, middle class and nationalist, which was especially to be found in Calcutta and after 1885 in the Congress Party.[11] One reason Congress hated the Raj was because its intrusive imperialism took the form of reverence for tradition and hierarchy. How ironic, Nehru observed, in a formulation that has been regularly repeated ever since, that the representatives of the dynamic, progressive west should ally themselves with the most conservative and oppressive elements of the static, backward east. But the British responded by dismissing these 'infernal Baboos' as 'unrepresentative extremists', as Leninist intellectuals in thrall to the masses and incorrigibly hostile to the established order.[12] Throughout its existence, the Raj preferred tradition to modernity, hierarchy to democracy, as exemplified in Lord Lytton's remark to the queen–empress at the time of the 1877 durbar that 'if we have with us the princes, we shall have with us the people'. And the same view underlay the decision taken in 1911, to move the capital 'from the premier city of politics and business, Calcutta, to Delhi, the noncommercial, nonpolitical centre of ancient Imperial splendour'.[13]

There were similar illusions regarding the colonial empire, where the tribal and chiefly world of indirect rule, with its ordered hierarchies and venerable structures, was often based, as Andrew Porter has observed, 'on skewed or imperfect knowledge of local societies'. For the British knew very little, either historically or anthropologically, about the regions that they annexed. And (as in India) the analogies they drew between native tribes and country estates, and between native chiefs and country gentlemen, were often wildly misleading: 'self-deceptions and half-truths', as John Tosh has rightly called them.[14] Lugard might have had some success in Northern Nigeria, where the emirs presided over their authoritarian regimes. But the south and west were (unknown to Lugard) stateless, decentralized, small-scale societies, without emirs or hierarchy, and his attempt to create 'warrant chiefs' gave great offence in societies with no tradition of chieftainship.[15] In the Sudan, indirect rule worked with some success in the south, but not in the north, where once again the chiefs in whom the British had reposed their confidence turned out to have less authority than they had thought.[16] And in Tanganyika, Sir Donald Cameron's attempt to discover (and rule through) 'authentic', 'traditional', pre-German conquest tribes and chiefs was an equally ignorant and ill-fated enterprise, for 'many east Africans had no chiefs, let alone kings'.[17]

This mistaken belief that hierarchy was always unchangingly *there* led to further limitations of indirect rule. As in India, the British preference for agriculture over industry, for the country over the town, for tradition rather than change, and for individuals over collective groups, meant there was a general dislike of the progressive, city-dwelling middle classes. In 1873 Lord Kimberley thought it better in West Africa to 'have nothing to do with the "educated natives" as a body. I would treat with the hereditary chiefs only.' This remained British policy thereafter, which meant that towns like Khartoum, Lagos and Nairobi were increasingly outside the British imperial mind-set. Yet this was where change was most rapid and irreversible, and where nationalist politics and hostility to empire and hierarchy would one day blossom. As one administrator in the Sudan put it, in unintended corroboration of Nehru, 'The chiefs represent the Past. The educated classes represent the Present.' To disregard this was to 'make a fetish of tradition' – an analysis that may be taken to apply to much of the British Empire in its heyday. That was certainly the progressive opinion in the section of the Colonial Office concerned with the administration of Malaya. 'From the democratic point of view,' noted Dr T. D. Shiels in 1931, 'it would be a retrograde step to enhance the position of the Rulers.'[18] Indeed, by then administrators and politicians were more widely criticizing the whole idea of indirect rule as anachronistic, undemocratic and too resistant to change.[19]

With appropriate local variations, the same limitations of perceptions and of policy characterized Britain's cultivation (and creation) of royal regimes in the Middle East. They may have been modelled on the princely states of India, and they may have been the expression of genuine imperial veneration for Arab hierarchies and Bedouin chiefs, but they lacked the stabilizing accoutrements of tradition and antiquity, and they were not well grounded in the affections of their subjects. There, as in Africa, the British were relying, out of necessity and out of ignorance, on partners whose powers and legitimacy did not always match their privileges or their pomp. In Egypt, 'the princes' and 'the pashas' were widely disliked as British stooges and puppets, and were seen as agents of empire rather than as beneficiaries of the people. The Hashemite rulers in Jordan and Iraq were equally vulnerable, since they owed their thrones entirely to the British and, as one official observed, they had 'never succeeded in establishing themselves firmly in the hearts of the people'.[20] Indeed, according to Elie Kedourie, Iraq was little more than a 'make-believe kingdom, built on false premises', a 'hotbed of corrupt and greedy reactionaries', where the king lacked the support of the Kurds, the Jewish population, the Shi'ite tribes and the Baghdad middle class.[21]

Inevitably, this meant that the British were seen by a majority of the population as the allies of 'vested interests' (as in India and the colonies), which increasingly came to mean 'being regarded as an obstacle in the way of beneficial change'.[22] And they were resented for it. Change in the inter-war Middle East had an Indian rather than an African dynamic: westernization, modernization, urbanization and education were rapidly bringing into being, in Alexandria, Cairo, Baghdad and Amman, a literate, politicized, nationalist middle class. From their oppositional perspective, the British Empire appeared 'a true ally of reaction . . . depending as it did upon the alliance of sheikhs and princes, distrustful of urban values and intellectual taste'.[23] The Second World War, which witnessed an unprecedented British military presence from the Suez Canal to the Persian Gulf, intensified these nationalist feelings into something that Sir Orme Sargent feared 'the ruling classes [could] no longer control'. He was not alone in this opinion. 'I do not believe,' Ernest Bevin remarked in 1946, 'that the Pashas will maintain for ever undisputed sway over Egypt.' 'Nationalism has come to stay' agreed one Foreign Office hand in Iraq two years later. But, he went on, 'the Regent is not the man to lead it'.[24] From this unsettling perspective, Britain's continued attachment to the Middle Eastern monarchies and the 'old gang' was more a sign of imperial weakness than of colonial cunning.[25]

Such were the local limitations on the hierarchical structures and sentiments of empire. There were also more general constraints, inadequacies and incompleteness that limited the reach and effectiveness of impulses emanating from the metropolis. In part this was because the social conservatism that was characteristic of the empire did not necessarily translate into political acquiescence. Dominion leaders might hanker after imperial titles and honours, and revere the royal family, but that did not prevent them from asserting their nations' independence and autonomy, thereby undermining the 'organic unity' of the empire. Before the First World War they had roundly rejected imperial federation, and during the 1920s and 1930s both General Smuts in South Africa and W. T. Cosgrave in the Irish Free State were ardent campaigners for recognition – ultimately embodied in the Statute of Westminster in 1931 – that the dominions were 'free and equal' to Britain.[26] And even so fervent a believer in Britain and in hierarchy as Robert Menzies would play the nationalist hand when it suited him. He was prepared to try to topple Churchill in the darkest days of 1941; he was a jealous defender of prime ministerial power even from the British governors-general he brought to Australia with such relish; and in signing the Anzus treaty (which involved the United States and New Zealand, but kept the United Kingdom out), he recognized the need to move his country away from the traditional British connection towards closer ties with America.[27]

It was the same in 'traditional' India, where collaboration between the Raj and the maharajas was rarely as cordial or as complete as was suggested by the cosy image of princes and proconsuls sharing equal membership of imperial orders of chivalry. Despite their public acquiescence in this post-Disraelian extravaganza, some rulers inwardly (and sometimes outwardly) rejected this whole enterprise as false and demeaning. Although they enjoyed a deserved reputation as model and loyal princes, the maharajas of Jaipur were silently protesting collaborators, who used Indo-Saracenic architecture for public buildings, but rejected it for their private palaces as smacking too much of complicity in British domination. Less subtly, the maharaja Sayajirao III of Baroda, who was second in rank among all the ruling princes after the nizam of Hyderabad and had been a GCSI since the days of Lord Dufferin, publicly snubbed the king–emperor at the 1911 durbar by doing homage insolently rather than obsequiously. Thereafter he was viewed by the British (with good cause) as a seditious nationalist.[28] According to Mahatma Gandhi, many princes resented being compelled to dress up, to wear stars and sashes, and to perform like circus animals in pantomimes of colonial devising – a mood of princely alienation that helps to explain their refusal to accede to the provisions of the Government of India Act of 1935 (well captured by Gita Mehta in her novel *Raj*).[29]

A similar picture emerges in the colonial empire, where collaborating emirs, sultans and notables could assert their own authority and defy the empire in the same manner as dominion leaders or Indian princes. Before the First World War the British presence in tropical Africa was generally weak and dispersed, which enabled ambitious native chiefs, like Chilongozi Gondwe of the Tumbuka, to enhance their position by using the title 'king', even when the local district commissioner disapproved. By the inter-war years the imperial presence was stronger and more systematic, but with that there came a growing yet reluctant recognition that, in places like the Sokoto Province of Nigeria, the most successful African chiefs – those with popular legitimacy, selected by the tribal kingmakers rather than the British administrators, who were relied upon for 'good native administration' – could also be the most difficult and independent-minded.[30] It was the same in Malaya where, in the early 1930s, the new high commissioner, Sir Cecil Clementi, sought to bring the sultans' states into closer association; but the rulers opposed the scheme so vehemently that it was eventually abandoned. And as the first stirrings of African nationalism began, royal visits and ceremonial events were increasingly manipulated by educated and 'progressive' Africans, so that within an ostensibly obsequious pattern of behaviour, opposition to empire was expressed. This was true of the visits of the prince of Wales and King George VI to Northern Rhodesia in 1925 and 1947; and by 1953 the country's Congress Party was openly boycotting Queen Elizabeth II's coronation festivities.[31]

But it was in the Middle East, where the new monarchies were insecurely grounded, and where the sovereigns needed to distance themselves from the British if they were to have any hope of conciliating the nationalists, that relations were the most difficult. Throughout the 1920s King Faisal of Iraq was the despair of British high commissioners: he was weak, devious, indecisive and unreliable, and he often sided with anti-British groups against the empire. His successor, King Ghazi, was another figure of 'total irresponsibility': he ran a broadcasting station from his palace that attacked the British, he flirted with Hitler, and laid claim to Kuwait.[32] It was no better in Egypt, where the pasha-dominated governments refused to sign a treaty with the Empire between 1922 and 1936, and where King Farouk made no secret of his pro-Axis sympathies. He was, according to Churchill, 'a poor friend of England'. During the Second World War the British were obliged to intervene in Iraq to restore the Regent Abdulillah to his throne after he had been deposed in a pro-Nazi coup in 1941, and in Egypt in the following year, when they effectively coerced Farouk into supporting the Allied war effort. Unsurprisingly, matters did not improve thereafter. An attempted treaty with Egypt failed in 1946, when Farouk laid claim to the Sudan; and in 1948 a new treaty negotiated by the Foreign Office and Iraq was repudiated by the regent because of popular nationalist pressure.[33]

All of which is simply to say that the British Empire as a social structure and hierarchical vision was not always in accord with the realities of imperial power politics; and so it was hardly surprising that the two greatest unifying forces of imperial hierarchy were also less effective than their most ardent supporters would have wished. For all its range, reach and inclusive inventiveness, the system of imperial honours never fully succeeded in unifying and ordering imperial society across the oceans and around the world. In the more egalitarian dominions of settlement, they were only ever embraced by a minority, and they never gained the prestige or resonance they were thought to have in Britain.[34] Back in the 1840s Governor Sir Charles Metcalfe had observed that the 'democratic or anti-British spirit' in parts of Canada meant people would 'strive to turn such honours into ridicule' and this prediction was often well borne out. 'Making titles,' Frederick Elliot agreed, 'does not make aristocracies. It is vain to give hereditary titles where fortunes are ephemeral.' The schemes for separate colonial peerages in Canada and Australia (and for hereditary upper houses in the colonial legislatures) never materialized: they were generally unpopular, and there were few people who would have been eligible. Few 'British' peerages were ever awarded to colonials, and some, such as Beaverbrook's, were very controversial.[35]

In any case, as the dominions became more conscious of their own nationalities, they became less eager to accept honours emanating from London, especially peerages. This was partly because they did not want to remain in this subservient imperial embrace, and partly because (*pace* Trollope) they believed their egalitarian ethos was against titles, especially hereditary ones. Accordingly, in 1919 Canada presented an address to the crown, asking that the king 'refrain hereafter from conferring any title of honour or titular distinction on any of your subjects domiciled or ordinarily resident in Canada'. It was because of this provision that the award of the Garter to the Anglophile and royalty-adoring Vincent Massey in the 1950s was vetoed (he was later consoled by Queen Elizabeth II with the non-title-conferring Royal Victorian Chain) and the proposed British life peerage for Conrad Black was recently opposed. South Africa adopted a similar practice in 1925. Although there was no official expression of disapproval from inter-war Australia, the Labour governments there simply stopped making any recommendations to London.[36] Elsewhere in the empire, the honours system was less contentious: but there were certainly some Indian princes who looked down on them as empty baubles; and, like any such system, it gave rise to envy and resentment as well as delight.

In such a climate, even the imperial monarchy legitimated hierarchy less effectively in the empire than it did in Britain. Notwithstanding the ubiquitous signs and symbols and signifiers of sovereignty, many Africans, South Asians, French Canadians and Afrikaners were, as Terence Ranger has rightly observed, simply not interested in British royalty.[37] Developing nationalist sentiments combined with more egalitarian impulses meant that in the melting-pot matrix of competing identities, the British imperial monarchy was not universally revered. In Australia, Irish-Catholics and radical labour did not buy into the hierarchical festival and kingly incorporation of Empire Day: they preferred St Patrick's Day, and after the First World War, Anzac Day became more popular.[38] In South Africa the Afrikaner nationalists remained more loyal to their own nationalist saints and heroes than to the Union or empire: the Great Trek meant more to them than Empire Day. Under these circumstances, royal proconsuls could be liabilities as well as assets, and they often had to tread more delicately than they knew how. The duke of Connaught's arrival in Canada met with an 'undercurrent of criticism' based on fears of too rigid a court at Rideau Hall; the appointment of Lord Athlone to South Africa was dismissed as 'an expensive survival of old and threadbare customs'; and the duke of Gloucester's term in Australia was cut short after two years, when he was replaced by W. J. McKell, at that time the Labour premier of New South Wales.[39]

In the same way, the royal tours to the empire were reported in Britain as triumphant progresses, evoking effusive displays of loyalty and devotion; but the reality was not always thus. In Australia a demented Irishman tried to assassinate the duke of Edinburgh during his visit in 1868; and when the duke of York toured in 1901, there were criticisms of 'the polluting finger marks of old-world royalty' and of 'bowing to crests and monograms . . . baubles and titles and . . . all such humbug and flummery', with the whole thing written off as 'anti-Australian, caste-perpetuating and toadstool-germinating'.[40] In India the duke of Connaught disliked being 'agitated against' by Gandhi and the Congress, and the future Edward VIII failed to win over the nationalists: 'I must tell you at once,' he wrote to his father, 'that I'm very depressed about my work in British India as I don't feel that I am doing a scrap of good; in fact I can say that I know I am not.' Thereafter, the situation deteriorated still further, so that the planning of the durbar that should have been for Edward VIII, and was subsequently intended for George VI, was abandoned.[41] In South Africa two royal governors-general had failed to stem the rising tide of Afrikaner nationalism, and the royal tour of 1947 was no more successful, with hostile reactions from the Nationalist Party and their supporters in the press. Even Queen Elizabeth II's tour of Australia in 1953/4 was sceptically greeted by radicals who thought it was all an upper-class racket, and by Catholic-Irish-Australians who found Menzies's snobbish sycophancy nauseating.[42]

In any case, by this time the position of the crown vis-à-vis the dominions had been fundamentally altered, and this carried deeply subversive implications for the idea that the British sovereign was at the apex of a single, all-embracing imperial hierarchy. In 1926 the Balfour 'Definition' recognized that the dominions were 'autonomous communities', no longer in any way subservient to Britain, but equal in all respects to it and 'united by a common allegiance to the crown', wording later embodied in the Statute of Westminster of 1931.[43] One consequence of this was the creation of the new concept of the 'divisible crown', with the king as separate sovereign of each of his dominions. This in turn implied (but they were implications that only the Irish Free State and South Africa at the time wished to make explicit) that the unitary British imperial monarchy was over, and with it the unitary imperial hierarchy of which the monarch was the apex and legitimator.[44] Another was that dominion governors-general, as the monarch's overseas representative, had their powers substantially reduced, and were now chosen by the king on the advice of the dominion government, rather than on that of the British prime minister. Hence the appointment of Sir Isaac Isaacs in Australia in 1931, an Australian and a Jew, and of the native-born Sir Patrick Duncan in South Africa in 1937, both portents that the days of integrated imperial hierarchy, as embodied in royal and aristocratic proconsuls, were numbered.[45]

As these qualifications and caveats suggest, there was a substantial element of ignorance, self-deception and make-believe in this hierarchical vision of the British Empire. This, in turn, meant the ornamental spectaculars that were famously and globally associated with it did not carry conviction everywhere. For some people the whole attempt to make empire and monarchy seem transcendently splendid was just a sham, which meant that there was conflict as well as consensus on these ceremonial occasions. So, when Queen Victoria celebrated her Diamond Jubilee, there may have been widespread imperial rapture, but the Irish protested vigorously and publicly that they had been starved to death, and that was all the record of her sixty years had to show.[46] In India the nationalists expressed their disdain for the Raj by appropriating its rituals for their own purposes, so that their Congress leaders might be placed 'on an equal plane with those of the imperial hierarchy'.[47] In Britain, Keir Hardie thought all this monarchy, empire and flummery absurd, and (along with the *Manchester Guardian*) supported the maharajah of Gwalior in the correspondence columns of *The Times* in 1911.[48] There was the 'Dreadnought Hoax' in February 1910 when, with five friends, including Duncan Grant and Horace de Vere Cole, Virginia Woolf paid an official visit to the flagship of the British Home Fleet, with the emperor of Abyssinia impersonated by Anthony Buxton. In Britain, as in many parts of the empire, the urban, middle-class intellectuals disliked spectacle as much as the empire it exaggeratedly celebrated. Like Woolf, they resented what Quentin Bell called the 'gold-laced masculine pomposity' of it all.[49]

This make-believe and illusion of the ornamental empire went deeper than that. For its essentially conservative imperial culture, stressing tradition and continuity, was in many ways very new and very innovative. The supposedly settled hierarchies of the great dominions, with ancestries stretching back to before the Conqueror, were recent creations, and *Burke's Colonial Gentry* was full of inconsistencies, inventions and mistakes.[50] The apparently 'timeless' India of caste and villages and ruling princes, with their 'traditional' Indo-Saracenic palaces, was not only a partial vision in that it ignored the towns, the middle classes and the nationalists; it also mistakenly assumed that these three pillars of 'timeless' India were unchanging, when in reality they were changing a great deal between the Mutiny and independence.[51] In the same way, the Malayan sultans whom the British cultivated were very different sorts of sovereign from those that had existed before; some of the 'traditional chiefs' identified by the British Colonial Service in parts of East and West Africa were actually no such thing; and the monarchies created in the Middle East were completely parvenu when compared to such authentic royal dynasties as the kings of Morocco. Orders of knighthood, the whole paraphernalia of the imperial monarchy and the imperial spectacles that were generated along with it – these were all attempts to give the impression that something very new was in fact something very old. From this perspective, the British Empire of Disraeli, Curzon, Milner, Lugard and Churchill was, like the earlier empire of Pitt, Dundas and Wellesley, built around innovation disguised as antiquity.[52]

But this was not the only way in which an empire, ostensibly dedicated to supporting the established order and denying disruptive change, was in fact the agent of great transformations that in the long run would help bring about the subversion and termination of the whole imperial enterprise. For while British officialdom generally rejected the Dalhousie–Bentinck–Palmerston–Chamberlain–Bevin view that their overseas rule should bring with it improvement and reform, modernization and progress, the reality of empire was that improvement was inevitable, reform was unavoidable, modernization was inexorable, and progress was irreversible – the law of unintended consequences operating on an epic scale. From railways to steamships, from telegraphs to aeroplanes, from Gatling guns to dreadnoughts, from dams to bridges, from gold mines to stock exchanges, the British Empire was held together functionally, and driven forward economically, by the most advanced technologies available; and in this version and vision of empire, there was little space (or scope) for the *faux* anachronistic paraphernalia of old–new hierarchies, chivalric sovereigns and glittering ceremonies.[53]

These technological transformations were intrinsically significant as the agents and avatars of imperial modernity rather than of imperial conservatism; they were, in addition, the harbingers of social developments and political changes, as the provision of irrigation, sanitation, epidemiology, mass primary education in the vernacular and university education in English reached India after 1857, and the rest of the colonies thereafter. For the effect of these improvements was not merely to enhance the material conditions of life for many on the periphery of empire in terms of health and schooling, and thus of life-expectancy in more senses than one; it was also to accelerate the creation, and increase the number, of those urban-based, university-educated, middle-class nationalists, whom the British so disliked, and whose anti-colonial agitations, mounted in the name of democracy, freedom and collective action, would eventually bring the empire to an end and replace its unified and interconnected hierarchies with separate, sovereign nations based on very different principles of political organization and social association.[54]

PART FOUR

ENDINGS

II

Dissolution

On 7 December 1936, at the height of the Abdication crisis, Virginia Woolf confided to her diary that it looked as though Edward VIII, 'this one little insignificant man had moved a pebble which dislodges an avalanche'. 'Things,' she went on, by which she meant 'empires, hierarchies, moralities', in short everything that Bloomsbury detested, would 'never be the same again'.[1] In retrospect, this may seem a misleadingly apocalyptic prediction, which ignored the conservative culture of the dominions; which disregarded ruling princes, native chiefs, traditional societies and indirect rule; and which failed to appreciate the allure of titles and baubles, honours and coats of arms, sovereigns and emperors. It also underestimated the monarchy's (and the empire's) powers of resistance and recovery, as instanced by George VI and his queen during the Second World War, by the determination of successive governments to keep Britain an imperial power in the ten years after 1945, and by the sensational success of the coronation of Elizabeth II and her subsequent world tour. Yet a longer perspective suggests that while Woolf was wrong in the timing of her remarks, she was emphatically right in their substance. For within a generation her predictions were borne out, as the British empire and the British hierarchy (and British morality too: remember the Profumo scandal of 1963?) were transformed and eroded beyond recognition.[2]

The end of empire has been written about many times as both a local and a global phenomenon: but except (and instructively) in the case of the American colonies, it has rarely been treated in a sustained and systematic way as witnessing, embodying, portending and meaning the end of hierarchy. Yet since this 'one vast interconnected world' had been constructed and envisaged on the basis of hierarchical homogeneity and social subordination, it should scarcely come as any surprise that it was eventually undermined by the politics of nationalism and the ideology of equality.[3] For when it happened, the achievement of autonomy and independence meant the rejection of Britain's empire *and* the rejection of Britain's transoceanically extended social order: locally, in the sense that domestic social structures were changed, modified, sometimes overturned; and globally, in that the imperial connection, imperial honours and the imperial monarchy were all repudiated. In most countries, sometimes rapidly, sometimes more slowly, independence was thus simultaneously a political and social revolution, as empire and hierarchy, indeed as empire *as* hierarchy, were rejected. In the era of decolonization, these themes played themselves out again and again: the way the empire faltered and fell thus tells us much, by way of retrospective commentary and corroboration, about the way it had flourished and functioned.

In one part of the empire these changes were already well under way when Virginia Woolf penned her lines. For the beginnings of the end of the British Empire as a unified, hierarchical realm took place close to home rather than at the ends of the earth: in inter-war Ireland, where, prototypically as it turned out, political and social revolution went hand in hand. One sign of this was that the British abandoned their high-status collaborators to their fate at the hands of nationalist agitators between 1918 and 1922. Notwithstanding the assurances the southern grandees and gentry had earlier been given, there were almost no safeguards provided for them in the legislation that set up the Irish Free State in 1922. As befitted a lifelong opponent of aristocracy, Lloyd George cheerfully sold the Irish landowners down the river, the first of many 'betrayals' of traditional elites that litter the history of the end of empire. Their estates were bought up by the peasantry under the provisions of the earlier Land Purchase Acts; their houses were burned to the ground by nationalist agitators; and many of them fled the country, defeated and dispossessed. And while the upper house of the new Irish parliament included some specific provisions for members of the former Ascendancy, its powers were limited, and no one took any notice of its debates.[4]

But this dismantling of aristocracy was not the only way in which the social hierarchy of southern Ireland was deliberately done away with. For it was also 'sceptres and thrones' that 'came tumbling down', as the royal-cum-ceremonial cynosure at Dublin Castle, which had provided the exemplary viceregal regime for the whole of the British Empire, was dismantled in its entirety. Already by the late nineteenth century Irish nationalists had largely ceased to attend social functions at the Castle, and these plumed parades of hierarchy were indefinitely suspended during the First World War. By then, indeed, the once-pre-eminent proconsular position of Irish viceroy had become little more than a 'transient and embarrassed phantom', surrounded by the 'outworn dignities of office'. When Viscount Fitzalan departed as the last lord-lieutenant in 1922, he left in a private car, and he was replaced by a low-key functionary as governor-general. Dublin Castle was closed down, there were no more state entries, levees or presentations, and no further non-royal appointments were made to the Order of St Patrick, which thus became the first British order of chivalry to go into desuetude, as the empire for which it was designed, the elite whom it was intended to recognize, and the social hierarchy it was supposed to legitimate all disappeared.[5]

With the advent to power of Eamon de Valera in 1932, these trends towards a democratic polity, egalitarian society and independent nation intensified, as the last, lingering vestiges of imperial hierarchy and control were one by one removed. The British government was asked to recall its governor-general; he was replaced by 'a nonentity who lived in a suburban house' and 'undertook no public duties'; and even that job was formally abolished in 1937, when the post was replaced by a president. This was a deliberate repudiation of royalty and of empire, and it had been made possible because at the time of the abdication of Edward VIII, de Valera (in inadvertent but coincidental corroboration of Virginia Woolf's prediction) took the occasion to remove any reference to the crown from the domestic affairs of the Irish nation. After the Second World War, the Irish Free State formally severed any remaining ties with Britain, and in April 1949 it became a sovereign, independent republic.[6] As with the revolt of the American colonists, this was a complete repudiation of the British Empire, for as

James Morris rightly noted, 'an Ireland run from Dublin' was 'an affront to the hierarchy of Empire'.[7]

But this disavowal was not only intrinsically important: for all these anti-hierarchical rejections, except the very last, would be replicated around the world as and when the rest of the empire was closed down and wound up. The next such episode, namely the independence of India in 1947, provides the textbook example. In negotiating an acceptable settlement, Mountbatten's overriding priority as the last viceroy was to reach accommodation with Nehru, Jinnah and Gandhi, the leaders of mass, organized nationalist opinion. Only very late in the day did he interest himself in what he saw as the lesser problem of the 'feudal relics' of the ruling princes and their states.[8] The result was that independence was a triumph for the middle-class, urban-based radicals the Raj had so detested, and it dealt many mortal blows to the British Empire as a traditional, hierarchical organism. At the midnight hour, the British monarch's imperial title disappeared; the matchless splendours of the viceroyalty, in New Delhi, and at Simla, vanished; the Indian orders of chivalry were no longer awarded to princes or proconsuls; and the whole ceremonial carapace of durbars and state elephants and loyal toasts and Empire Day was swept away. So too were the statues of the viceroys, queen–empress and king–emperors, which were removed from the open spaces and great intersections of Bombay, Calcutta, Madras and New Delhi (as they had already been in Dublin), exiled to unfrequented enclaves or the back quarters of museums. And streets called Kingsway or Queensway, or commemorating proconsular worthies and heroes, were suitably renamed.[9]

At the same time the rulers of the native states – who had, once again, been both loyal and generous during the Second World War – were forced by Mountbatten to accede to India or Pakistan, as the British abruptly withdrew their protection from their once-prized allies on the rather spurious grounds that 'paramountcy could not be transferred'. Within two years of independence, they lost their freedom and their independence, and eventually, in 1971, their revenues and their titles, in this brave new world of post-imperial egalitarianism. Many old hands in the Indian Political Service, which had provided the residents for the princely states, thought their friends had been

32. Removal of statue of Lord Curzon from Calcutta
after Indian independence.

betrayed, by Britain's cynical repudiation of 'inviolate and inviolable' treaties, and by Mountbatten's Lloyd George-like unconcern for their fate. 'It was,' Philip Mason recalls, 'distasteful in the extreme that the British should behave to these people with such contempt for past obligations, and such callous disregard for the decencies of diplomacy.'[10] Spurned by their old allies, rejected by their new leaders and 'consigned to the dustbin of history', many princes behaved as the Irish aristocracy, placed in a similar unenviable position, had done a generation before, disappearing into private life, managing what remained of their lands or going into business.

It is easy to see why they did so. For the whole ethos of Nehru's post-independence government was 'rampantly republican' and 'democratic and egalitarian', and thus hostile to what he regarded as the unacceptably conservative remnants of the Raj: to a hierarchical ordering of society, to the ruling princes and the British monarchy, and to everything about the 'traditional' or 'timeless' India that the British had favoured and supported.[11] And so, having marginalized and discredited the nawabs and the maharajas, Nehru turned his attention to the crown. In 1949, despite the British government's best efforts to the contrary, India definitively rejected the British-cum-imperial monarchy and proclaimed itself a republic within the Commonwealth. It was, Nehru insisted, 'quite impossible' to preserve any vestige of monarchical presence in the Indian constitution, because it would provoke so much 'division and controversy'. This was a doubly portentous decision. It ushered in a wholly new (and post-imperial) ordering and perception of Indian society and politics, stressing progress, modernity and equality. And it paved the way for the overwhelmingly multiracial and *republican* membership of the Commonwealth over the next twenty years. This change of name was indicative of a significant change in substance. 'The British Empire' had been a royal realm. 'The Commonwealth' (the prefix 'British' was removed in 1948) would soon be an association of republics.[12]

For all the euphoria of her coronation in 1953, the independence of Ireland and of India and their espousal of republican government inevitably meant that Queen Elizabeth's was in many ways the first post-imperial crowning – a change in circumstance (and in pomp) well caught by Sir William Walton in the titles and the tone of his two coronation marches: 'Crown Imperial' for George VI had been Elgarian *nobilmente*, redolent of chivalry, history and tradition; but 'Orb and Sceptre' for Elizabeth II verged on the jauntily irreverent, with raspberries and banana-skins deftly inserted. This, in turn, was indicative of deeper changes. For the new Royal Titles Act, which had been passed earlier in coronation year, recognized that Elizabeth was no longer empress of India and ruler of the British dominions beyond the seas. Instead, she was merely 'head of the Commonwealth', the symbol of the 'free association' of fully independent member nations.[13] In the republican regimes that would soon become the majority, she would have no constitutional standing or social pre-eminence; and even in those former colonies of which she remained head of state, she was now separately queen of Canada, Australia, New Zealand, South Africa and so on. Instead of being, as her forebears had been, a unitary imperial monarch, Elizabeth was simply the symbol of association, and the wearer of a crown that was shared around between different, separate sovereign states.[14] The divisible monarchy, implicit in the empire since the 1920s, had finally arrived.

From Victoria to George VI, the revived and reinvented British monarchy had been essential in giving the British imperial hierarchy its unity, coherence and legitimacy. Now all that was going, and right-wing Tories like Enoch Powell, the self-appointed defenders of the traditional empire, were much put out. But their rearguard action in parliament had been to no avail and, as they feared, this new doctrine of the divisible crown was the prelude to further moves in the former dominions (another term, along with the '*British* Commonwealth', that had lapsed in 1948) towards disassociation and diversity.[15] For since the 'British' queen was also the separate sovereign in those realms of which she remained head of state, there were growing demands that she should be represented by a native-born governor-general, rather than an exported British aristocrat or British royal. This change had already been portended in Australia in 1931 (Isaacs) and had taken place irreversibly in South Africa in 1937 (Duncan), and after the Second World War the rest of the former dominions followed suit: Canada in 1952, Australia in 1965 and New Zealand in 1967.[16]

Inevitably, these post-imperial regimes were less British and less grand than their predecessors – shorn of viceregal pretensions, devoid of aristocratic lineage or royal family connection, they no longer completed or legitimated a mimetic social-cum-imperial hierarchy subordinated to Britain. Instead of stressing ordered deference, rural values, courtly exclusiveness and white superiority, they increasingly came to stand for national autonomy, open access, social equality, economic modernity, ethnic diversity and multiculturalism.[17]

These changes in India and the old dominions were paralleled by developments in the colonial empire and the former League of Nations Mandates. For imperial government through the 'timeless' tribes and 'traditional' hierarchies of Africa and the Middle East did not long survive the Second World War. Indirect rule had already been widely criticized in the 1930s, and the entry of the United States into the conflict, lead by a president strongly aware of his nation's proud anti-colonial heritage, and unafraid of putting this point of view to the beleaguered British prime minister, only reinforced these concerns. 'It is absurd,' noted Sir Arthur Dawe, assistant under-secretary at the Colonial Office, 'to erect what is an ephemeral expedient into a sacrosanct principle.' 'Things,' he went on, 'are moving so fast in Africa that the doctrinaire adherents of the indirect rule principle may find themselves outmoded much quicker than anyone would have thought possible a few years ago.'[18] So, indeed, they did. For in a fundamental act of imperial reappraisal, the colonial secretary, Malcolm Macdonald, asked Lord Hailey, formerly governor of the Punjab and the United Provinces, to undertake a wartime survey of Britain's African colonies, and in so doing to answer the by-now inescapable question: where was indirect rule going? Hailey's answer, though carefully hedged about with qualifications as befitted a champion of the Indian princes, was, essentially, nowhere: it was too static, too conservative and of no relevance to educated Africans or their future.[19]

And so in Africa, as they had previously done in Ireland and in India, the British withdrew their support from the traditional hierarchies and tried to 'democratize the Empire' – by dismantling indirect rule and setting up representative local government, and by shifting their attention from the rural chiefs to the city-dwelling bourgeoisie to whom they hoped to hand over power.[20] This turnabout is vividly illustrated in the case of Ghana. Among the urban middle class, with whom the British began to negotiate in the late 1940s, it seemed that Dr Joseph Danquah would be the first African to head the government of the Gold Coast. He was a member of chiefly family, and his half-brother Nana Sir Ofori Atta had been a paramount Ashanti chief (CBE 1918, KBE 1927). Then in the early 1950s Kwame Nkrumah, a Marxist revolutionary, became the effective leader of the nationalists, and the British (especially the governor, Sir Charles Arden-Clarke) transferred their attention and allegiance to him. But the up-country Ashanti chiefs had no wish to support independence if it meant having their power taken away by the urban radicals of Accra: they, however, were abandoned to their fate. As Brian Lapping concludes, London 'gave independence to the modern, popular party over the protests of the traditional chiefs whom British rule had formerly encouraged'.[21] It was the same in Nigeria, where the British corralled the emirs and sheikhs of the north into a federation that would be dominated by the Lagos-based south; and in Uganda, where the kabaka of Buganda was deported from 1953 to 1955 so as to make possible the integration of his kingdom with the rest of the country, and to encourage the growth of an authentic Ugandan national identity.[22]

In Africa, as previously in India and southern Ireland, independence was thus not just the end of imperial control: it was also the end of the ornamental proconsular regimes that had been the means and expression of that control, and of the domestic social hierarchies in collaboration with which that control had been exercised. Like the Indian Empire, the colonial empire had existed as a pageant, and so it was entirely appropriate that it expired in a succession of valedictory spectacles. At independence ceremonials around the globe, modelled on those first devised by Mountbatten in 1947, the British flag was hauled down for the last time in the presence of a member of the royal family, witnessing the end of empire, hierarchy and monarchy.[23] In all these new countries, as previously in India, proconsular splendour, resident advisers, plumed hats, ribbons and orders, royal statues and Empire Day very soon disappeared, to be replaced by middle-class

33. The end of empire, Nairobi, 1963.

leaders of western-style political parties. Most of these new nation states joined the Commonwealth and, in so doing, further transformed it. Following the precedent set by India, they became republics, thereby proclaiming their commitment to modernity and equality, and their rejection of hierarchy and tradition.

In many of these new nations, this rejection was as complete as it had been in Ireland and in India. In Uganda, the by-now-returned Kabaka Mutesa II of Buganda had been given the KBE in 1962 (just as his father had been in 1937), and he became the first president of the newly independent nation in the following year. But in 1966 he was unceremoniously bundled out by an unholy alliance of Milton Obote and General Amin, and he died in exile in London three years later. In Zanzibar, which became independent in December 1963, the sultan whose father had been congratulated by King George VI for his dynasty's endurance was overthrown within a month by an African-organized coup, and by 1964 the new regime had negotiated a full union with Nyerere's Tanganyika.[24] And in Malta there was a similar revolution, albeit by more peaceful means. After Lord Strickland's death in 1940, the political mantle descended to his redoubtable daughter, Mabel. But her passionate pro-British views found little support on the island in the era of decolonization and independence, and power passed to Dom Mintoff, the Labour leader, who steered Malta to independence in 1964 and republican status ten years later. By the time she died in 1988, the Stricklands had ceased to be a power in the land, and Mabel had outlived the aristocratic, Anglo-Maltese world into which she had been born.[25]

It was almost the same in the Middle East, where the alliances between the British and the monarchies they had created or cultivated broke down, as 'the people' finally triumphed over 'the pashas', and the nationalists over the empire.[26] But it was not quite the same: for within this recognizable framework of imperial withdrawal and domestic transformation, there were significant local variations. In Ireland, India and much of Africa, the British had understood the way the winds of change were blowing and had largely abandoned the notables, the princes and the chiefs to their fate: they transferred their attention and their allegiance to the middle-class nationalists, to whose leaders they eventually (and with evident relief) transferred power. In Egypt, Jordan and Iraq, the same winds were blowing, and with even greater ferocity, but the British were powerless to adapt to them. They were too closely identified with the princes and the pashas to forge links with the new generation of nationalist leaders, who increasingly looked to Moscow for ideology and inspiration. This failure to win over the middle and working classes meant the British had no choice but to continue supporting the 'old regimes', even though they saw that they were now 'the wrong kind of people', and that in the era of decolonization this was the wrong kind of policy. For as Ernest Bevin had recognized, the princes and the pashas 'would not stand up to revolutionary conditions, and would be swept away'.[27]

Soon after he left the Foreign Office, Bevin's predictions were amply (and violently) vindicated, as the old regimes buckled before the full onslaught of Arab nationalism, and their imperial partners were repudiated. In Egypt, King Farouk was forced by popular protest to dismiss his prime minister Nahas Pasha, and was himself deposed in a military coup in 1952. This was led by Colonel Gamal Abdel Nasser, who was determined to rid the country of its antiquated social structure and also of British domination, and the greater Arab world of those he regarded as imperialist stooges. Within four years he had achieved most of these objectives: he exiled the king to Italy, rid his country of British troops, created a republic and nationalized the Suez Canal.[28] In Jordan, King Abdullah was assassinated in 1951, and his son, Talal, reigned for barely a year, being generally regarded as mentally unbalanced and unfit for the succession. Abdullah's grandson, the young King Hussein, found it difficult to keep his throne, and he was able to appease nationalist agitations only by distancing himself from empire, by forging closer links with Egypt and Saudi Arabia, and by dismissing the British officers of the Arab Legion in 1956, including Sir John Glubb, who had been commander since 1939. And in Iraq there was a 'pro-Nasser, anti-western coup' in July 1958, led by Abd al-Karim Quasim, which saw the brutal murder of the young King Faisal II, the former regent Abdulillah and Nuri Pasha, and the institution of a republic that swept away 'an entrenched aristocracy' and the existing social order.[29]

34. A smashed picture of King Farouk lying on an Egyptian pavement.

Only a decade after it seemed that Britain's imperial position in the Middle East was of greater amplitude than ever before, the Bedouin romance had collapsed in the face of rampant pan-Arab nationalism and widespread Soviet infiltration. Thereafter, the last British bastions in the region, dependent on the collaboration of the sheikhs, soon fell. In Aden, the South Asian solution of backing the ruling princes against the urban nationalists was no more successful than it had been in the nation of its inception. Faced with the incorrigible hostility of the Egypt- and Yemen-backed National Liberation Front, the British abandoned their previous support for the sheikhs and the sultans and, having failed to negotiate an independence deal with the nationalists, ignominiously withdrew in the 'worst shambles of the end of Empire', leaving their stores behind, in 1967. Thereupon a People's Democratic Republic of South Yemen, a Marxist Soviet satellite, was established.[30] And between 1961 and 1971, beginning with Kuwait and ending with Bahrain and Qatar, Britain repudiated its remaining alliances in the Gulf, and withdrew its residents and its regiments from the sheikhdoms. Nowhere in the Middle East was there the last, dignified retreat of independence ceremonials, and for all the supposed kinship between British mandarins and Bedouin chiefs, none of these independent Arab countries subsequently joined the Commonwealth.[31]

Accordingly, and within scarcely a generation, the whole hierarchical embrace of empire – Virginia Woolf's 'things' – had been rapidly dismantled. The coherent and ordered vision of transoceanic dominion that the British and their collaborators had sought to sustain and project had vanished into thin air with extraordinary speed. In 1903 Curzon had banned the singing of the hymn 'Onward Christian Soldiers' from his great durbar, because it contained the words 'Crowns and thrones may perish, kingdoms rise and wane' – a subversive line for a believer in imperial hierarchy and imperial permanence.[32] Seventy years on, that was just what had happened. The British Empire had been about subordination and homogeneity, replication and analogy; the Commonwealth was about equality and diversity, repudiation and autonomy: there was, then, much more than simply a change of name being recognized when, in 1958, Empire Day became Commonwealth

Day. For, notwithstanding many pious and platitudinous observations to the contrary, the 'post-Britannic', 'de-Britannicized' Commonwealth was not the fulfilment, but the antithesis (indeed, negation) of empire – a voluntary organization run by a secretary-general and pledged to promote equality, rather than a mandatory organization presided over by king–emperor and pledged to uphold hierarchy.[33]

This transformation was also reflected in the further downsizing, dismantling and discrediting of the system of imperial honours, more gradually than in Ireland or in India, but cumulatively with similar results. As long as a limited number of proconsular postings remained, from the late 1940s to the mid 1960s, there were still some figures in the traditional Lansdowne–Curzon–Willingdon mode, festooned with titles and laden with orders: Lords Mountbatten (viceroy of India), Alexander (governor-general of Canada) and Slim (governor-general of Australia).[34] Even in the 1960s there were still some former Indian princes holding the GCSI and the GCIE, such as the nizam of Hyderabad, the maharaja of Mysore and the nawab of Rampur (as well as the sultan of Muscat and Oman). But they were increasingly viewed as imperial-cum-Ruritanian relics, and since the late 1960s few Britons have been decorated for services to their empire. Today there are no proconsuls or residents to be given the Order of St Michael and St George, which is now bestowed almost exclusively on ambassadors, diplomats and members of the Foreign Office. No appointments have been made to the Imperial Service Order since 1993, and many people now feel that the continued use of an order of chivalry named after the British Empire is absurd – partly because the empire has long since gone, and partly because so few of these honours are now awarded to people who live overseas.[35]

These honorific changes in Britain have been paralleled by (and in part driven by) changes in attitudes and practices in the former dominions in the years since 1945. Instead of being sought after by those who wanted incorporation in, and recognition by, the empire, imperial honours were increasingly seen as intrusive and outdated emblems of British condescension and colonial subordination. Very few hereditary peerages were given out to those in the empire during and after the Second World War (Bennett of Canada, Bruce of

Australia, Freyberg of New Zealand, Huggins of Rhodesia and Thomson of Canada), and the life peerages for Lords Casey (Australia) and Elworthy (New Zealand) were the first and the last of their kind. Australia formally abolished titles in 1983, and even in New Zealand, once the most conservative of the former dominions, they were repudiated in 2000.[36] The other side of this is that since the 1960s the former dominions have given out their own honours: the Order of Canada since 1967, the Order of Australia since 1975 and the New Zealand Order of Merit since 1996.[37] True to their nations' by now much vaunted egalitarian traditions, they do not carry with them any title, nor do they command that much prestige. And this policy of imperial repudiation and domestic reinvention has also been followed in the former British colonies in Africa and Asia.

This dismantled honorific hierarchy has been accompanied by the transformation, and the weakening, of the position of the British-cum-imperial monarchy. For however seriously Queen Elizabeth II takes her role as head of the Commonwealth, the House of Windsor inevitably counts for less overseas than it did in the heyday of empire. One sign of this has been the disappearance of royal proconsuls, those exported Disraelian icons of hierarchy and monarchy. To be sure, Lord Mountbatten was the king–emperor's cousin: but he was sent to India in 1947 to close the Raj down rather than to keep it going. He did so rapidly, ruthlessly, and unsentimentally, backing (unlike Lord Lytton) the people against the princes. Thereafter, as the old dominions opted for native-born governors-general, these plumage positions in Canada, Australia, New Zealand and South Africa ceased to be available to British royals – even to Prince Charles. At a lower level of proconsular grandeur, the last quasi-royal imperial notable was Sir Henry Abel-Smith, who was governor of Queensland from 1958 to 1966. Although himself a commoner, Abel-Smith was the husband of Lady Mary Cambridge, and thus the son-in-law of the earl of Athlone, who in an earlier era had governed Canada and South Africa. But this was the end of a dynasty, and the end of the line.

At the same time the standing and significance, resonance and meaning of royal tours to parts of what was once the empire have also markedly diminished. The head of the Commonwealth and the divisible

35. Lord and Lady Mountbatten as the last viceroy
and vicereine of India, 1947.

sovereign is no longer the iconic king–emperor of old, a symbol of unity and order and subordination; and while the advent of air travel has made such visits more easy and more frequent, familiarity has also served to undermine their mystery and magic. The six-month voyages in British battleships, the transcontinental journeys in splendid trains, the massed throngs of eager and expectant crowds, the obsequious behaviour of colonial princes and premiers, the hushed and reverent tones of journalists and authors: all this has long since gone, like the royal yacht itself, and along with it the very notion that the monarch was the supreme embodiment of imperial unity and hierarchy. The queen's tours of Australia in 1963 and India in 1997 were pale shadows of the imperial progresses of 1954 or 1910, and her visits to the Commonwealth heads-of-government conferences are deliberately low-key affairs.[38] Indeed, the prime and paradoxical effect of these more frequent and less spectacular royal visits has been to draw attention in Canada, New Zealand and Australia to the anomaly of having a non-native born head of state who lives half a world away in Britain. Hence the growth of republicanism in all three countries.[39]

What conclusions may we draw from this account of the ending of empire as the ending of hierarchy? One is that, despite Trollope's observation (and prediction) to the contrary, the four former British dominions *have* increasingly come to resemble the United States – not by means of sudden political and social revolutions, replicating 1776, but rather as a result of slower, long-term evolution. Nor should this occasion any surprise: for as 'new' nations, they bore a certain resemblance to America from the outset; and as the United Kingdom has waned as world force, while the United States has waxed, those resemblances were bound to grow and deepen. Like America, the former dominions are large countries, with dense populations in some areas, but also with vast tracts of open space and abundant natural resources. They also contain substantial indigenous populations and, following the civil rights legislation in the United States, they have all outlawed discrimination on the grounds of race or colour – Canada in 1962, Australia in 1973, New Zealand in 1987 and South Africa with the collapse of apartheid in 1990.[40] Today these countries see themselves (in some senses realistically, in others mythologically) as dynamic, egalitarian, democratic, multicultural and anti-hierarchical societies, following the American rather than the British model. The period in their past when they were the setting for the export and replication of the metropolitan social order may have lasted longer than domestic critics wanted, and than historians have generally allowed. But it is now definitely over.[41]

While the former dominions have freed up their once imperial polities and relaxed their once hierarchical societies in the direction of the United States, the former colonies and mandates have followed the rather different precedents set by Ireland and India. This, again, is unsurprising. On the contrary, it is both logical and chronological. Unlike America and the dominions, the colonies and mandates were not societies settled and created by the British, but merely occupied by them, and governed through 'traditional' social structures and elites. Accordingly, the repudiation of the imperial connection and the overthrow of 'traditional' hierarchies went hand in hand. In some former colonies and mandates this process was as thorough as in Ireland. Burma, the Sudan, Egypt, Iraq and the Yemen completely repudiated Britain, empire and hierarchy, establishing peoples' republics that rejected the idea of Commonwealth membership. But Zimbabwe, Nigeria, Ghana, Kenya and Uganda preferred the milder Indian variant of independence and social revolution, while remaining in the Commonwealth and recognizing the queen as its head.[42]

As imperial links were severed, and as social hierarchies were undermined, there were many people in the former empire who, with ample justification, felt abandoned and betrayed. In its heyday the empire had depended on collaboration between the British and the social elites in the dominions, in India, in the colonies and in the mandates – a lengthy and mutually beneficial encounter that had been based more on class than on colour. And in this regard, the imperial ending was all of a piece with the imperial existence. For as the empire was dismantled, British policy-makers understood, with a ruthless lack of sentiment, that they must now do business with those nationalist leaders who generally came from lower down the social scale – and this less-enduring collaboration was, once again, more concerned with rank than with race.[43] But this repudiation of their traditional allies atop local hierarchies left many former notables adrift and alone: the old ascendancies in Ireland, Melbourne and Toronto; the gentry settlers in the White Highlands of Kenya; the nawabs and maharajas in India; and the sultans, emirs and chiefs in Africa and the Middle East. 'English gentlemen, Indian Princes, African Knights of the British Empire': whatever the colour of their skin, many of them felt aggrieved, disappointed, let down. In this, as in so much of the empire story, the 'really important category' was not race: it was status.[44]

It was not only English gentlemen (of whatever colour) out there in what had once been the empire who were thus affected and diminished by its ending. As John Darwin has rightly remarked, the United Kingdom was no less 'a successor state of the old imperial system', and it has also been obliged to make adjustments.[45] For as the imperial hierarchy faltered and fell abroad, the domestic hierarchy, which empire had both replicated and reinforced, also began to lose credibility and conviction. That, at least, was the argument advanced by the young Peregrine Worsthorne in the immediate aftermath of the Suez fiasco of 1956. 'What,' he wanted to know, 'is the point of maintaining a Queen Empress without an Empire to rule over?' 'Everything,' he concluded, 'about the British class system begins to look foolish and tacky when related to a second-class power on the decline.' These views were echoed and amplified in the attacks on the class-bound nature of the monarchy that were launched at the same time by Lord Altrincham and Malcolm Muggeridge, and they were amply borne out by subsequent events. For as the empire waned in the 1960s, and as the whole culture of ornamentalism fell victim to satire and scepticism and scorn, Britain *did* become (as Virginia Woolf had foreseen) a less hierarchical, less 'moral' and more open society, a trend that has intensified in the 1980s and 1990s. This 'decline of deference' and lessened respect for established institutions has undoubtedly been the most significant domestic consequence of the loss of empire – though it is a large and complex subject that still awaits its historian.[46]

But some of the outlines are already clear. One indication of this, as conspicuous in the former metropolis as on the former periphery, has been the deliberate diminution of the high Victorian, Disraelian monarchy, as the whole paraphernalia of ostentatious living – royal yachts, royal trains, royal tax exemptions, royal ceremonials – have been cut down and scaled back, so as to create a reduced, post-imperial crown in better alignment with the diminished, post-imperial power that Britain has become during the present queen's reign.[47] Another has been the virtual disappearance by the aristocracy from the corridors of power. The Conservative governments of 1951 to 1964 were themselves unprecedentedly unaristocratic; but they still had their share of grandees and gentry, like the marquess of Salisbury, who wished to maintain and govern the empire. They wished in vain. The late 1950s and the early 1960s witnessed both the end of the British Empire, and the end of the British aristocracy's claims to be the national and imperial ruling class by hereditary right. The fact that these developments occurred simultaneously was not accidental.[48] Today, Britain is a less hierarchical nation and society than it was in the days when it was the imperial metropolis, just as the former dominions are less hierarchical nations and societies than they were in the days when they were a prime part of the imperial periphery. Once again, these simultaneous trends are not mere coincidence. In its ending, as in its making and in its heyday, the history of the empire and the history of Britain are inseparable.

12

Epilogue

All this is rightly written of in the past tense: for it describes the hierarchical-cum-imperial world – 'an entire interactive system' – we have lost.[1] Or does it? And have we? To both questions, the answer must be: yes, but not entirely. Things change; but survivors survive and residues endure. To be sure, the 'vast interconnected world' that flourished between the 1850s and 1950s, and reached its zenith between Victoria's Diamond Jubilee of 1897 and George V's Silver Jubilee of 1935, has gone – an historical revolution aptly recognized by Robin Cook's reported decision, on becoming foreign secretary in May 1997, to remove the pictures *both* of British proconsuls *and* Indian ruling princes from his office.[2] But in what was once the British Empire, in the metropolis and on the periphery, traces of hierarchy linger, as structure and sentiment, and as institutions and ideology, and they sometimes do so in the most surprising and unexpected of places.[3] In South Asia, and notwithstanding their treatment at the hands of the Raj and the Congress Party, the former ruling princes of India have retained some of their wealth and status, and some of them remain involved in the country's public life, as diplomats, governors, cabinet ministers or elected representatives; and the president of India is surrounded by many of the ceremonial trappings originally invented for the British viceroy.[4]

Near by, in Malaya, the ruling sultans did even better, surviving the invasion and occupation of the Japanese, the unprecedented disruption from Communist insurgents, and the deliberate attempt of the British to renounce their historic treaty obligations and to withdraw its support for them: in short, to abandon them as they had earlier abandoned the ruling princes of India. Accordingly, between 1945 and 1948 the Colonial Office attempted to create a Malayan Union, in which the power and position of the sultans would be much curtailed, and Britain would transfer its support to other groups in society. But, unlike India, there was no indigenous demand for a reduction in the authority of the native rulers, and such was the level of protest from both the sultans and their subjects that – as in the 1930s – the emasculation scheme was abandoned. Thereafter, by judicious collaboration with the emerging nationalists, the rulers maintained their authority, and independence negotiations proceeded smoothly (and unusually), without nationalist agitation and with the sultans still in charge.[5] As a result, when independence came in 1957 the 'safeguarding of the position and prestige of Their Highnesses as Constitutional Rulers of their Respective States' was an essential element in the new constitution; the rulers agreed to elect one of their number on a system of rotation to act as king of the new nation for five-year periods. Far from being, as the British had hoped (and note the use of analogy again), somewhere 'between an eighteenth-century Bishop and an hereditary Lord Lieutenant', they have maintained their powers, virtually unimpaired, until very recently.[6]

As these very different examples of India and Malaya serve to show, independence from Britain might encourage the ending of social hierarchy and princely dominion, or it might witness its preservation. Between these extremes, a picture emerges in some parts of the former empire of the limited survival of traditional social hierarchies and social perceptions. The monarchies that the British created or protected in Brunei, Jordan, Buganda, Tonga, Lesotho, Kuwait, Oman and Swaziland still function; and chiefly prestige and tribal identities endure (or have been recovered) elsewhere in some parts of what was once British Africa, from Nigeria (where one quarter of the members of the Federal Executive Council are chiefs) to Zimbabwe (where among the Hwesa chiefly power has re-emerged in the aftermath of the collapse of the ruling party at local level).[7] Nor are these the only signs. On the queen's recent visit to Ghana, she participated in durbars to meet native Ashanti chiefs that would have gladdened the heart of Lord Lugard;

Nelson Mandela clearly draws some of his authority from his inherited position as a southern Nguni minor chief; and the previous secretary-general of the Commonwealth was Chief Emeka Anyaoku of Nigeria. Meanwhile, in Canada and New Zealand, Inuit and Maori chiefs are now accorded attention and deference, which their forebears never received in the days of empire.[8]

Even for the British, and in their former colonies of settlement, empire as hierarchy is not entirely over: there is still some overdue adjustment and belated dismantling going on – or (since there is nothing inevitable about this) not going on. In November 1999 the hereditary peerage in the British House of Lords was largely removed – a definite blow against landed aristocracy, unwritten tradition and the organic, Burkeian constitution in what had once been the imperial metropolis, and a blow that had been portended and promised in the Parliament Act passed in 1911. But for virtually the whole of the remainder of the twentieth century, nothing substantive had happened: as long as Britain remained an imperial power, the traditional, hereditary peers survived in the traditional House of Lords. But once the empire was finally seen to be irrevocably gone, the hereditary peerage soon followed: two years after the handover of Hong Kong, to be precise. This near-simultaneous termination of the last great colonial outpost overseas, and of the last great bastion of hierarchy in the metropolis, cannot be accidental. And there have also been calls for a thorough review and rationalization of the honours system which, even allowing for the demise of the Orders of St Patrick, the Star of India and the Indian Empire, and for the ending of overseas awards, remains stubbornly (and ever more implausibly) stuck in a late-Victorian and early-twentieth-century time-warp.[9]

The same argument has been made in the three former dominions of settlement that retain Queen Elizabeth II as head of state. To be sure, she is separately and divisibly the queen of Canada, Australia and New Zealand. But these positions are not only intrinsically anomalous in that she lives half a world away and only pays occasional visits to these overseas realms: they are also a hangover from the old imperial monarchy rather than an expression of vibrant, independent nationhood. How long will they survive? At almost the very same time that the hereditary peers were expelled from the British House of

Lords, but with what looked like the opposite outcome, Australia voted in its referendum to retain the queen as its head of state by a majority of 55 to 45 per cent. In conformity with the view of empire as being primarily (and wholesomely) rural and agrarian, the most vociferous supporters of the monarchy came from Queensland, Tasmania and Western Australia, the least urbanized states, from whom there was much criticism of the 'Chardonnay republicans' living in Sydney, Melbourne and Adelaide, the direct descendants of those middle-class city-dwellers who had never found favour in imperial circles. But while the traditionalists may have triumphed in the short run, the general feeling seemed to be a recognition that the monarchy would eventually go – and not just in Australia but elsewhere in the Commonwealth where the Queen remained head of state. If and when that is done, the vestiges of empire-as-hierarchy will largely have disappeared. But who can be certain this will happen? Or confidently predict when?[10]

Meanwhile, such attitudes and perceptions certainly survive at what was once the top of the national-cum-imperial hierarchy, in part in the person of the queen. To be sure, it is only 'in part'. She operates well as a post-imperial, low-key player at the Commonwealth heads-of-government meetings, she had acquiesced in the downsizing of the still-imperial crown that she inherited in 1952, and in her millennial tour of Australia she expressed affection for the people, but insisted that it was for them alone to decide the future of their monarchy and of their constitution. On the other hand, her grandparents and her parents *were* emperor and empress of India, she likes the traditional world of landed grandees and landed estates, and she shares her forebears' passion for medals, uniforms, decorations, investitures and ceremonial. Not surprisingly, as someone at the apex of what remains of the imperial hierarchy, she likes things ordered, and she likes things not to change.[11] As befits a person born in 1926, and who was nine at the time of King George V's Silver Jubilee, she is a child of the empire to which she pledged her life on her twenty-first birthday in South Africa in 1947. And she seems to have a particular affection for those monarchs whose forebears were sovereigns of dependent territories in

36. Queen Elizabeth II greeted by King Hussein on her 1984 visit to Jordan.

the heyday of the British Empire, such as the late King Hussein of Jordan (Hon. GCB, GCVO and the Royal Victorian Chain), or the sultan of Brunei (Hon. GCMG), or the king of Tonga (Hon. GCMG, GCVO and KBE).

Perhaps more surprisingly, it is not only in the person of the queen that these traditional views and perceptions linger, but also in the next generation in the person of Prince Charles. As the owner of Highgrove and the creator of Poundbury, he believes in the 'natural' ordering of things, be it in a regiment or on a landed estate, where everyone knows their place, and where deference and hierarchy rule.[12] And these domestic perceptions and presuppositions clearly influence him, as they did his forebears, in his views of those nations and peoples that were once part of the British Empire. He thinks that the thirteen American colonies would not have revolted if George III had undertaken a royal tour, which would have enabled the colonists to realize how decent he was. He had hoped to follow his uncle and become governor-general of Australia, and was much disappointed when he learned this was something many Australians did not want and would not welcome. And in his eulogy of King Hussein of Jordan, at a memorial service held in St Paul's Cathedral, he recognized him (as an earlier prince of Wales had recognized the king of Hawaii) as a social equal whose high rank dissolved racial differences: 'a wonderful combination of the virtues of the Bedouin Arab and, if I may say so, the English gentleman'. The British Empire may have vanished from the map, but it has not entirely vanished from the mind: in Buckingham Palace, and elsewhere too, its hierarchical sentiments, and some of its structures, still endure.[13]

An Imperial Childhood?

For anyone who is professionally interested in Britain's imperial past – and I must stress at the outset that, for reasons that will soon become clear, it is from the perspective of the British imperial metropolis that I am very largely writing – 1997 was the most important year for historical reflection and commemorative retrospection since the bicentennial of the American Declaration of Independence was observed in 1976. It marked the centenary of Queen Victoria's Diamond Jubilee, when imperial consciousness (though not imperial dominion) was probably at its zenith, and when the British discovered and displayed their empire to themselves in London in an uncharacteristic fit of imperial presence of mind. But it also witnessed the fiftieth anniversary of the end of the British Raj in India – an intrinsically momentous event, as the 'jewel in the crown', the veritable keystone of the imperial arch, the land of Robert Clive and Lord Curzon, of Rudyard Kipling and Sir Edwin Lutyens, was given away; and a no-less momentous portent, since in the aftermath of Indian independence, the maintenance of much of the rest of the British Empire in Africa and Asia was rendered both unnecessary and, as it soon turned out, impossible.

But 1997 was not only retrospectively resonant in the British imperial story: it was also an intrinsic part of that story. Indeed, it saw the *end* of that story, as British dominion was terminated in the last great colony, Hong Kong, and as the recently decommissioned royal yacht *Britannia* sailed away, over the waves the British Navy had long since ceased to rule, into what was, beyond any doubt, the final, definitive, irreversible imperial sunset. That these three events – the Diamond Jubilee, Indian independence and the Hong Kong handover – should have been separated by two fifty-year intervals is a calendrical coincidence that would be wildly implausible, did it not happen to be true. But to move from the zenith of empire to the beginning of the end of empire in the space of one half century, and then to move from the beginning of the end of empire to the end of the end of empire within the span of another, is not only a convenient accident of chronology: it also reminds us how short-lived was this heyday of Britain's imperial history, and how rapidly and completely that empire declined and fell.

Because I was born in 1950, my life coincides almost exactly with this second fifty-year period: this is personal time as historic time, and *vice versa*. From one perspective, this means that I never knew the empire when its far-flung existence really did seem to many to be a permanent, indissoluble part of the providential order of things, and when the ultimate responsibility for the government of more than one quarter of the world's land surface and population actually did reside in London. But from another, it means that I belong to the last generation of Britons for whom their empire was something like a real presence in their formative years and imaginative life. But what sort of a presence was it? And how much of a presence was it? Some of the most influential recent writing has been concerned to tell us what it was like to grow up in the colonies and dependencies of this empire as the sun went down, and in the years immediately after it had set. But empires, by their nature, mean different things to different people in different places, and in this regard the British Empire was no exception. What, then, did it mean to me, and how did it impinge on my consciousness, as I lived out what there was of my imperial childhood, not in the empire, but in Britain itself?

I must begin by making plain that such imperial childhood as I had was not because I came from what would then have been termed 'an imperial family'. So far as I know, my parents and their forebears had no personal or professional connection with the empire and, with one exception, of which more soon, they had never visited any part of it, and had no first-hand experience of it. Nor, being born and brought up in Birmingham, at the very centre of the British Midlands, did I come from an imperial city in ways that would have been true had I been born and brought up in Glasgow or Belfast or Liverpool or London – great, outward-looking, maritime communities, with their shipyards and warehouses, their docks and harbours and beckoning horizons, which were still in the 1950s closely linked to the old imperial realms across and beyond the seas. To be sure, Birmingham had claimed as its own the two pre-eminent imperialist politicians of their time: Joseph Chamberlain and Leopold Amery, both of whom were MPs for the city, and both long-serving colonial secretaries in Conservative governments. But Chamberlain had died in 1914, three years before my parents had been born, and Amery was a spent force in politics by 1945, half a decade before I came into the world.

Not surprisingly, then, the first imperial moment that made any impact on me had nothing specific to do with Birmingham and, in a way, nothing specific to do with empire. But it was a sort of imperial moment, none the less. Just as many late Victorians began their autobiographies with recollections of the Diamond Jubilee of the Great White Queen, so I suspect that many of my contemporaries will begin theirs with their recollections of the coronation of Queen Elizabeth II in 1953, and the extraordinary feelings of hope and euphoria it generated. I was too young to remember the day or the event itself, and my parents did not then own a television on which I might have watched the proceedings. But my childhood was certainly suffused by what seemed to be the warm after-glow of what for years was simply called 'the Coronation'. So while I have no recollection of the deprivations of food rationing, I vividly remember playing with cardboard cut-outs of soldiers and horses and golden coaches; I know my sister's first doll was named Queenie after the queen of Tonga, one of the overseas celebrities of the coronation; and I later learned that Mount Everest had been successfully conquered by a British-led expedition on the very day the queen had been crowned, a Henty-like adventure story that was regularly retold throughout the 1950s, and especially to my generation of schoolchildren.

Because I was in these ways a Coronation child, I think I did acquire the vague impression that there was a greater Britain, somewhere beyond Birmingham and beyond the seas, that had sent its representatives to London to join the queen in Westminster Abbey, and that this was how things always had been and always would be. Initially, I had no notion of what this greater Britain looked like, or where, indeed, it was. But this unfocused idea of empire gradually became more concrete as I absorbed my father's recollections of his time in India, the one first-hand piece of imperial experience to which my family could lay claim, which meant that for me, as for hundreds of thousands of Britons between 1757 and 1947, the British Empire primarily meant the Indian Empire. Of course, India had become independent three years before I was born, but the country I learned about was one over which the king–emperor had still reigned. My father had served there in the Royal Engineers between 1942 and 1945, and this was the greatest adventure of his life. It was nearly the *last* adventure of his life, because he caught malaria, and had he not been near Calcutta, where he got the best medical treatment then available, he would have died, and I would not have lived.

But he survived to bring back his memories – and more than his memories. While in India, he compiled a scrapbook, with a vivid black and green cover, full of pictures of what seemed to me this strange, exotic, far-off land: of the Gateway of India in Bombay, the Victoria Memorial Hall in Calcutta, the Taj Mahal at Agra and the Kanchenjunga Mountains. He sent home rugs, tablecloths, ornaments and small pieces of furniture: fabrics and artifacts of empire that were an everyday part of my young life. And he talked endlessly about India: the journey out, via Cape Town, on the *Franconia*; the torrential rains at Cherrapunji; mongooses and snakes and scorpions; standing up in the presence of the vicereine at Simla; travelling on trains where tea was made with boiling water from the engine; the voyage back, through the Suez Canal, on the *Cape Town Castle*; and the stormy passage in the Bay of Biscay, when he was obliged to eat tripe. He admired Lord Wavell as a wise and patient viceroy, and thought Mountbatten by comparison a glib and self-serving adventurer. His last memory was bitter: leaving India to the jeers of those he believed owed their freedom *to* the British, but who now wanted freedom *from* the British. He regretted independence and partition, feared India would subsequently go Communist, and was delighted that it did not.

I have no recollection that I learned from my father's stories that military force was an important element in the maintenance of empire, perhaps because he had himself so disliked the petty regimentation of army life. But I can say that India meant more to me than it would have done if he had not gone there: it was not just a place on the map, but became a place in my mind. In one guise, Mount Everest was the peak that had been climbed at the queen's coronation, by the appropriately imperial duo of Edmund Hillary and Sherpa Tenzing. In another, it was part of the Himalayan range that my father had seen and photographed for himself. In the same way, Jawaharlal Nehru and Ayub Khan seemed as much a real presence in my early life as Harold Macmillan or Hugh Gaitskell, and since the one had attended Harrow School and Trinity College, Cambridge, and the other had been to the Royal Military College at Sandhurst, they provided some sort of reassurance that the old imperial connection remained strong and close. Then, in 1961, the queen paid a state visit to India, a kind of post-imperial durbar complete with elephant processions and tiger shoots, which was very different in tone and reception from her recent, fiftieth-anniversary tour. At my primary school we made a map to trace this royal progress, and because of my father's experiences, I claimed to be an expert on the subject – though while I think I knew more than my contemporaries, it didn't amount to very much.

My primary school also possessed a large world map, on which the British Empire was coloured red, as in those days it invariably was. It was at least ten years out of date, which meant it depicted the empire as it had existed at its territorial zenith between the First and the Second World Wars. It was an extraordinary vista of earthly dominion for a Birmingham boy of nine or ten to behold, though I was far too young to have any idea of what earthly dominion actually meant or entailed – for the dominators let alone for the dominated. But it provided a geographical context in which to fit the India my father talked about, and also Canada, Australia, New Zealand and South Africa, the old dominions of empire, which were then much closer both in sentiment and in substance to Britain than they are today. The British press reported events there as though they were domestic news, and figures such as Lester Pearson and Vincent Massey in Canada, Keith Holyoake in New Zealand and Robert Menzies in Australia were household names (at least, they were in my household). So too were Lords Slim and Cobham, both latter-day proconsuls with strong local links. Slim was a self-made Birmingham boy, my father's 'old boss' in India during the war, and governor-general of Australia from 1953 to 1960. Cobham was an authentic aristocrat, and owned a great country house near by at Hagley, which was opened to the public while he was away as governor-general of New Zealand from 1957 to 1962.

This seemed to bring empire close to home, and it came home in more concrete ways too. The gifts my father had sent back from India gave me some notion that one of the purposes of empire was to produce goods that were exported to Britain, and during my childhood I encountered many more examples of this imperial provisioning. There was lamb and butter from New Zealand, tea from India, chocolate from Nigeria, coffee from Kenya, and apples, pears and grapes from South Africa. My mother went to a dressmaker named Miss Halfpenny, who was Canadian, and her house was full of souvenirs of her homeland: postcards of Niagara Falls, craftwork by Indians, and so on. And I played with toys that were identified as 'Empire Made' – an explicit acknowledgement that the empire still existed, but a euphemism for the fact that such goods invariably originated in Hong Kong. As this suggests, there were also some imperial ambiguities here, of which I gradually became aware, but did not fully comprehend. New Zealand lamb and butter were regarded as 'inferior' to English provisions; 'Empire Made' goods were low-quality plastic such as was found only in Woolworths; and when South Africa left the Commonwealth in 1961, my mother promptly stopped buying its produce.

There was a second physical sense of empire that was much more powerful for me than chocolate or apples. As a schoolboy, my imagination was captivated by the marvels of civil engineering, and it was scarcely coincidence that many of these man-made wonders were located in the empire. There was the Suez Canal in Egypt, the Aswan Dam on the Nile and the Kariba Dam, which was being built at just this time on the Zambezi. There was the St Lawrence Seaway, which the queen opened with President Dwight D. Eisenhower in 1957. There were the P & O liners that still plied to the Antipodes, including the newly built *Canberra* and *Oriana*, and there was the Canadian Pacific fleet, including the *Empress of Canada*, which I saw on a school outing to the Liverpool docks. There were the great imperial bridges – over Sydney Harbour, across the Zambezi at Victoria Falls and across the St Lawrence at Quebec – the details and dimensions of which I learned by heart. And there were the great imperial trains: the *Spirit of Progress* in Australia, the *Blue Train* in South Africa and the Canadian Pacific transcontinentals. Indeed, in the middle of Birmingham, there was a Canadian Pacific branch office, and in the window were displayed models of its ships and trains. I regularly dreamed of travelling on them; but I never did. For my first visit to any part of what had been the British Empire did not take place until I went to Canada in 1973.

This was my private, childhood sense of empire: first- and second-hand experiences as I absorbed and elaborated them in Birmingham during the 1950s and early 1960s. As I look back on it now, it seems an extremely superficial and limited picture – superficial in the way that childhood knowledge invariably is, and limited because I knew nothing of the empire itself at first hand. It was also a comforting picture: as I envisaged and understood it, the empire seemed good and friendly and big and strong, and I simply took it for granted that it was right that Britain had it, without thinking what it might be like for the people who actually lived in it. But this was also a picture that became harder to reconcile with what was actually happening to the empire in the real, grown-up world outside my imagination. After the coronation, the next imperial episode I remember was very different: the Suez crisis of 1956. I was too young to know what it was all about, or to appreciate the bitter passions and divisions that it provoked. But I *do* remember that my father was emphatically on the side of Eden against Nasser; that one of the greatest marvels of imperial engineering had first been nationalized and then been damaged; that for some time after I thought committing suicide meant jumping in a canal; and that Britain had been defeated and the idea of imperialism discredited. A mere three years on, the coronation and the feelings to which it had given rise had been turned upside down or inside out.

Thereafter, my life seemed to coincide with a succession of anti-imperial or de-imperializing episodes. By the late 1950s and early

1960s *imperialism* had become a very dirty word indeed – in the Congo, in Indonesia, in Algeria. All round the globe, 'the end of European primacy' was being proclaimed, the colonial powers were in retreat, and the British Empire was no exception to this rule. On the contrary, it exemplified this rule: as the greatest empire, there was the most to give away. I don't think I had any understanding of why it was coming to an end at this time, except a vague idea, which my father did not share, that these people wanted 'freedom' and 'independence'. Nor did I connect it in my own mind with the independence of India three years before I was born, as the next stage in a continuing historical process of imperial dissolution. *That* was the past, *this* was the present, and I had no understanding that these things were linked together in a seamless web. But I could not disguise the fact that it was happening, and while part of me thought that if colonial people wanted 'freedom' or 'independence' they ought to have it, another part of me found it all very sad – for me, not for them.

I soon began to notice that there was a general pattern to this end of empire, which went roughly as follows. At some point from the mid 1950s to the mid 1960s, there would be 'trouble' in a colony: the Communist insurgence in Malaya, Mau Mau in Kenya, guerrilla warfare in Cyprus. Thereupon a state of emergency was declared by the hard-pressed British governor, and the nationalist leaders were arrested and put in prison. Sometime later, they were released, and soon after that, one of them became the colony's first prime minister, with whom the British then began negotiations for a speedy advance to independence. At the agreed date, there was a ceremonial handover in the stadium of the capital city, attended by a member of the royal family, though never by the queen herself. On the stroke of midnight, the British flag was lowered for the final time, to the accompaniment of the 'Last Post', and the very different flag of the newly independent country was raised. The Sudan, Ghana and Nigeria; Sierra Leone, Malaya and British Guiana; Kenya, Uganda and Tanganyika; Malta, Cyprus and Singapore; Northern Rhodesia and Nyasaland: one by one, these colonies went their own way, their roll-call of names sounding the death-knell of empire.

No wonder that when Harold Macmillan visited South Africa in

February 1960, he observed that 'the wind of change is blowing through this continent and, whether we like it or not, this growth of national consciousness is a political fact'. I vividly remember the broadcast of that speech, and indeed the whole of his tour of the British Empire in Africa, which was, by the standards of the time, an extraordinary and unprecedented prime ministerial progress. So rapidly did this wind of change blow in the next few years that Britons had to learn the names of newly independent nations, as Northern Rhodesia became Zambia, and Nyasaland became Malawi. And there were also the names of new black leaders – Kwame Nkrumah, Hastings Banda, Julius Nyerere, Tunku Abdul Rahman, Sir Abubakar Tafawa Balewa – to set alongside the live white males from the old dominions. But not everyone liked these winds of change. British settlers in the White Highlands in Kenya felt they were being abandoned by their 'kith and kin' in Britain, and television programmes regularly reported their plight and rage. And in 1961 South Africa was forced to leave the Commonwealth because of objections from among the new member nations to its racist policy of apartheid.

'The Commonwealth': that was the phrase and the concept held up to those who felt regret or simply bewilderment that the empire was ending so rapidly. By this time, 'the Commonwealth' had long since superseded 'the Empire' in official terminology, and it carried with it a new historical narrative (devised by politicians rather than by historians) that superseded the old imperial story of trusteeship, the white man's burden, or dominion over palm and pine. According to this revised account, which was in full flower by the mid 1960s, the British had always intended to prepare their colonies for independence. This path was pioneered by the great overseas dominions, which were to all intents and purposes self-governing by the inter-war years, though they still recognized the British monarch as their head of state. Then, in 1947, India, Pakistan and Burma all became independent, and decided to become republics. With the exception of Burma, they too joined the Commonwealth, and recognized the British monarch as the head of this new, post-imperial community. Finally came the third phase, with the independence of most of the remaining colonies in Asia and Africa, and they in turn joined the club, most as republics.

This was a comforting and reassuring story, which sought to present the *end* of the British Empire as the whole *point* of the British Empire – by calling it the Commonwealth. But, like many others, I was not entirely convinced by this. The empire had been about power; the Commonwealth was about sentiment – an alumni association of a university that seemed to be rapidly going under. In the mid 1950s the Commonwealth had still been primarily British and white; ten years later it was overwhelmingly multiracial. And as Britain's influence invariably lessened, the unity and coherence of the Commonwealth were correspondingly attenuated. For there was not only the fierce disagreement about South Africa. As Harold Macmillan sought to turn Britain away from its imperial past and towards a European future by applying for membership of the Common Market, both Australia and New Zealand felt that the mother country was turning her back on them, and they were right. For much of this time India and Pakistan were also at loggerheads, and the 'Kashmir problem' remained unresolved. (It still does.) There was a terrible civil war in Nigeria, and many of the newly independent African nations soon became one-party states. I regularly told myself that none of this compared with the dreadful things that were going on in Indonesia, Indo-China, Algeria or the Congo: but they did suggest that 'the Commonwealth' was less of a success story than was often implied.

Nevertheless, it was clear that, once this final phase in the dissolution of empire was begun, it was going to be irreversible. There were those on the far right of the Conservative Party, like Lord Salisbury, who disapproved of what Macmillan was doing, and who disapproved even more of the brilliant, controversial colonial secretary, Iain Macleod, whom they accused of pushing the colonies to independence with unjustified speed, and of abandoning the British settlers to the Africans. Although part of me was saddened by this ending of empire, and by the recognition that the map I had seen at my primary school was now impossibly out of date, I was also clear that in this matter I was on the side of Macleod. The alternative line of criticism, voiced by Dean Acheson in his famously wounding comment of 1962, was that 'Britain has lost an Empire but not yet found a role.' It was wounding because it was true – both in terms of what had happened and what had not. I don't remember when in the 1960s I first came across this remark: but ever since, it has been impossible for me to forget it. In the years of Harold Wilson's premiership, from 1964 to 1970, Acheson's words became more applicable, not less, as the last outposts of empire, the military bases east of Suez, were given up.

But there was one part of empire that went neither quickly nor quietly during the Wilson years, and that was Southern Rhodesia, by then the last large British colony left in Africa. The white settlers, led by Ian Smith, were appalled by the prospect of black majority rule, and unilaterally declared independence from Britain in November 1965. They were determined that Britain should not sell them out (as they felt had been the case with the settlers in Kenya), and they were convinced that the only way to do so was to go it alone. Wilson was no less convinced that economic sanctions would bring the rebel regime to its knees in a matter of weeks rather than months. He could not have been more wrong. By the end of his prime ministership, the matter was still unresolved, and it dragged on throughout the 1970s. But soon after Mrs Thatcher came to power, a settlement was finally reached, and Southern Rhodesia became independent as Zimbabwe, with African majority rule. By then, all that was left of my once-mighty British Empire were a few islands in the Atlantic and the Pacific, plus Gibraltar, the Falklands and Hong Kong – along with Test Match cricket (which, strange to record, I don't remember thinking of at the time as an imperial relic), the Order of the British Empire (the last use of this phrase in official parlance) and the BBC World Service (appropriately enough, the Empire of the Air).

I realize that these two narratives I have unfolded are in many ways very discrepant and disconnected, both in terms of the type of recollection, and in terms of the substance of the recollection. The first might best be described as an amalgam of paternal memories handed on, my own personal experiences, and my inner life of dreams and fantasies. This was all very private, self-centred and solipsistic: it at no stage and in no sense involved me directly with the British Empire beyond Britain. I gradually acquired some geographical understanding of *where* it was, but no operational understanding of *what* it was in terms of dominion over other peoples. And it was an essentially backward-looking and unchanging vision, oriented towards the empire as it had been in 1939 rather than as it was – or as it was becoming – in 1959, let alone 1969. Thus remembered, this was the British Empire as *my* imagined community: far-off places rather than far-off people. The second set of recollections tells a very different story, which was going in a very different direction: the public, political and international events associated with the ending of empire, as I recall they impinged on me at the time. This was a forward-looking, disruptive, uncertain and dynamic vision: not an imagined community existing comfortably inside my own head, but a real community dissolving uncomfortably in the world outside and beyond it.

At this point I must complicate the picture still further by introducing the third and final narrative of my imperial childhood: what was I reading about empire, and what was it telling me? Once again, I go back to my father, who provided me with another imperial story, only this time not his own. When he left his primary school in Birmingham in 1926, he was presented with a book by his headmaster. It was the second of a three-volume work entitled *The Outline of the World Today*, published by George Newnes and edited by Sir Harry Johnston and Dr Hayden Guest, and it was called *The British Empire*. I cannot remember how old I was when I first came upon it on my parents' bookshelves, but I do remember that for a time I was enthralled by it. Here is the *fortissimo* opening paragraph:

The British Empire is only three hundred years old, but it has already outrun all the records of history. The Roman Empire never reached one seventh, the Arab, Mongolian, Spanish and Chinese Empires never more than one third, even the Empire of the Tsars did not account to much more than one half of the British Empire, which covers a quarter of the land of the globe. It is three times greater than Europe, twice as great as South America, a hundred times greater than the United Kingdom.

'What,' the authors went on to inquire, with not a trace of irony or self-doubt, 'is the secret of Britain's greatness?'[1]

In fact, the book (which I have beside me as I write) made no pretence at answering this question: it simply took this greatness for granted, and assumed it would be permanent, in ways that were no longer possible or plausible by the time I came to read it. I think that I vaguely understood this: but for a time that made the book more appealing, not less. Beginning with Britain itself, it provided a grand tour of the whole inter-war imperial agglomeration: dominion by dominion, colony by colony, protectorate by protectorate, naval base by naval base – the empire at its greatest extent, on which the sun truly did not set. Part history, part travelogue, part evocation, part propaganda, it was lavishly illustrated with pictures of the empire's natural wonders (lakes, rivers, waterfalls, mountains) and the man-made marvels (temples, churches, parliament houses, dams and bridges). As a panoramic survey, it was an irresistible read, and for many years such detailed knowledge as I had of the British Empire was derived from its undeniably self-congratulatory pages. The dominions and colonies were depicted as places that produced raw materials for the mother country, where good government flourished and good administration thrived, where the benefits of British civilization were widely available, and where, as a result, the people were happy and contented. If the book had a hero, it was probably Cecil Rhodes.

This view of empire was reinforced (though it probably should have been questioned) by the fiction I was beginning to read: Henty and Haggard, Conan Doyle and John Buchan, C. S. Forester and Ian Fleming. The 1950s and 1960s may have been a period in which new writing was experimental, undeferential and in revolt against Britain's Victorian and imperial past. But for a significant part of that time, I was reading about heroic adventurers in far-off locations, latter-day St Georges slaying innumerable dragons, and I rather suspect that most schoolboys of my generation (I cannot speak for schoolgirls) were doing the same. Of course, these writers were spinning their yarns over a span of eighty years, during which the world and the British Empire had changed a great deal; and it is hard to imagine the stiff-upper-lip heroes of Henty or Buchan at ease in James Bond's more indulgent era of sex, gambling and good living. But all these authors took it for granted that Britain was a great imperial power, and they all seemed to be saying that the empire had only been won, and could only be maintained, by constant struggle and unceasing vigilance on its frontiers. This was hardly the same picture as that conveyed in the calmly confident pages of Johnston and Guest. I would like to report that I was troubled by this discrepancy between what I thought of as imperial fact and imperial fiction. But I do not think that I was.

Imperial fact reappeared in a more rigorous guise when I took my O-level exam in history in the summer of 1966. The course that was offered at my school was not (as I think was more generally the case) on Britain or Europe, but on the British Empire and Commonwealth from the loss of the American colonies to Indian independence. I was extremely well taught by an inspired schoolmaster – so well, indeed, that the notebooks I compiled stood me in excellent stead when I returned to this subject in my final year as a Cambridge undergraduate. The textbook we read was by Sidney Reed Brett, who had been born in 1893, when Queen Victoria had another seven years to reign, and who had first published his *History of the British Empire* in 1941. In 1959 he produced a revised edition, *A History of the British Empire and Commonwealth*, and it was this that I used six years later.[2] It had been written in the immediate aftermath of Suez, but before decolonization had begun, or South Africa had left the Commonwealth, and its treatment reflected this. The history of the great dominions was a Whiggish progress from settlement, via union or federation, to responsible government; the history of India presented independence and partition as triumph; and the history of the colonial empire had not yet ended. None of these nations had separate or autonomous histories outside the British imperial embrace.

Self-evidently, this did not altogether square with the decolonizing story that was unfolding before my eyes, and nor did the imperial history that I later studied at Cambridge between 1969 and 1972. In Part One of the History Tripos I took a paper entitled 'The Expansion of Europe' and in Part Two another paper on 'The Commonwealth'. As its title suggested, the first was concerned with the impulses to empire emanating from the European metropolis, rather than with extra-European responses to them: theories of imperialism from Hobson to Lenin, the partition of Africa, and so on. As for the Commonwealth paper, this represented little advance on my O-level syllabus.

The basic story was the same, albeit treated with much more scholarly sophistication, and, once again, decolonization did not loom large. This was less surprising then than it may seem now. When I took this paper, the empire had been gone for less than a decade, and historical scholarship and teaching had not yet absorbed the implications of these revolutionary changes. Moreover, the dominant figures in the field – Nicholas Mansergh, Jack Gallagher, Eric Stokes and Ronald Robinson – had all known something of the empire first hand: Mansergh had worked in the Dominions Office, Gallagher had driven tanks in the North African desert, Robinson had been in the Colonial Office, and Stokes had taught at university colleges in Singapore and Rhodesia.

Thus described, these men belonged to the last British generation among whom it was possible to believe that the empire had a serious future. To this extent, their views had something in common with Reed Brett and even Harry Johnston, and some of this must have rubbed off on me. For their histories of the empire were still written from the viewpoint of the British metropolis: Mansergh described the evolution from empire to commonwealth in sophisticated Whig terms; Robinson and Gallagher analysed the partition of Africa from the perspective of what they called 'the official mind of imperialism'; and Eric Stokes followed the English Utilitarians out to India to see what they did when they got there.[3] In retrospect, this was the last and fullest flowering of British imperial history from the British point of view. For already, the focus of scholarly interests was beginning to change, away from the British metropolis to those on the receiving end of the empire. Robinson began to explore the 'collaborating elites' on the periphery; Stokes turned to study agrarian society in India; and the way was open for histories of Africa and South Asia in which the British imperial presence was re-presented as an ephemeral episode of external European intrusion, rather than as the defining, permanent framework of people's lives or historical scholarship.[4]

I became aware of these developments only after my graduation from Cambridge in 1972, the point at which my imperial childhood (and adolescence) finally came to an end. To be sure, the Rhodesian settlement, the Falklands War, and the Hong Kong handover were still to

come, as well as the overthrow of apartheid and the return of South
Africa to the Commonwealth. But had I not gone on to study its history
at school and university, the British Empire would effectively have
ended for me, as it did for most Britons, with the death of Winston
Churchill in 1965. His state funeral was the most magnificent public
spectacle since the coronation, but it sent out a very different message,
as the last rites of the great man himself were also a requiem for Britain
as a great imperial power. I cannot remember by which of these endings
I was more distressed. But the fact that I was so upset reinforces my
claim that I belong to the last generation to whom the British Empire
really meant something. If you were born in 1950, this was still – just
– true; but if you were born in 1960, it was – already – too late. I have
tried to set down here, as fully and honestly as I can, such imperial
recollections as I have, and to separate them off from the imperial
history I later learned at school and university. Inevitably, I have
dredged up these memories in a less structured and more incoherent
way than I have presented them here. But, as I look back on them, they
seem a contradictory amalgam of private and public, fact and fiction,
past and present, sentiment and scholarship, from which no single
'imperial experience' can be plausibly extracted.

This brings me to a final matter that I must mention, which does not
form any part of the three narratives I have so far related, but which
should certainly be included here, since it was my only first-hand
experience, not so much of empire, but of the aftermath of empire:
and that is the issue of immigration. By the late 1960s Birmingham
contained a large community of Africans, West Indians and South
Asians, post-imperial immigrants who had often settled in the least
attractive parts of the city, and who were doing many of the least
attractive jobs. They also settled in nearby Wolverhampton, one of
whose MPs, Enoch Powell, made his infamously apocalyptic speech,
in April 1968, predicting that there would be 'rivers of blood'. There
was an outcry at the time; Powell was sacked from the Tory shadow
cabinet; and thereafter he was a marked man in British politics. But,
once again, my direct involvement with this most emotive post-imperial
issue was small. I did not live in a part of Birmingham where immigrants
settled, although some of my relatives did; I recall but one dark-skinned

pupil at my grammar school during my time there, and he was very much younger than I was; and I once took part in an undergraduate demonstration at Cambridge against Enoch Powell, whose speeches I thought outrageous. Beyond that, all I can now recall is that it seemed to me strange that the British had never minded having dark-skinned people living in their empire, but that they did not want them living in Britain.

How, then, do these limited childhood memories of empire strike me, from the professional perspective of the middle-aged historian I have since become? I note that there are many things that are *not* here: heat and dust, palm and pine, the P & O. And I seem to have had no military or strategic perception of empire, and no awareness of the people who lived in the empire, whatever the colour of their skin. As such, this is a very domestic, metropolis-based story, from which ignorance of empire, rather than knowledge of it, emerges as its most marked feature. This means, in turn, that my recollections are wholly devoid of the searing, wrenching episodes of independence and partition, massacre and murder, imperial resentment and post-imperial trauma, which are so vividly recounted in the writings of post-colonial contemporaries such as Salman Rushdie and Sara Suleri, in whose writings the British Empire looms much larger and more malevolent than it does in mine. This is my version of the empire and the imperial events of my childhood, and that is theirs, and there is a massive discrepancy between them. But such discrepancies should occasion no surprise, although they often do. For the British experience of empire in the metropolis *was* very different from the British or the colonial experience of empire on the periphery. In Britain, empire was often disregarded, or taken rather ignorantly for granted, or (just occasionally and no-less ignorantly) delighted in; and since for most people none of this was the result of first-hand experience, their sense of empire was more an internal state of mind than an external way of life.

All this leads me to wonder whether I should describe myself as having been drenched in 'the imperial project', in the way that many post-colonial scholars argue was characteristic of the British throughout (and beyond?) the existence of empire itself. One answer is that I am not sure there was ever such a thing as 'the imperial project': even at its apogee, the British Empire was far too ramshackle a thing ever to display such unanimity of action and consistency of purpose. Another would be to say that there might have been 'an imperial project' in the heyday of empire, but that it had long ceased to be pursued in any vigorous or recognizable way by the time my generation happened upon the scene. But if I wasn't 'drenched' in a coherently monolithic 'project', then was I 'drenched' in an incoherently unmonolithic 'empire'? Did these imperial experiences loom large in my life at the time? And how far were they typical of the last imperial generation to which I belonged? I have to say, with a certain amount of regret, that my answers are, respectively, 'no', 'not much' and 'more than most'. I was not 'drenched' in empire; it was not all that important to me; but it was probably more important to me than to many, perhaps most, of my contemporaries.

These are hardly resounding conclusions, but I do not think that necessarily makes them insignificant or unimportant. For me, the imperial dog sometimes did bark in the night, but not very often, and not very loudly and, while I heard the bark, I never saw the dog. I *was* a child of empire, though empire was only a small and distant part of my childhood. I studied the history of the empire, though empire was only a small part of the history I studied. Perhaps it would be more accurate to say that as I grew up, I realized that I *had been* a child of an empire that had been – a realization that was prompted by the recognition that the empire in question was going, indeed had all but gone, even as it was being brought back from the dead in some of the history that I was studying. But to the extent that the British Empire existed primarily inside my head rather than outside, it did not do so on a very large scale, or in a particularly profound or influential way, and if I hadn't learned more about empire at school and university, in ways that were, I suspect, very atypical among my contemporaries, it would have meant even less to me than it did. Paradoxical though it may superficially seem, the only people 'drenched' in the British 'imperial project' among my generation were not Britons, but the nationalist opponents of empire and its post-colonial commentators and critics.

Hence the question mark at the end of my title: perhaps it would have been better to call this essay 'imperial coat-tails'. When James

Morris concluded his history of the British Empire, he used some words that seem no less pertinent as I draw this piece to its close. 'Is that the truth?' he asked, of the account he had unfolded. 'Is that how it was?' And he gave the only answer he could: 'It is *my* truth.'[5] I have addressed the same questions, and come up with an answer that is in one sense exactly the same (this is the truth of empire for *me*), but, in another sense, very different (it is not the same truth of empire as for *him*). How could it have been otherwise, given that we belong to two very different generations, and that empire was, inevitably, a much bigger thing for him than it has ever been, or could ever have been, for me? All I can say is that this is what I remember of these things and those times as we recall 1997 – the year of the centenary of Queen Victoria's Diamond Jubilee, the fiftieth anniversary of Indian independence and the return of Hong Kong to China. It is these commemorations and these events, combined with a reawakening of a sense of end-of-empire occasioned by a visit to Russia earlier that year, that have prompted me to try to recall the imperial childhood I had – and didn't have. I wonder if they have prompted similar (or different) recollections in anyone else who belongs, like me, to the last generation that hung, by its finger ends, on the coat-tails of empire?

Notes

ABBREVIATIONS

The following abbreviations have been used throughout the notes:

AHR	*American Historical Review*
AHS	*Australian Historical Studies*
CSSH	*Comparative Studies in Society and History*
HJ	*Historical Journal*
JBS	*Journal of British Studies*
JICH	*Journal of Imperial and Commonwealth History*
JMRAS	*Journal of the Malaysian Branch of the Royal Asiatic Society*
MAS	*Modern Asian Studies*
OHBE	W. R. Louis (ed.), *The Oxford History of the British Empire*, 5 vols.:
i	N. Canny (ed.), *The Origins of Empire* (Oxford, 1998)
ii	P. J. Marshall (ed.), *The Eighteenth Century* (Oxford, 1998)
iii	A. N. Porter (ed.), *The Nineteenth Century* (Oxford, 1999)
iv	J. M. Brown and W. R. Louis (eds.), *The Twentieth Century* (Oxford, 1999)
v	R. W. Winks (ed.), *Historiography* (Oxford, 1999)
P & P	*Past and Present*
TRHS	*Transactions of the Royal Historical Society*
W&MQ	*William and Mary Quarterly*

I have not included a comprehensive list of further reading, since the references constitute what is in effect a running bibliography. All works are cited in full in their first entry in the notes to each chapter.

Preface

1. For the dates of independence, and a list of the very few colonies remaining, see W. D. McIntyre, *British Decolonization, 1946–1997* (London, 1998), pp. ix–x; A. H. M. Kirk-Greene, *On Crown Service: A History of HM Colonial and Overseas Civil Services, 1837–1997* (London, 1999), pp. 81, 91.

2. *OHBE* v gives an admirably full account.

3. D. Cannadine, 'The Empire Strikes Back', *P & P*, no. 147 (1995), pp. 180–84. There was also a debased version of the ethos of religion and duty, for which see R. Hyam, *Empire and Sexuality: The British Experience* (Manchester, 1990).

4. A. B. Keith, *The Sovereignty of the British Dominions* (Oxford, 1929); K. C. Wheare, *The Statute of Westminster and Dominion Status* (Oxford, 1938).

5. P. N. S. Mansergh, *The Commonwealth Experience* (London, 1969).

6. D. K. Fieldhouse, 'Can Humpty-Dumpty be Put Together Again?', *JICH*, xii (1984), pp. 9–23; B. R. Tomlinson, ' "The Contraction of England": National Decline and the Loss of Empire', *JICH*, xi (1982), pp. 58–72; D. A. Low, '*The Contraction of England*' (Cambridge, 1984).

7. D. Kennedy, 'Imperial History and Post-Colonial Theory', *JICH*, xxiv (1996), pp. 345–63.

8. A. G. Hopkins, 'Development and the Utopian Ideal, 1960–1999', in *OHBE* v, pp. 647–9.

9. A. G. Hopkins, *The Future of the Imperial Past* (Cambridge, 1997); *idem*, 'Back to the Future: From National History to Imperial History', *P & P*, no. 164 (1999), pp. 198–220.

10. *OHBE* i–v; B. Porter, 'An Awfully Big Colonial Adventure', *TLS*, 14 January 2000, pp. 4–5; G. Johnson, 'Watching the Sun Go Down', *The Higher*, 10 March 2000, pp. 24–5.

11. P. Buckner, 'Whatever Happened to the British Empire?', *Journal of the Canadian History Association*, new ser., iv (1993), pp. 3–32; C. A. Bayly, 'Returning the British to South Asian History: The Limits of Colonial Hegemony', *South Asia*, xvii (1994), pp. 1–25. For an honourable (and strangely neglected) exception, who sought explicitly to link British and imperial history, see A. P. Thornton, *The Imperial Idea and Its Enemies: A Study in British Power* (London, 1959); *idem, The Habit of Authority: Paternalism in British History* (London, 1966).

12. For a pioneering example, never fully followed up, see A. Briggs's chapter on Melbourne in *Victorian Cities* (Harmondsworth, 1968), pp. 277–310.

13. J. A. Schumpeter, *Imperialism and Social Classes* (Oxford, 1951). See also J. Darwin, 'Civility and Empire', in P. Burke, B. Harrison, and P. Slack (eds.),

Civil Histories: Essays Presented to Sir Keith Thomas (Oxford, 2000), pp. 321–6.

14. On the need 'to see connections between things', see, as well as the first epigraph to this book, also S. Marks, 'History, the Nation and Empire: Sniping from the Periphery', *History Workshop*, no. 29 (1990), pp. 114–16; A. L. Stoler, *Race and the Education of Desire: Foucault's History of Sexuality and the Colonial Order of Things* (London, 1995), pp. xi–xii.

15. H. Liebersohn, 'Discovering Indigenous Nobility: Tocqueville, Chamisso, and Romantic Travel Writing', *AHR*, lxxxxix (1994), p. 749; L. H. Guest, 'Curiously Marked: Tattooing, Masculinity, and Nationality in Eighteenth-Century British Perceptions of the South Pacific', in J. Barrell (ed.), *Painting and the Politics of Culture: Nine Essays on British Art, 1700–1850* (Oxford, 1992), p. 101. For other discussions of these similar–dissimilar polarities, see: T. Todorov, *The Conquest of America: The Question of the Other* (New York, 1992), p. 42; M. Malia, *Russia Under Western Eyes: From the Bronze Horseman to the Lenin Mausoleum* (Cambridge, Mass., 1999), pp. 6–7.

16. P. J. Marshall, *'A Free Though Conquering People': Britain and Asia in the Eighteenth Century* (London, 1981), p. 2; *idem*, 'Imperial Britain', *JICH*, xxiii (1995), pp. 379–94; Hopkins, 'Back to the Future', pp. 207–8, 214–20.

PART ONE: BEGINNINGS

1. Prologue

1. B. Anderson, *Imagined Communities: Reflections on the Origin and Spread of Nationalism* (London, 1983); E. J. Hobsbawm and T. O. Ranger (eds.), *The Invention of Tradition* (Cambridge, 1983).

2. J. Morris, *Pax Britannica: The Climax of an Empire* (London, 1968), p. 9; R. Hyam, *Britain's Imperial Century, 1815–1914* (London, 1976), p. 15; A. J. Stockwell, 'Power, Authority and Freedom', in P. J. Marshall (ed.), *The Cambridge Illustrated History of the British Empire* (Cambridge, 1996), pp. 154–6.

3. E. Hinderaker, 'The "Four Indian Kings" and the Imaginative Construction of the First British Empire', *W & MQ*, 3rd ser., liii (1996), p. 487.

4. M. Malia, *Russia Under Western Eyes: From the Bronze Horseman to the Lenin Mausoleum* (Cambridge, Mass., 1990), p. 9.

5. D. A. Washbrook, 'Economic Depression and the Making of "Traditional" Society in Colonial India, 1820–1855', *TRHS*, 6th ser., iii (1993), p. 239;

E. W. Said, *Orientalism: Western Conceptions of the Orient* (Harmondsworth, 1995 edn.). For the most well-grounded historical critiques of the Said thesis, see J. M. MacKenzie, *Orientalism: History, Theory and the Arts* (Manchester, 1995); D. A. Washbrook, 'Orients and Occidents: Colonial Discourse Theory and the Historiography of the British Empire', in *OHBE* v, pp. 596–611. This contrast between an 'egalitarian' west and a 'hierarchical' orient has also been made by L. Dumont, *Homo Hierarchicus: The Caste System and Its Implications* (Chicago, 1991). See S. Barnett, L. Fruzzetti and A. Stor, 'Hierarchy Purified: Notes on Dumont and His Critics', *Journal of Asian Studies*, xxxv (1976), pp. 627–46.

6. D. Cannadine, *Class in Britain* (London, 1998); *idem*, 'Beyond Class? Social Structures and Social Perceptions in Modern England', *Proceedings of the British Academy*, xcvii (1997), pp. 95–118.

7. G. W. Stocking, *Race, Culture and Evolution: Essays in the History of Anthropology* (Chicago, 1982), p. 45; K. Malik, *The Meaning of Race: Race, History and Culture in Western Society* (London, 1996), pp. 5–6.

8. V. Kiernan, *The Lords of Human Kind: European Attitudes towards the Outside World in the Imperial Age* (London, 1969); A. Pagden, *Lords of All the World: Ideologies of Empire in Spain, Britain and France, c. 1500–c. 1800* (London, 1995); P. J. Marshall and G. Williams, *The Great Map of Mankind: British Perceptions of the World in the Age of Enlightenment* (London, 1982); C. A. Bayly, *Imperial Meridian: The British Empire and the World, 1780–1830* (London, 1989), pp. 147–55, 222; T. R. Metcalf, *Ideologies of the Raj* (Cambridge, 1995), pp. 30–34.

9. Hyam, *Britain's Imperial Century*, pp. 37–40, 78–85, 156–62; Lord Cromer, *Political and Literary Essays, 1908–1913* (Freeport, NY, 1969 edn.), pp. 12–14, 40–43.

10. P. J. Marshall, 'Imperial Britain', *JICH*, xxiii (1995), p. 385; *idem*, 'Britain without America – A Second Empire?', in *OHBE* ii, pp. 591–2; A. N. Porter, 'Introduction', in *OHBE* iii, pp. 21–5. For similar views, see J. Harris, *Private Lives, Public Spirit: A Social History of Britain, 1870–1914* (Oxford, 1993), pp. 6, 234–5; A. Marwick, *Class: Image and Reality in Britain, France and the USA since 1930* (London, 1980), p. 30.

11. A. Briggs, *Victorian Cities* (Harmondsworth, 1968), pp. 62–4, 313–16; G. Stedman Jones, *Outcast London: A Study in the Relationship between the Classes in Victorian Society* (Oxford, 1971); G. Himmelfarb, *The Idea of Poverty: England in the Early Industrial Age* (London, 1984), pp. 307–70; Malik, *The Meaning of Race*, pp. 92–100; M. J. Daunton and R. Halpern, 'Introduction: British Identities, Indigenous Peoples, and the Empire', and C. A. Bayly, 'The British and Indigenous Peoples, 1760–1860: Power, Perception

and Identity', both in M. J. Daunton and R. Halpern (eds.), *Empire and Others: British Encounters with Indigenous Peoples, 1600–1850* (London, 1999), pp. 12, 33.

12. K. O. Kupperman, *Settling with the Indians: The Meeting of English and Indian Cultures in America, 1580–1640* (Totowa, NJ, 1980), pp. vii, 2–5, 35–8, 47–54, 120–27, 143–8.

13. This argument has been well made for the first half of the nineteenth century by D. Lorimer, *Colour, Class and the Victorians: Attitudes to the Negro in the Mid-Nineteenth Century* (Leicester, 1978), esp. pp. 67–8. But it underestimates the extent to which later Victorians persisted in seeing coloured people in this way. See B. Brereton, *Race Relations in Colonial Trinidad, 1870–1900* (Cambridge, 1979), p. 211; J. Fingard, 'Race and Respectability in Victorian Halifax', *JICH*, xx (1992), pp. 169–95.

14. P. Magnus, *King Edward the Seventh* (Harmondsworth, 1967), pp. 217–18. For an earlier instance of the prince of Wales's encounter with ruling monarchs, see F. Harcourt, 'The Queen, the Sultan and the Viceroy: A Victorian State Occasion', *The London Journal*, v (1979), pp. 35–56.

15. Malia, *Russia Under Western Eyes*, pp. 36–9. P. Mason, *Prospero's Magic: Some Thoughts on Class and Race* (London, 1962), p. 4, also noted the 'tacit alliance across a race barrier between top people'. See below, pp. 123–6.

16. H. Spurling, 'Paul Scott: Novelist and Historian', in W. R. Louis (ed.), *Adventures with Britannia: Personalities, Politics and Culture in Britain* (London, 1995), pp. 35–6; M. Gorra, *After Empire: Scott, Naipaul, Rushdie* (Chicago, 1997), pp. 35–6. In this regard, it is also worth noting this Colonial Office confidential memorandum on appointments: 'He must above all not be infected with racial snobbery. Colour prejudice in the colonial civil servant is the one unforgivable sin.': A. H. M. Kirk-Greene, *On Crown Service: A History of HM Colonial and Overseas Civil Services, 1837–1997* (London, 1999), p. 99. There was also, of course, a third imperial hierarchy, built around gender. For a suggestive discussion of the interrelatedness on these class, race and gender hierarchies, see A. McClintock, *Imperial Leather: Race, Gender and Sexuality in the Colonial Contest* (London, 1995), pp. 4–9.

17. Kupperman, *Settling with the Indians*, p. 4.

18. P. J. Marshall, 'Empire and Authority in the Later Eighteenth Century', *JICH*, xv (1987), pp. 105–22.

2. Precursors

1. A. P. Thornton, *The Habit of Authority: Paternalism in British History* (London, 1966); D. Roberts, *Paternalism in Early Victorian England* (New Brunswick, NJ, 1979); D. Cannadine, *The Decline and Fall of the British Aristocracy* (London, 1990), pp. 8–24.

2. J. G. A. Pocock, 'The Limits and Divisions of British History: In Search of the Unknown Subject', *AHR*, lxxxvii (1982), pp. 311–36; D. Armitage, 'Greater Britain: A Useful Category of Historical Analysis?', *AHR*, civ (1999), pp. 427–43; N. Canny, 'Writing Atlantic History; or, Reconfiguring the History of Colonial British America', *Journal of American History*, lxxxvi (1999), pp. 1,093–1,114.

3. C. Barnett, *The Collapse of British Power* (London, 1972), pp. 74–5; T. R. Metcalf, *Ideologies of the Raj* (Cambridge, 1995), p. 54; A. J. Stockwell, 'Power, Authority and Freedom', in P. J. Marshall (ed.), *The Cambridge Illustrated History of the British Empire* (Cambridge, 1996), p. 173; P. J. Marshall, 'Introduction', in *OHBE* ii, p. 16; W. R. Louis, 'Introduction', in *OHBE* iv, p. 7; R. E. Robinson, 'Imperial Theory and the Question of Imperialism after Empire', *JICH*, xii (1984), p. 45. Though it ought also to be said that before 1848, this difference would have been much less clear: see M. Taylor, 'The 1848 Revolutions and the British Empire', *P & P*, no. 166 (2000), pp. 146–80.

4. L. Hartz et al., *The Founding of New Societies: Studies in the History of the United States, Latin America, South Africa, Canada and Australia* (New York, 1969); W. H. McNeill, *The Great Frontier: Freedom and Hierarchy in Modern Times* (Princeton, NJ, 1983); H. Temperley, 'Frontierism, Capital, and the American Loyalists in Canada', *Journal of American Studies*, xiii (1979), pp. 5–27.

5. F. G. Hutchins, *The Illusion of Permanence: British Imperialism in India* (Princeton, NJ, 1967), pp. vii–xiv; Metcalf, *Ideologies of the Raj*, pp. ix–x.

6. W. M. Elofson and J. A. Woods (eds.), *The Writings and Speeches of Edmund Burke*, vol. iii, *Party, Parliament and the American War, 1774–1780* (Oxford, 1996), pp. 267–8, 365. For similar hostile views on the part of the settlers, see G. B. Nash, 'The Image of the Indian in the Southern Colonial Mind', *W & MQ*, 3rd ser., xxix (1972), pp. 197–230; J. O'Brien, ' "They are So Frequently Shifting Their Place of Residence": Land and the Construction of Social Place of Indians in Colonial Massachusetts', in M. J. Daunton and R. Halpern (eds.), *Empire and Others: British Encounters with Indigenous Peoples, 1600–1850* (London, 1999), pp. 204–16.

7. E. Hindraker, 'The "Four Indian Kings" and the Imaginative Construction

of the First British Empire', *W & MQ*, 3rd ser., liii (1996), pp. 487–526; D. C. Richter, 'Native Peoples of North America and the Eighteenth-Century British Empire', in *OHBE* ii, pp. 358–9.

8. A. D. Kriegel, 'A Convergence of Ethics: Saints and Whigs in British Anti-Slavery', *JBS*, xxvi (1987), pp. 441, 449; D. Brion Davis, *The Problem of Slavery in the Age of Revolution, 1770–1823* (Ithaca, NY, 1975), p. 377; C. A. Bayly, 'The British and Indigenous Peoples, 1760–1860: Power, Perception and Identity', in Daunton and Halpern, *Empire and Others*, pp. 19–41.

9. M. J. Braddick, 'The English Government, War, Trade and Settlement, 1625–1688', in *OHBE* i, p. 297; R. M. Weir, ' "Shaftesbury's Darling": British Settlement in the Carolinas at the Close of the Seventeenth Century', in *OHBE* i, p. 375; R. R. Johnson, 'Growth and Mastery: British North America, 1690–1748', in *OHBE* ii, pp. 290–91; D. Cannadine, *Class in Britain* (London, 1998), pp. 35–7.

10. Sir I. de la Bere, *The Queen's Orders of Chivalry* (London, 1964), pp. 174–5; J. R. Hill, 'National Festivals, the State and Protestant Ascendancy in Ireland, 1790–1829', *Irish Historical Studies*, xxiv (1984), pp. 30–51; C. A. Bayly, *Imperial Meridian: The British Empire and the World, 1780–1830* (London, 1989), p. 196; E. Brynn, *Crown & Castle: British Rule in Ireland, 1800–1830* (Dublin, 1978), pp. 20–30, 96–112; R. B. McDowell, *The Irish Administration, 1801–1914* (London, 1964), pp. 52–6.

11. J. Thurston, ' "The Dust of Toryism": Monarchism and Republicanism in Upper Canadian Travel and Immigration Texts', *Journal of Canadian Studies*, xxx (1996), p. 80; Thornton, *Habit of Authority*, pp. 139–44.

12. G. Martin, *Bunyip Aristocracy: The New South Wales Constitution Debate of 1853 and Hereditary Institutions in the British Colonies* (Beckenham, 1986), pp. 3, 18–27; Bayly, *Imperial Meridian*, pp. 111–12, 135, 196–206; P. J. Marshall, 'British North America, 1760–1815', in *OHBE* ii, pp. 384–5, 391. For South Africa at this time, see R. Ross, *Status and Respectability in the Cape Colony, 1750–1870: A Tragedy of Manners* (Cambridge, 1999), pp. 9–69.

13. D. M. Peers, ' "That Habitual Nobility of Being": British Officers and the Social Construction of the Bengal Army in the Early Nineteenth Century', *MAS*, xxv (1991), pp. 548–9: 'The use of class in British India in the early nineteenth century, as befitted an officer corps drawn largely from rural England, was one of natural orders and ranks in society. Class, and therefore caste, for such individuals was largely understood to be occupational and hereditary, organic and unchanging. This was a vision of social ordering which harked back to an idealized eighteenth-century rural Britain and which came to be used as a means of coming to grips with Indian social structures in such a way as to meet administrative requirements.' See also B. S. Cohn, 'Notes on the History

of the Study of Indian Society and Culture', in M. Singer and B. S. Cohn (eds.), *Structure and Change in Indian Society* (Chicago, 1968), pp. 6–11; N. Dirks, 'Castes of Mind', *Representations*, no. 37 (1992), pp. 61–6.

14. B. Stein, *Thomas Munro: The Origins of the Colonial State and His Vision of Empire* (New Delhi, 1989), p. 127.

15. Metcalf, *Ideologies of the Raj*, pp. 20–21; M. H. Fisher, 'The Resident in Court Ritual, 1764–1858', *MAS*, xxiv (1990), pp. 419–58; British Library India Office Library MS, Home Misc./104, f. 409.

16. Bayly, *Imperial Meridian*, pp. 111, 209–16; T. R. Metcalf, *An Imperial Vision: Indian Architecture and Britain's Raj* (London, 1989), p. 13.

17. R. E. Robinson, 'European Imperialism and Indigenous Reactions in British West Africa, 1880–1914', in H. L. Wesseling (ed.), *Expansion and Reaction* (Leiden, 1978), p. 145.

18. N. Penny (ed.), *Reynolds* (London, 1986), pp. 271–2; B. Smith, *European Vision and the South Pacific* (2nd edn., London, 1985), pp. 81–2, 114–16; *idem, Imagining the Pacific: In the Wake of the Cook Voyages* (London, 1992), pp. 45–6.

19. E. M. Weeks, 'About Face: Sir David Wilkie's Portrait of Mehemet Ali, Pasha of Egypt', in J. F. Codell and D. Sachko Macleod (eds.), *Orientalism Transposed: The Impact of the Colonies on British Culture* (Aldershot, 1998), pp. 46–62; T. C. McCaskie, 'Cultural Encounters: Britain and Africa in the Nineteenth Century', in *OHBE* iii, p. 675. For British admiration for other native African rulers, such as Cetewayo and Lobenguala, see C. Bolt, *Victorian Attitudes to Race* (London, 1971), pp. 144–7, 151–2.

20. Bayly, *Imperial Meridian*, p. 112; J. Benyon, 'Overlords of Empire? British "Proconsular Imperialism" in Comparative Perspective', *JICH*, xix (1991), p. 187; D. Cannadine, *Aspects of Aristocracy: Grandeur and Decline in Modern Britain* (London, 1994), pp. 29–32.

21. I. K. Steele, 'The Anointed, the Appointed and the Elected: Governance of the British Empire, 1689–1794', in *OHBE* ii, p. 105; T. Falola and A. D. Roberts, 'West Africa', in *OHBE* iv, p. 518.

22. R. S. Dunn, 'The Glorious Revolution and America', in *OHBE* i, p. 455; R. L. Bushman, *King and People in Provincial Massachusetts* (Chapel Hill, NC, 1985); I. K. Steele, 'The Empire and Provincial Elites: An Interpretation of Some Recent Writings on the English Atlantic, 1675–1740', in P. J. Marshall and G. Williams (eds.), *The British Atlantic Empire before the American Revolution* (London, 1980), p. 2.

23. L. J. Colley, 'The Apotheosis of George III: Loyalty, Royalty and the British Nation, 1760–1820', *P & P*, no. 102 (1984), pp. 94–129; *idem, Britons: Forging the Nation, 1707–1837* (London, 1992), pp. 194–236; Bayly, *Imperial*

Meridian, pp. 111–12. This subject will be further treated by C. Janigo, 'Cultural Politics: Ceremony, Celebration and the Crown in Canada, 1763–1867' (University of Alberta, Ph.D., forthcoming).

24. Hartz, *Founding of New Societies*, pp. 3–10; Temperley, 'Frontiersmen, Capital, and the American Loyalists', pp. 9, 11; Hutchins, *Illusion of Permanence*, pp. 1–78; Metcalf, *Ideologies of the Raj*, pp. 28–43. The two classic books that originally advanced this interpretation were E. T. Stokes, *The English Utilitarians and India* (London, 1959); A. T. Embree, *Charles Grant and British Rule in India* (New York, 1962).

25. R. E. Robinson and J. A. Gallagher with A. Denny, *Africa and the Victorians: The Official Mind of Imperialism* (London, 1961), pp. 1–5; A. J. Stockwell, 'British Expansion and Rule in South East Asia', in *OHBE* iii, p. 374. As such, Raffles and Palmerston embraced the alternative views of native chiefs as ugly and stupid primitives that had underlain very different images of Omai from that popularized by Reynolds. See Smith, *European Vision and the South Pacific*, pp. 82, 144–5; L. H. Guest, 'Curiously Marked: Tattooing, Masculinity, and Nationality in Eighteenth-Century British Perceptions of the South Pacific', in J. Barrell (ed.), *Painting and the Politics of Culture: New Essays on British Art, 1700–1850* (Oxford, 1992), pp. 102–6, 111–14.

26. P. J. Marshall, 'Empire and Authority in the Later Eighteenth Century', *JICH*, xv (1987), p. 112; D. Cannadine, 'The Context, Performance and Meaning of Ritual: The British Monarchy and the "Invention of Tradition", *c.* 1820–1977', in E. J. Hobsbawm and T. O. Ranger (eds.), *The Invention of Tradition* (Cambridge, 1983), pp. 109, 117–18. Schemes to establish cadet branches of the British monarchy in the colonies also came to nothing: Martin, *Bunyip Aristocracy*, pp. 30, 174, 177, 188–9.

27. C. A. Bayly, *Indian Society and the Making of the British Empire* (Cambridge, 1987), p. 158; D. A. Washbrook, 'India, 1818–1860: The Two Faces of Colonialism', in *OHBE* iii, pp. 412–51.

28. Bayly, *Imperial Meridian*, pp. 133–4; Marshall, 'Empire and Authority in the Later Eighteenth Century', p. 106.

29. G. Watson, *The English Ideology: Studies in the Language of Victorian Politics* (London, 1973), p. 174.

PART TWO: LOCALITIES

3. Dominions

1. G. S. R. Kitson Clark, *An Expanding Society: Britain, 1830–1900* (Cambridge, 1967), pp. 5–7; A. G. Hopkins, 'Back to the Future: From National History to Imperial History', *P & P*, no. 164 (1999), pp. 218–19, 235–6; D. McCaughey, N. Perkins and A. Trumble, *Victoria's Colonial Governors, 1839–1900* (Melbourne, 1993), p. 8.

2. A. N. Porter, 'Introduction', in *OHBE* iii, pp. 22–3.

3. O. P. Dickason, *Canada's First Nations: A History of Founding Peoples from the Earliest Times* (London, 1992); G. Martin, 'Canada from 1815', in *OHBE* iii, p. 533; D. Denoon with M. Wyndham, 'Australia and the Western Pacific', in *OHBE* iii, pp. 563–4; A. G. L. Shaw, 'British Policy towards the Australian Aborigines, 1830–1850', *AHS*, xxv (1992–3), pp. 265–85; T. Clarke and B. Galligan, ' "Aboriginal Native": and the Institutional Construction of the Australian Citizen', *AHS*, xxvi (1994–5), pp. 523–43; R. Dalziel, 'Southern Islands: New Zealand and Polynesia', in *OHBE* iii, pp. 578–82; J. Belich, *The New Zealand Land Wars and the Victorian Interpretation of Racial Conflict* (Oxford, 1986); C. Ornge, *The Treaty of Waitangi* (Wellington, 1987).

4. A. N. Porter, 'Trusteeship, Anti-Slavery and Humanitarianism', in *OHBE* iii, p. 213; C. Saunders and I. R. Smith, 'Southern Africa, 1795–1910', in *OHBE* iii, pp. 598–603, 621–2; S. Marks, 'Southern Africa', in *OHBE* iv, p. 552; A. Bank, 'Losing Faith in the Civilizing Mission: The Premature Decline of Humanitarian Liberalism at the Cape, 1840–1860', in M. J. Daunton and R. Halpern (eds.), *Empire and Others: British Encounters with Indigenous Peoples, 1600–1850* (London, 1999), pp. 364–83.

5. G. Martin, *Bunyip Aristocracy: The New South Wales Constitution Debate of 1853 and Hereditary Institutions in the British Colonies* (Beckenham, 1986), p. 196; W. D. Rubinstein, 'The End of "Old Corruption" in Britain, 1780–1860', *P & P* no. 101 (1983), pp. 55–86; P. Harling, *The Waning of 'Old Corruption': Politics and Economic Reform in Britain, 1779–1846* (Oxford, 1996).

6. J. B. Hirst, *Convict Society and Its Enemies: A History of Early New South Wales* (Sydney, 1983), pp. 150–68; G. C. Bolton, 'The Idea of a Colonial Gentry', *Historical Studies*, xiii (1968), p. 318; Martin, *Bunyip Aristocracy*, pp. 66–7.

7. P. de Serville, *Pounds and Pedigrees: The Upper Class in Victoria, 1850–*

1880 (Melbourne, 1991); D. van Dissel, 'The Adelaide Gentry, 1850–1920', in E. Richards (ed.), *The Flinders History of South Australia: Social History* (Adelaide, 1992), pp. 333–68; H. Reynolds, ' "Men of Substance and Deservedly Good Repute": The Tasmanian Gentry, 1856–1875', *Australian Journal of Politics and History*, xv, no. 3 (1969), pp. 65–7; Bolton, 'Colonial Gentry', p. 320; A. Trollope, *Australia and New Zealand* (2 vols., London, 1873), vol. i, pp. 466, 469.

8. S. Eldred-Grigg, *A Southern Gentry: New Zealanders Who Inherited the Earth* (Wellington, 1980); J. Graham, 'Settler Society', in G. W. Rice (ed.), *The Oxford History of New Zealand* (2nd edn., Auckland, 1992), pp. 125, 133–5.

9. Bolton, 'Colonial Gentry', pp. 317–19; J. Thurston, ' "The Dust of Toryism": Monarchism and Republicanism in Upper Canadian Travel and Immigration Texts', *Journal of Canadian Studies*, xxx (1996), pp. 76, 81; J. Burroughs, 'Loyalists and Lairds: The Politics and Society of Upper Canada Reconsidered', *JICH*, xix (1991), pp. 70–82.

10. P. Russell, *Attitudes to Social Structure and Mobility in Upper Canada, 1815–1840: 'Here We Are Laird Ourselves'* (Queenstown, 1990), pp. 2, 201; P. McCanin, 'Culture, State Formation and the Invention of Tradition: Newfoundland, 1832–1855', *Journal of Canadian Studies*, xxiii (1988), pp. 86–103.

11. Martin, *Bunyip Aristocracy*, p. 197; Graham, 'Settler Society', p. 134; J. K. Chapman, *The Career of Arthur Hamilton Gordon, First Lord Stanmore, 1829–1912* (Toronto, 1964), pp. 6–7.

12. Martin, *Bunyip Aristocracy*, pp. 53–4, 57, 124; Bolton, 'Colonial Gentry', pp. 317–19; J. B. Hirst, 'Egalitarianism', in S. L. Goldberg and F. B. Smith (eds.), *Australian Cultural History* (Cambridge, 1988), pp. 61–7.

13. J. M. Main, 'Men of Capital', in Richards, *Flinders History of South Australia*, p. 102; Martin, *Bunyip Aristocracy*, p. 95; Reynolds, ' "Men of Substance" ', p. 61; R. M. Crawford, *An Australian Perspective* (Melbourne, 1960), p. 5.

14. Martin, *Bunyip Aristocracy*, pp. 27–37, 75; R. Hubbard, *Rideau Hall* (London, 1977), p. 56; B. Knox, 'Democracy, Aristocracy and Empire: The Provision of Colonial Honours, 1818–1870', *AHS*, xxv (1992–3), pp. 248, 261.

15. Martin, *Bunyip Aristocracy*, pp. 31, 44; idem, 'Canada from 1815', in *OHBE* iii, p. 529; A. P. Thornton, *The Habit of Authority: Paternalism in British History* (London, 1966), p. 22.

16. M. Francis, *Governors and Settlers: Images of Authority in the British Colonies, 1820–1860* (London, 1992), pp. 9, 30–31, 33, 57–8, 62; McCaughey, Perkins and Trumble, *Victoria's Colonial Governors*, pp. 8–9,

91–3; de Serville, *Pounds and Pedigrees*, pp. 102–3; Sir B. Burke, *The Book of Precedence* (London, 1881), pp. 83–4; Lord Willoughby de Broke, *The Passing Years* (London, 1924), pp. 56–8.

17. J. B. Hirst, *Adelaide and the Country, 1870–1917: Their Social and Political Relationship* (Melbourne, 1973), pp. 37–50; *idem*, 'Egalitarianism', p. 69; M. Girouard, *The Return to Camelot: Chivalry and the English Gentleman* (London, 1981), p. 226; Bolton, 'Colonial Gentry', p. 321.

18. D. Cannadine, *The Decline and Fall of the British Aristocracy* (London, 1990), pp. 432–3; P. Duane, *Gentlemen Emigrants: From the British Public Schools to the Canadian Frontier* (Vancouver, 1981), pp. 82–90, 102–4, 168–9; Bolton, 'Colonial Gentry', p. 317.

19. A. Briggs, *Victorian Cities* (Harmondsworth, 1968), p. 300; Girouard, *Return to Camelot*, p. 226.

20. Kitson Clark, *An Expanding Society*, p. 1; P. J. Gibbons, 'The Climate of Opinion', in Rice, *Oxford History of New Zealand*, pp. 310–11; E. Olssen, 'Towards a New Society', in ibid., p. 261; de Serville, *Pounds and Pedigrees*, p. 137; E. Jones, 'English Canadian Culture in the Nineteenth Century: Love, History and Politics', *Journal of Canadian Studies*, xxv (1990), pp. 162–9.

21. R. A. J. McDonald, 'Vancouver's "Four Hundred": The Quest for Wealth and Status in Canada's Urban West, 1886–1914', *Journal of Canadian Studies*, xv (1990), pp. 55–73; Briggs, *Victorian Cities*, p. 305.

22. J. Burke, *A Genealogical and Heraldic Dictionary of the Peerage and Baronetage of the British Empire* (4th edn., 2 vols., London, 1832), vol. i, p. xiv; Sir B. Burke, *A Genealogical and Heraldic History of the Colonial Gentry* (2 vols., London, 1891–5), vol. ii, p. i.

23. Burke, *Colonial Gentry*, vol. i, pp. 4, 95, 97, 211; vol. ii, p. 406; Bolton, 'Colonial Gentry', pp. 323–4; de Serville, *Pounds and Pedigrees*, pp. 197–204.

24. See below, pp. 45–54, 101–20.

25. D. Cannadine, 'Imperial Canada: Old History, New Problems', in C. M. Coates (ed.), *Imperial Canada, 1867–1917* (Edinburgh, 1997), pp. 1–19; McCaughey, Perkins and Trumble, *Victoria's Colonial Governors*, pp. 206–9, 268–9.

26. C. Cunneen, *Kings' Men: Australia's Governors-General from Hopetoun to Isaacs* (Sydney, 1983), p. 34; A. Adonis, *Making Aristocracy Work: The Peerage and the Political System in Britain, 1884–1914* (Oxford, 1993), p. 223; Cannadine, *Decline and Fall*, p. 589; Hubbard, *Rideau Hall*, p. 35.

27. Cannadine, *Decline and Fall*, pp. 601, 723–5; McCaughey, Perkins and Trumble, *Victoria's Colonial Governors*, pp. 201–42, 283–316.

28. Adonis, *Making Aristocracy Work*, p. 225; A. L. Lowell, *The Government of England* (2 vols., New York, 1912), vol. ii, pp. 412–13, 420.

29. Cannadine, *Decline and Fall*, pp. 103–12; F. M. L. Thompson, *English Landed Society in the Nineteenth Century* (London, 1963), pp. 327–45.

30. Cannadine, *Decline and Fall*, pp. 438–42; E. J. Hobsbawm, *Industry and Empire* (Harmondsworth, 1969), p. 202; E. Waugh, *Remote People* (London, 1931), pp. 179, 183–5; E. Huxley, *White Man's Country: Lord Delamere and the Making of Kenya* (2 vols., London, 1935), vol. i, p. 6.

31. Hirst, 'Egalitarianism', p. 70.

32. Bolton, 'Colonial Gentry', pp. 324–7; Hopkins, 'Back to the Future', pp. 218–19; Gibbons, 'The Climate of Opinion', pp. 308–10, 335; McCaughey, Perkins and Trumble, *Victoria's Colonial Governors*, pp. 194–5; de Serville, *Pounds and Pedigrees*, p. 112.

4. India

1. F. G. Hutchins, *The Illusion of Permanence: British Imperialism in India* (Princeton, NJ, 1967), p. xi; T. R. Metcalf, *Ideologies of the Raj* (Cambridge, 1995), pp. 43–65.

2. Metcalf, *Ideologies of the Raj*, p. 50.

3. D. A. Washbrook, 'India, 1818–1860: The Two Faces of Colonialism', in *OHBE* iii, p. 415; *idem*, 'Economic Depression and the Making of "Traditional" Society in Colonial India, 1820–1855', *TRHS*, 6th ser., iii (1993), pp. 237–63; B. S. Cohn, 'Notes on the History of the Study of Indian Society and Culture', in M. Singer and B. S. Cohn (eds.), *Structure and Change in Indian Society* (Chicago, 1968), pp. 15–18; L. Carroll, 'Colonial Perceptions of Indian Society and the Emergence of Caste(s) Associations', *Journal of Asian Studies*, xxxvii (1978), pp. 233–50; N. Dirks, 'Castes of Mind', *Representations*, no. 37 (1992), pp. 66–72; S. Bayly, *Caste, Society and Politics in India from the Eighteenth Century to the Modern Age* (Cambridge, 1999), pp. 64–97, 124.

4. Metcalf, *Ideologies of the Raj*, pp. 117–22; B. S. Cohn, 'The Census, Social Structure and Objectification in South Asia', in *idem, An Anthropologist among Historians and Other Essays* (New Delhi, 1990), pp. 224–54; *idem, Colonialism and Its Forms of Knowledge: The British in India* (Princeton, NJ, 1996), pp. 48, 53; C. Pinney, 'Colonial Anthropology in the "Laboratory of Mankind"', in C. A. Bayly (ed.), *The Raj: India and the British, 1600–1947* (London, 1990), pp. 252–63; S. Bayly, 'The Evolution of Colonial Cultures: Nineteenth-Century Asia', in *OHBE* iii, p. 448.

5. J. W. Cell, *Hailey: A Study in British Imperialism, 1872–1969* (Cambridge, 1992), p. 18; *idem*, 'Colonial Rule', in *OHBE* iv, pp. 244–7; T. R. Metcalf,

An Imperial Vision: Victorian Architecture and Britain's Raj (London, 1989), p. 151; *idem, Ideologies of the Raj*, pp. 70–73; Hutchins, *Illusion of Permanence*, p. 156; R. Inden, *Imagining India* (Oxford, 1990), pp. 137–40. See also C. Dewey, 'Images of the Village Community: A Study in Anglo-Indian Ideology', *MAS*, vi (1972), pp. 291–328.

6. L. D. Wurgraft, *The Imperial Imagination: Magic and Myth in Kipling's India* (Middletown, CT, 1983); I. Copland, *The Princes of India in the Endgame of Empire, 1917–1947* (Cambridge, 1997), p. 22; P. Mason, *A Shaft of Sunlight: Memories of a Varied Life* (London, 1978), p. 97; J. W. Burrow, 'The Village Community and the Uses of History in Late Nineteenth Century England', in N. McKendrick (ed.), *Historical Perspectives: Studies in English Thought and Society in Honour of J. H. Plumb* (London, 1974), pp. 255–84.

7. Sir B. Burke, *The Book of Precedence* (London, 1881), pp. 85–8; E. W. Said, *Orientalism: Western Conceptions of the Orient* (Harmondsworth, 1995 edn.), p. 45; P. Woodruff, *The Men Who Ruled India*, vol. ii, *The Guardians* (London, 1963), pp. 193–4; S. Khilnani, *The Idea of India* (London, 1997), pp. 122, 134; Hutchins, *Illusion of Permanence*, p. 117; P. Scott, *Staying On* (London, 1994 edn.), p. 169; Mason, *Shaft of Sunlight*, pp. 77, 80, 97; Cell, *Hailey*, pp. 30–31.

8. R. J. Moore, 'Imperial India, 1858–1914', in *OHBE* iii, p. 431; P. Burroughs, 'Imperial Institutions and the Government of Empire', in *OHBE* iii, pp. 181–2.

9. Mason, *Shaft of Sunlight*, p. 94 (my italics); J. Brown, 'India', in *OHBE* iv, p. 425; Cell, *Hailey*, pp. 156, 161, 202; Metcalf, *Ideologies of the Raj*, pp. 191–2.

10. R. Hyam, *Britain's Imperial Century, 1815–1914* (London, 1976), pp. 227–8.

11. I. Copland, *The British Raj and the Indian Princes: Paramountcy in Western India, 1857–1930* (New Delhi, 1982), p. 93; *idem, Princes of India*, pp. 17, 24; R. J. Moore, 'Imperial India, 1858–1914', in *OHBE* iii, pp. 422–7.

12. D. A. Washbrook, 'Caste, Class and Dominance in Modern Tamil Nadu: Non-Brahmanism, Dravidianism and Tamil Nationalism', in F. R. Frankel and M. S. A. Rao (eds.), *Dominance and State Power in Modern India: Decline of a Social Order* (Delhi, 1989), p. 248.

13. I. Butler (ed.), *The Viceroy's Wife: Letters of Alice, Countess of Reading, from India, 1921–1925* (London, 1969), p. 43.

14. J. W. Cell, 'Colonial Rule', in *OHBE* iv, p. 237; Metcalf, *Ideologies of the Raj*, pp. 195–6; *idem, Imperial Vision*, p. 105. The eighty-three states deserving between 11 and 21 guns are listed in R. Jeffrey (ed.), *People, Princes and Paramount Power: Society and Politics in the Indian Princely States* (Delhi, 1978), pp. 389–90.

15. J. Morris, *Pax Britannica: The Climax of an Empire* (London, 1968), p. 272. Two editions of Lethbridge's work were produced, in 1893 and 1900. A promised third edition never appeared.

16. Washbrook, ' "Traditional" Society in Colonial India', p. 240.

17. Butler, *Viceroy's Wife*, p. 27.

18. Copland, *British Raj and the Indian Princes*, pp. 154–5; L. A. Knight, 'The Royal Titles Act and India', *HJ*, xi (1986), p. 488; M. Lutyens, *The Lyttons of India: Lord Lytton's Viceroyalty* (London, 1979), pp. 74–89; B. S. Cohn, 'Representing Authority in Victorian India', in E. J. Hobsbawm and T. O. Ranger (eds.), *The Invention of Tradition* (Cambridge, 1983), pp. 165–210; J. C. Masselos, 'Lytton's "Great Tamasha" and Indian Unity', *Journal of Indian History*, xliv (1966), pp. 737–60; J. P. Waghorne, *The Raja's Magic Clothes: Re-Visioning Kingship and Divinity in England's India* (Philadelphia, PA, 1994), pp. 7–10.

19. Cohn, 'Representing Authority in Victorian India', p. 188; Waghorne, *Raja's Magic Clothes*, pp. 23–6, 33–6; D. Haynes, 'Imperial Ritual in a Local Setting: The Ceremonial Order in Seurat, 1890–1939', *MAS*, xxiv (1990), pp. 495–511. For one contemporary evocation of princely magnificence, see T. Morison, *Imperial Rule in India* (London, 1899), pp. 48–9.

20. Metcalf, *Imperial Vision*, pp. 105–40; P. Davies, *Splendours of the Raj* (London, 1995), pp. 202–3.

21. Lord Ronaldshay, *The Life of Lord Curzon* (3 vols., London, 1928), vol. ii, pp. 86–95; D. Gilmour, *Curzon* (London, 1994), p. 186; S. Bayly, 'The Evolution of Colonial Cultures: Nineteenth-Century Asia', in *OHBE* iii, p. 468; R. J. Moore, 'Imperial India, 1858–1914', in *OHBE* iii, p. 437; Metcalf, *Imperial Vision*, pp. 23, 199–202; Copland, *British Raj and the Indian Princes*, p. 190; C. S. Sundram, ' "Martial" Indian Aristocrats and the Military System of the Raj: The Imperial Cadet Corps, 1900–1914', *JICH*, xxv (1997), pp. 417–18.

22. Metcalf, *Imperial Vision*, pp. 55–104; J. Morris, *Stones of Empire: The Building of the Raj* (Oxford, 1983), pp. 105, 111–12, 133–5; Davies, *Splendours of the Raj*, pp. 14, 183–214.

23. Davies, *Splendours of the Raj*, pp. 117–18, 163; Morris, *Stones of Empire*, pp. 105–6; T. P. Issar, *Mysore: The Royal City* (Bangalore, 1991), pp. 18–33.

24. Metcalf, *Imperial Vision*, pp. 129–40.

25. A. Trevithick, 'Some Structural and Sequential Aspects of the British Imperial Assemblages at Delhi: 1877–1911', *MAS*, xxiv (1990), p. 570.

26. R. E. Frykenberg, 'The Coronation Durbar of 1911: Some Implications', in idem (ed.), *Delhi through the Ages: Essays in Urban History, Culture and Society* (Delhi, 1986), pp. 369–90; K. Rose, *King George V* (London, 1983),

pp. 131-6; H. Nicolson, *King George V: His Life and Reign* (London, 1967), pp. 228-38.

27. B. N. Ramusack, *The Princes of India in the Twilight of Empire* (Columbus, OH, 1978), pp. 38-40; Rose, *King George V*, p. 349; Copland, *Princes of India*, pp. 33, 41-2; D. A. Low, 'Laissez-Faire and Traditional Rulership in Princely India', in Jeffrey, *People, Princes and Paramount Power*, p. 377; Woodruff, *The Guardians*, pp. 288-9; Cell, *Hailey*, pp. 210, 213.

28. D. A. Low, *Eclipse of Empire* (Cambridge, 1991), p. 87; J. Rudoe, *Cartier, 1900-1939* (London, 1997), pp. 31-6, 156-87; Ramusack, *Princes of India* pp. 43, 91-4. But compare the alternative argument advanced in N. Dirks, *The Hollow Crown: Ethnohistory of an Indian Kingdom* (Cambridge, 1987).

29. *Whitaker's Almanack* (London, 1926), p. 601; J. Manor, 'Princely Mysore before the Storm: The State-Level Political System of India's Model State, 1920-1936', *MAS*, ix (1975), pp. 31-58; Issar, *Mysore*, pp. 44-7, 69-71, 101, 104-6, 136-7; Davies, *Splendours of the Raj*, p. 206.

30. These are reproduced in D. V. Devaraj, *The Magnificent Mysore Dasara* (Mysore, 1994). See also S. Sivapriyanand, *Mysore: Royal Dasara* (New Delhi, 1995).

31. Woodruff, *The Guardians*, pp. 281, 284-5; Khilnani, *Idea of India*, pp. 122, 134.

32. R. G. Irving, *Indian Summer: Lutyens, Baker and Imperial Delhi* (London, 1981), pp. 26-32. The meaning and success of New Delhi as an imperial capital is still debated. Those who think it was unconfident and unsuccessful, thereby prefiguring the end of the Raj, include Metcalf, *Imperial Vision*, pp. 211-51; Morris, *Stones of Empire*, pp. 32, 76-81, 216-22. Those who see it as a masterly synthesis of east and west and a majestic expression of the British will to rule permanently include Davies, *Splendours of the Raj*, pp. 15-16, 215-41; J. Ridley, 'Edwin Lutyens, New Delhi, and the Architecture of Imperialism', *JICH*, xxvi (1998), pp. 67-83.

33. Cohn, *Colonialism and Its Forms of Knowledge*, p. 121; Butler, *Viceroy's Wife*, p. 27.

34. Morris, *Stones of Empire*, p. 17; J. Charmley, *Lord Lloyd and the Decline of the British Empire* (London, 1987), p. 127.

35. V. C. P. Chaudhry, *Imperial Honeymoon with Indian Aristocracy*, K. P. Jayaswal Research Institute, Historical Research Series, no. xviii (Patna, 1980), p. 154; Copland, *Princes of India*, p. 21; Hutchins, *Illusion of Permanence*, p. 199.

36. Metcalf, *Ideologies of the Raj*, p. 56; *idem*, *Imperial Vision*, p. 242.

5. Colonies

1. D. van Dissel, 'The Adelaide Gentry, 1850–1920', in E. Richards (ed.), *The Flinders History of South Australia: Social History* (Adelaide, 1992), pp. 335, 363.

2. J. M. Gullick, *Rulers and Residents: Influence and Power in the Malay States, 1870–1920* (Singapore, 1992); A. J. Stockwell, 'Expansion and Rule in South East Asia', in *OHBE* iii, pp. 383–4; S. C. Smith, 'The Rise, Decline and Survival of the Malay Rulers during the Colonial Period, 1874–1957', *JICH*, xxii (1994), pp. 84–92; idem, *British Relations with the Malay Rulers from Decentralization to Malayan Independence, 1930–1957* (Kuala Lumpur, 1995), pp. 1–41; J. De Vere Allen, 'Malayan Civil Service, 1874–1941: Colonial Bureaucracy/Malayan Elite', *CSSH*, xii (1970), p. 153; A. V. M. Horton, 'British Administration in Brunei, 1906–1959', *MAS*, xx (1986), pp. 353–74.

3. J. K. Chapman, *The Career of Arthur Hamilton Gordon, First Lord Stanmore, 1829–1912* (Toronto, 1964), pp. 163, 181–202, 226; D. Denoon with M. Wyndham, 'Australia and the Western Pacific', in *OHBE* iii, pp. 556–7, 571.

4. J. G. Carrier, 'Introduction', in J. G. Carrier (ed.), *Occidentalism: Images of the West* (Oxford, 1995), p. 22; Chapman, *Arthur Hamilton Gordon*, p. 337; S. Bayly, 'The Evolution of Colonial Cultures: Nineteenth-Century Asia', in *OHBE* iii, p. 468.

5. R. E. Robinson, 'European Imperialism and Indigenous Reactions in British West Africa, 1880–1914', in H. L. Wesseling (ed.), *Expansion and Reaction* (Leiden, 1978), pp. 151–2; J. E. Flint, 'Nigeria: The Colonial Experience from 1880 to 1914', in L. H. Gann and P. Duignan (eds.), *Colonialism in Africa, 1870–1960*, vol. i, *The History and Politics of Colonialism, 1870–1914* (Cambridge, 1969), p. 246; P. Gifford, 'Indirect Rule: Touchstone or Tombstone for Colonial Policy?', in P. Gifford and W. R. Louis (eds.), *Britain and Germany in Africa: Imperial Rivalry and Colonial Rule* (New Haven, CT, 1967), p. 355.

6. Gifford, 'Indirect Rule', pp. 375–6; R. L. Tignor, *The Colonial Transformation of Kenya* (Princeton, NJ, 1976), pp. 42–3; A. N. Porter, 'Introduction', in *OHBE* iii, p. 18; D. A. Low and R. C. Pratt, *Buganda and British Overrule, 1900–1955* (Oxford, 1960), pp. 136–59, 163–78; C. Saunders and I. R. Smith, 'Southern Africa, 1795–1910', in *OHBE* iii, pp. 608–9; R. Hyam, *The Failure of South African Expansion, 1908–1948* (London, 1972), pp. 98–100.

7. M. Lynn, 'British Policy, Trade and Informal Empire in the Mid-Nineteenth Century', in *OHBE* iii, pp. 107–8, 118–19.

8. Smith, 'Rise, Decline and Survival of the Malay Rulers', p. 85; Robinson, 'European Imperialism and Indigenous Reactions', pp. 141–63.

9. Gifford, 'Indirect Rule', p. 355; J. De Vere Allen, 'Two Imperialists: A Study of Sir Frank Swettenham and Sir Hugh Clifford', *JMRAS*, xxxvii (1964), p. 49; P. Burroughs, 'Imperial Institutions and the Government of Empire', in *OHBE* iii, p. 196.

10. M. Bull, 'Indirect Rule in Northern Nigeria, 1906–1911', in K. Robinson and F. Madden (eds.), *Essays in Imperial Government Presented to Margery Perham* (Oxford, 1963), p. 50; M. Perham, *Native Administration in Nigeria* (London, 1937); idem, *Lugard: The Years of Authority, 1898–1945* (London, 1960), pp. 128–9, 138, 140, 144; J. W. Cell, 'Colonial Rule', in *OHBE* iv, p. 240 (my italics).

11. T. Falola and A. D. Roberts, 'West Africa', in *OHBE* iv, p. 518; Gifford, 'Indirect Rule', pp. 362, 383; F. Robinson, 'The British Empire and the Muslim World', in *OHBE* iv, p. 407; D. M. Wai, 'Pax Britannica and the Southern Sudan: The View from the Theatre', *African Affairs*, lxxix (1980), pp. 378–82; M. W. Daly, *Empire on the Nile: The Anglo-Egyptian Sudan, 1898–1934* (Cambridge, 1986), pp. 360–79; idem, *Imperial Sudan: The Anglo-Egyptian Condominium, 1934–1956* (Cambridge, 1991), pp. 25–45.

12. H. A. Gailey, *Sir Donald Cameron: Colonial Governor* (Stanford, CA, 1974), pp. 67–86; R. A. Austen, 'The Official Mind of Indirect Rule: British Policy in Tanganyika, 1916–1939', in Gifford and Louis, *Britain and Germany in Africa*, pp. 580–92; J. Iliffe, *A Modern History of Tanganyika* (Cambridge, 1979), pp. 318–41.

13. T. Falola and A. D. Roberts, 'West Africa', in *OHBE* iv, p. 518; Gifford, 'Indirect Rule', pp. 383–8; H. Kuklick, *The Imperial Bureaucrat: The Colonial Administrative Service in the Gold Coast, 1920–1939* (Stanford, CA, 1979), pp. 53–4.

14. T. O. Ranger, 'The Invention of Tradition in Colonial Africa', in E. J. Hobsbawm and T. O. Ranger (eds.), *The Invention of Tradition* (Cambridge, 1983), pp. 211–12, 221.

15. Gullick, *Rulers and Residents*, pp. 231–40; H. S. Barlow, *Swettenham* (Kuala Lumpur, 1997), pp. 467–81. Ranger, 'Invention of Tradition in Colonial Africa', pp. 221–3.

16. Perham, *Lugard*, pp. 128–30, 214–15, 218, 398–401; L. H. Gann and P. Duignan, *The Rulers of British Tropical Africa, 1870–1914* (London, 1978), pp. 154–64; A. H. M. Kirk-Greene, 'On Governorship and Governors in British Africa', in L. H. Gann and P. Duignan (eds.), *African Proconsuls* (New York, 1978), pp. 214–29.

17. W. R. Louis, 'The Coming of Independence in the Sudan', *JICH*, xix (1991), pp. 139, 149; Ranger, 'Invention of Tradition in Colonial Africa',

pp. 233–4; D. Bates, *A Gust of Plumes: A Biography of Lord Twining of Godalming and Tanganyika* (London, 1972).

18. Q. Letts, 'End of White Tie and Glory Days', *The Times*, 30 May 2000; A. H. M. Kirk-Greene, *On Crown Service: A History of HM Colonial and Overseas Civil Services, 1837–1997* (London, 1999), p. 67.

19. T. O. Ranger, 'Making Northern Rhodesia Imperial: Variations on a Royal Theme, 1924–1938', *African Affairs*, lxxix (1980), pp. 350, 367; B. Bush, *Imperialism, Race and Resistance: Africa and Britain, 1919–1945* (London, 1999), pp. 93–8; Iliffe, *Tanganyika*, p. 325.

20. D. A. Low, 'Lion Rampant', *Journal of Commonwealth Political Studies*, ii (1963–4), pp. 235–52; Bull, 'Indirect Rule in Northern Nigeria', p. 63; Iliffe, *Tanganyika*, p. 326.

21. M. Girouard, *The Return to Camelot: Chivalry and the English Gentleman* (London, 1981), p. 225; A. J. Stockwell, 'Sir Hugh Clifford's Early Career (1866–1903)', *JMRAS*, xlix (1976), p. 90; Low and Pratt, *Buganda*, pp. 167–8; Gifford, 'Indirect Rule', pp. 358, 361.

22. De Vere Allen, 'Two Imperialists', p. 44.

23. D. A. Low, 'Laissez-Faire and Traditional Rulership in Princely India', in R. Jeffrey (ed.), *People, Princes and Paramount Power: Society and Politics in the Indian Princely States* (New Delhi, 1978), p. 377; Flint, 'Nigeria: The Colonial Experience', p. 253.

24. Daly, *Empire on the Nile*, p. 452; M. Perham, 'A Re-Statement of Indirect Rule', *Africa*, vii (1934), pp. 326, 332; C. Gertzel, 'Margery Perham's Image of Africa', *JICS*, xix (1991), p. 33.

25. J. Darwin, *Britain and Decolonization: The Retreat from Empire in the Post-War World* (London, 1988), p. 105; W. R. Louis, 'The Dissolution of the British Empire', in *OHBE* iv, p. 338.

26. R. Heussler, *Yesterday's Rulers: The Making of the British Colonial Service* (Syracuse, NY, 1963), pp. 68–70, 82–3.

27. S. Howe, *Anti-Colonialism in British Politics: The Left and the End of Empire, 1918–1964* (Oxford, 1993), pp. 34–5.

28. *Who Was Who, 1961–70* (London, 1979), p. 61.

29. S. C. Smith, *British Relations with the Malay Rulers from Decentralization to Malayan Independence, 1930–1957* (Kuala Lumpur, 1995), pp. 18–19.

30. J. Darwin, *Britain and Decolonization: The Retreat from Empire in the Post-War World* (London, 1988), p. 30.

31. Darwin, *Britain and Decolonization*, pp. 283–5; A. J. Stockwell, 'Imperialism and Nationalism in South East Asia', *OHBE* iv, pp. 487–8; *idem*, 'Malaysia: The Making of a Neo-Colony?', *JICH*, xxvi (1998), pp. 138–56.

6. Mandates

1. J. Morris, *Farewell the Trumpets: An Imperial Retreat* (Harmondsworth, 1979), p. 250; D. Cannadine, *The Decline and Fall of the British Aristocracy* (London, 1990), pp. 381–3; M. Girouard, *The Return to Camelot: Chivalry and the English Gentleman* (London, 1981), pp. 271–2; S. J. Nasir, *The Arabs and the English* (London, 1979), pp. 53–115; J. MacKenzie, *Orientalism: History, Theory and the Arts* (Manchester, 1995), pp. 43–70. For an earlier example of similar attitudes by post-1789 French aristocrats towards North American Indians, see H. Liebersohn, *Aristocratic Encounters: European Travellers and North American Indians* (Cambridge, 1998).

2. Nasir, *Arabs and the English*, pp. 76–83; Cannadine, *Decline and Fall*, pp. 537–8; E. Longford, *A Pilgrimage of Passion: The Life of Wilfrid Scawen Blunt* (London, 1979), pp. 97–8, 103, 114–16, 123–51, 167–76, 230–34, 242, 274, 311, 342–5, 384–5, 406–9.

3. S. Leslie, *Mark Sykes: His Life and Letters* (London, 1923), pp. 71, 204–7; R. Adelson, *Mark Sykes: Portrait of an Amateur* (London, 1975), pp. 34–7, 42–4, 61–2, 77, 100–101, 126, 144, 259–60; M. Fitzherbert, *The Man Who was Greenmantle: A Biography of Aubrey Herbert* (London, 1985), pp. 1–2, 35–45, 54–67, 73, 121–2, 188.

4. J. Darwin, *Britain, Egypt and the Middle East: Imperial Policy in the Aftermath of War, 1918–1922* (London, 1981), pp. 53–5, 58; A. L. al-Sayyid-Marsot, 'The British Occupation of Egypt from 1882', in *OHBE* iii, pp. 655, 664.

5. J. B. Kelly, *Britain and the Persian Gulf, 1795–1880* (Oxford, 1991 edn.), pp. 831–7; F. Robinson, 'The British Empire and the Muslim World', in *OHBE* iv, p. 402; E. Kedourie, *England and the Middle East: The Destruction of the Ottoman Empire, 1914–1921* (London, 1987 edn.), pp. 49–52; [Lord Winterton], 'Arabian Nights and Days', *Blackwood's Magazine*, ccvii (1920), pp. 585–608, 750–68.

6. B. Westrate, *The Arab Bureau: British Policy in the Middle East, 1916–20* (University Park, PA, 1992), pp. 157–8; Kedourie, *England and the Middle East*, pp. 71, 86.

7. Morris, *Farewell the Trumpets*, p. 255; J. Wilson, *Lawrence of Arabia: The Authorized Biography of T. E. Lawrence* (London, 1990), pp. 621–2, 941–4; T. E. Lawrence, *Seven Pillars of Wisdom: A Triumph* (New York, 1991 edn.), p. 213.

8. Darwin, *Britain, Egypt and the Middle East*, p. 135; D. Cannadine, *Aspects of Aristocracy: Grandeur and Decline in Modern Britain* (London, 1994), pp. 156–9; idem, *Class in Britain* (London, 1998), pp. 127, 156; P. Ziegler,

'Churchill and the Monarchy', in R. Blake and W. R. Louis (eds.), *Churchill* (Oxford, 1994), pp. 187–8, 196.

9. Wilson, *Lawrence of Arabia*, pp. 643–55; U. Dann, 'Lawrence "of Arabia" – One More Appraisal', *Middle Eastern Studies*, xv (1979), pp. 154–62; R. Hyam, 'Churchill and the British Empire', in Blake and Louis, *Churchill*, pp. 174–5. The conference is well treated in A. S. Klieman, *Foundations of British Policy in the Arab World: The Cairo Conference of 1921* (London, 1970).

10. M. C. Wilson, *King Abdullah, Britain and the Making of Jordan* (Cambridge, 1987); Kedourie, *England and the Middle East*, pp. 175–213; Darwin, *Britain, Egypt and the Middle East*, pp. 215–23, 232–41; [G. Bell], 'Great Britain and the "Iraq": An Experiment in Anglo-Asiatic Relations', *The Round Table*, xiv (1923–4), pp. 64–83.

11. D. Silverfarb, *Britain's Informal Empire in the Middle East: A Case Study of Iraq, 1929–41* (Oxford, 1986); G. Balfour-Paul, 'Britain's Informal Empire in the Middle East', in *OHBE* iv, pp. 500–501.

12. E. Monroe, *Britain's Moment in the Middle East, 1914–1971* (London, 1981), pp. 74–5; B. Lapping, *End of Empire* (London, 1985), p. 240.

13. Wilson, *Lawrence*, pp. 655–63; G. Troeller, 'Ibn Sa'ud and Sharif Husain: A Comparison in Importance in the Early Years of the First World War', *HJ*, xiv (1971), pp. 627–33; S. Mousa, 'A Matter of Principle: King Hussein of the Hijaz and the Arabs of Palestine', *International Journal of Middle Eastern Studies*, ix (1978), pp. 183–94.

14. C. Leatherdale, *Britain and Saudi Arabia, 1925–1939: The Imperial Oasis* (London, 1983), esp. pp. 57–77; R. M. Burrell, 'Britain, Iran and the Persian Gulf: Some Aspects of the Situation in the 1920s and 1930s', in D. Hopwood (ed.), *The Arabian Peninsular: Society and Politics* (London, 1972), pp. 160–88; S. C. Smith, *British Relations with the Malay Rulers, from Decentralization to Malayan Independence, 1930–1957* (Kuala Lumpur, 1995), p. 13.

15. Lady Bell (ed.), *The Letters of Gertrude Bell* (2 vols., London, 1927), vol. ii, pp. 462–3, 561, 594, 609–10, 614–15, 619–21, 634, 676; H. Batatu, *The Old Social Classes and Revolutionary Movements of Iraq* (Princeton, NJ, 1978), pp. 31–2, 99–110; J. Charmley, *Lord Lloyd and the Decline of the British Empire* (London, 1987), p. 127; M. Elliot, 'Independent Iraq': The Monarchy and British Influence, 1941–1958 (London, 1996), p. 10; R. Wilson, 'Economic Aspects of Arab Nationalism', in M. J. Cohen and M. Kolinsky (eds.), *Demise of the British Empire in the Middle East: Britain's Response to Nationalist Movements, 1943–1955* (London, 1998), pp. 68–9.

16. Nasir, *The Arabs and the English*, pp. 125, 146–7, 161–3; W. Thesiger, *The Life of My Choice* (London, 1988), pp. 56, 95.

17. Monroe, *Britain's Moment in the Middle East*, p. 61.

18. W. R. Louis, *The British Empire in the Middle East, 1945–1951: Arab Nationalism, the United States, and Post-War Imperialism* (Oxford, 1984), p. 347; Monroe, *Britain's Moment in the Middle East*, p. 77; Morris, *Farewell the Trumpets*, pp. 259–72.

19. Louis, *British Empire in the Middle East*, pp. 124, 174, 179; Smith, *British Relations with the Malay Rulers*, pp. 12, 18.

20. W. R. Louis and R. E. Robinson, 'The Imperialism of Decolonization', *JICH*, xxii (1994), pp. 473–4.

21. J. Darwin, 'British Decolonization since 1945: A Pattern or a Puzzle?', *JICH*, xii (1984), pp. 193–4; Louis, *British Empire in the Middle East*, pp. 17–19; N. Owen, 'Britain and Decolonization: The Labour Governments and the Middle East, 1945–1951', in Cohen and Kolinsky, *Demise of the British Empire in the Middle East*, p. 3.

22. Louis, *British Empire in the Middle East*, pp. 228, 232, 347, 352–4, 358, 693.

23. Louis, *British Empire in the Middle East*, pp. 309–11, 315–16, 320.

24. W. R. Louis, 'The British and the Origins of the Iraqi Revolution', in R. A. Fernea and W. R. Louis (eds.), *The Iraqi Revolution of 1958: The Old Social Classes Revisited* (London, 1991), p. 41; R. J. Blyth, 'Britain Versus India in the Persian Gulf: The Struggle for Political Control, c. 1928–1948', *JICH*, xxviii (2000), pp. 90–111.

25. G. Balfour-Paul, *The End of Empire in the Middle East* (Cambridge, 1991), p. 75; W. D. McIntyre, *British Decolonization* (London, 1998), p. 64.

26. Morris, *Farewell the Trumpets*, pp. 532–5.

PART THREE: GENERALITIES

7. Honours

1. R. Jeffrey, 'The Politics of "Indirect Rule": Types of Relationship among Rulers, Ministers and Residents in a "Native State" ', *Journal of Commonwealth and Comparative Politics*, xiii (1975), pp. 261–81; D. A. Low, 'Lion Rampant', *Journal of Commonwealth Political Studies*, ii (1963–4), pp. 235–52; J. Benyon, 'Overlords of Empire? British "Proconsular Imperialism" in Comparative Perspective', *JICH*, xix (1991), pp. 164–202; A. J. Stockwell, 'Power, Authority and Freedom', in P. J. Marshall (ed.), *The Cambridge Illustrated History of the British Empire* (Cambridge, 1996), pp. 161–3.

2. *Debrett's Peerage* (London, 1924 edn.), p. 840.

3. Sir I. de la Bere, *The Queen's Orders of Chivalry* (London, 1964), pp. 116–20.

4. B. Knox, 'Democracy, Aristocracy and Empire: The Provision of Colonial Honours, 1818–1870', *AHS*, xxv (1992–3), pp. 244–64; Stockwell, 'Power, Authority and Freedom', p. 171.

5. A. H. M. Kirk-Greene, 'On Governorship and Governors in British Africa', in L. H. Gann and P. Duignan (eds.), *African Proconsuls* (New York, 1978), pp. 254–5; L. H. Gann and P. Duignan, *The Rulers of British Africa, 1870–1914* (London, 1978), pp. 163–4.

6. J. K. Chapman, *The Career of Arthur Hamilton Gordon, First Lord Stanmore, 1829–1912* (Toronto, 1964), pp. 108, 178; H. S. Barlow, *Swettenham* (Kuala Lumpur, 1995), pp. 328, 344, 391, 486, 613, 646, 667.

7. P. de Serville, *Pounds and Pedigrees: The Upper Class in Victoria, 1850–1880* (Melbourne, 1991), pp. 212–13; J. M. Gullick, *Rulers and Residents: Influence and Power in the Malay States, 1870–1920* (Singapore, 1992), pp. 236–7.

8. G. Martin, *Bunyip Aristocracy: The New South Wales Constitution Debate of 1853 and Hereditary Institutions in the British Colonies* (Beckenham, 1986), p. 186; A. B. Keith, *Responsible Government in the Dominions* (2nd edn., 2 vols., Oxford, 1928), vol. ii, p. 1,023.

9. F. Metcalf, *Ideologies of the Raj* (Cambridge, 1995), p. 77; B. S. Cohn, *Colonialism and Its Forms of Knowledge: The British in India* (Princeton, NJ, 1996), pp. 119–21.

10. C. L. Tupper, *Our Indian Protectorate: An Introduction to the Study of the Relations between the British Government and Its Indian Feudatories* (London, 1893), p. 360. Quoted in E. S. Haynes, 'Rajput Ceremonial Interactions as a Mirror of a Dying Indian State System, 1820–1947', *MAS*, xxiv (1990), pp. 487–8.

11. For honours given to officers of the Indian Army, see A. J. Guy and P. B. Boyden (eds.), *Soldiers of the Raj: The Indian Army, 1600–1947* (London, 1997), pp. 250–54, 283–8.

12. De la Bere, *Queen's Orders of Chivalry*, pp. 177–81; J. MacLeod, 'The English Honours System in Princely India, 1925–1947', *Journal of the Royal Asiatic Society*, 3rd ser., iv (1994), pp. 237–50.

13. Martin, *Bunyip Aristocracy*, pp. 165–6; British Library India Office Library MS, Home/Misc. 104, f. 409; Tupper, *Our Indian Protectorate*, p. 360.

14. R. Kipling, 'A Legend of the Foreign Office', in *Rudyard Kipling's Verse: Definitive Edition* (Garden City, NY, 1940), p. 8. Quoted in P. Davies, *Splendours of the Raj: British Architecture in India, 1660 to 1947* (London, 1985), p. 200.

15. De la Bere, *Queen's Orders of Chivalry*, pp. 83, 154, 180–81.

16. T. Falola and A. D. Roberts, 'West Africa', in *OHBE* iv, p. 518.

17. Gullick, *Rulers and Residents*, pp. 237, 259 n. 41.

18. A. W. Thorpe (ed.), *Handbook to the Most Excellent Order of the British Empire* (London, 1921).

19. T. P. Issar, *Mysore: The Royal City* (Bangalore, 1991), p. 136.

20. J. Charmley, *Lord Lloyd and the Decline of the British Empire* (London, 1987), p. 118.

21. D. Cannadine, *The Decline and Fall of the British Aristocracy* (London, 1990), pp. 591, 599–600. Other examples include Field Marshal the Earl Roberts of Kandahar and Waterford, VC, KG, KP, OM, GCB, GCSI, GCIE; Lord Hardinge of Penshurts, KG, GCB, GCSI, GCMG, GCIE, GCVO; the Earl of Halifax, KG, OM, GCSI, GCMG, GCIE; and the Marquess of Linlithgow, KG, KT, GCSI, GCIE.

22. H. Nicolson, *Helen's Tower* (London, 1937), pp. 77, 137, 207–8, 258; P. Magnus, *Kitchener: Portrait of an Imperialist* (New York, 1968), pp. 136, 191–2, 236, 240, 260, 275, 341, 378.

23. *Dictionary of National Biography, 1941–1950* (Oxford, 1959), p. 280.

24. Martin, *Bunyip Aristocracy*, p. 164; de Serville, *Pounds and Pedigrees*, p. 215.

25. D. Cannadine, *Aspects of Aristocracy: Grandeur and Decline in Modern Britain* (London, 1994), pp. 109–29.

26. J. Morris, *Pax Britannica: The Climax of an Empire* (London, 1968), p. 508.

27. D. Denoon with M. Wyndham, 'Australia and the Western Pacific', in *OHBE* iii, p. 570; K. Rose, *King George V* (London, 1983), p. 256.

28. P. Burroughs, 'Imperial Institutions and the Government of Empire', in *OHBE* iii, p. 183; E. Shuckburgh, *Descent to Suez: Diaries, 1951–1956* (London, 1986), p. 215.

29. *The Times*, 1 January 1920.

30. W. Lee-Warner, *The Protected Princes of India* (London, 1894), p. 305.

31. Morris, *Pax Britannica*, p. 508; P. Magnus, *King Edward the Seventh* (Harmondsworth, 1967), pp. 373–8; Rose, *King George V*, pp. 184–6, 245–64; S. Bradford, *The Reluctant King: The Life and Reign of George VI, 1895–1952* (New York, 1989), pp. 403–6.

32. De la Bere, *Queen's Orders of Chivalry*, pp. 83–4, 129–30, 143, 147, 158–61.

8. Monarchs

1. M. Francis, *Governors and Settlers: Images of Authority in the British Colonies, 1820–1860* (London, 1992), p. 248; D. Cannadine, 'The Context, Performance and Meaning of Ritual: The British Monarchy and the "Invention of Tradition"', c. 1820–1977', in E. J. Hobsbawm and T. O. Ranger (eds.), *The Invention of Tradition* (Cambridge, 1983), pp. 120–39.

2. A. B. Keith, *The King and the Imperial Crown: The Powers and Duties of His Majesty* (London, 1936), pp. 9–10, 400–452; T. O. Ranger, 'The Invention of Tradition in Colonial Africa', in Hobsbawm and Ranger, *The Invention of Tradition*, pp. 229–30.

3. There is no sustained or explicit treatment of monarchy in *OHBE* i–v, and most post-colonial writers ignore it completely.

4. J. Morris, *Pax Britannica: The Climax of an Empire* (London, 1968), p. 178; A. J. Stockwell, 'Power, Authority and Freedom', in P. J. Marshall (ed.), *The Cambridge Illustrated History of the British Empire* (Cambridge, 1996), p. 171. For this section, I am also much indebted to C. Geertz, *Negara: The Theatre-State in Nineteenth-Century Bali* (Princeton, NJ, 1980), esp. pp. 13–19, 102–4, 121–36.

5. Morris, *Pax Britannica*, p. 255.

6. J. Morris, *Stones of Empire: The Buildings of the Raj* (Oxford, 1983), pp. 182–4; idem, *The Spectacle of Empire* (London, 1982), pp. 185–6; P. Davies, *Splendours of the Raj* (London, 1985), pp. 211–14.

7. D. Armitage, *The Ideological Origins of the British Empire* (Cambridge, 2000), p. 174.

8. T. Falola and A. D. Roberts, 'West Africa', in *OHBE* iv, p. 518. For the importance of the monarch to the Indian Army, see D. Omissi, *The Sepoy and the Raj: The Indian Army, 1600–1940* (London, 1994), pp. 108–11.

9. J. Morris, *Farewell the Trumpets: An Imperial Retreat* (Harmondsworth, 1979), p. 312; idem, *Pax Britannica*, p. 178.

10. D. Haynes, 'Imperial Ritual in a Local Setting: The Ceremonial Order in Seurat, 1890–1939', *MAS*, xxiv (1990), p. 301.

11. T. O. Ranger, 'Making Northern Rhodesia Imperial: Variations on a Royal Theme, 1924–1938', *African Affairs*, lxxix (1980), p. 352; J. M. MacKenzie, 'The Popular Culture of Empire in Britain', in *OHBE* iv, pp. 218–19, 224–5; J. O. Springhall, 'Lord Meath, Youth and Empire', *Journal of Contemporary History*, v, 4 (1970), pp. 97–111.

12. N. Levy, 'The Mangled Mask of Empire: Ceremony and Political Motive in the Anglo-Egyptian Sudan, 1925–1937' (Columbia University senior thesis, 1991), pp. 17–19, 33–40, 43–5, 58, 77, 83–4, 103.

13. Morris, *Pax Britannica*, p. 29; E. Hammerton and D. Cannadine, 'Conflict and Consensus on a Ceremonial Occasion: The Diamond Jubilee in Cambridge in 1897', *HJ*, xxiv (1981), pp. 111–12; Stockwell, 'Power, Authority and Freedom', p. 170; Ranger, 'Invention of Tradition in Colonial Africa', p. 235.

14. L. J. Colley, 'The Apotheosis of George III: Loyalty, Royalty and the British Nation, 1760–1820', *P & P*, no. 102 (1984), pp. 94–129; *idem, Britons: Forging the Nation, 1707–1837* (London, 1992), pp. 194–236; M. Harrison, *Crowds and History: Mass Phenomena in English Towns, 1790–1835* (Cambridge, 1988), pp. 234–67; C. A. Bayly, *Imperial Meridian: The British Empire and the World, 1780–1830* (London, 1989), pp. 111–12.

15. See above, pp. 46–54.

16. S. Khilnani, *The Idea of India* (Harmondsworth, 1997), pp. 120–21; T. R. Metcalf, *An Imperial Vision: Indian Architecture and Britain's Raj* (London, 1989), p. 242; Cannadine, 'British Monarchy and the "Invention of Tradition"', pp. 120–55.

17. Morris, *Pax Britannica*, pp. 341–2; M. Kennedy, *Portrait of Elgar* (3rd edn., Oxford, 1987), pp. 60, 163–87.

18. Morris, *Stones of Empire*, p. 37; *idem, Pax Britannica*, pp. 29–33.

19. C. Geertz, 'Centers, Kings and Charisma: Reflections on the Symbolics of Power', in S. Wilentz (ed.), *Rites of Power: Symbolism, Ritual and Politics Since the Middle Ages* (Philadelphia, PA, 1985), pp. 14–33.

20. Morris, *Pax Britannica*, p. 502.

21. Hence the description of King George VI, when visiting Northern Rhodesia in 1947, as 'the biggest King in the world': Ranger, 'Invention of Tradition in Colonial Africa', p. 233.

22. *Who Was Who, 1916–1928* (5th edn., London, 1992), pp. 422–3.

23. J. M. Gullick, *Rulers and Residents: Influence and Power in the Malay States, 1870–1920* (Singapore, 1992), pp. 250–51.

24. Ranger, 'Invention of Tradition in Colonial Africa', pp. 239–41; *idem*, 'Making Northern Rhodesia Imperial', pp. 368–72.

25. Gullick, *Rulers and Residents*, pp. 231–75; J. K. Chapman, *The Career of Arthur Hamilton Gordon, First Lord Stanmore, 1829–1912* (Toronto, 1964), pp. 184, 227; B. N. Ramusack, *The Princes of India in the Twilight of Empire* (Columbus, OH, 1978), p. 31; Ranger, 'Making Northern Rhodesia Imperial', pp. 354–5.

26. W. R. Louis, *The British Empire in the Middle East, 1945–1951: Arab Nationalism, the United States and Post-War Imperialism* (Oxford, 1984), p. 692.

27. G. Martin, *Bunyip Aristocracy: The New South Wales Constitution Debate of 1853 and Hereditary Institutions in the British Colonies* (Beckenham, 1986), pp. 44–5, 136–7, 168–77, 191.

28. R. Hubbard, *Rideau Hall* (London, 1977), pp. 41–60.

29. Hubbard, *Rideau Hall*, pp. 125–39; N. Frankland, *Witness of a Century: The Life and Times of Prince Arthur, Duke of Connaught, 1850–1942* (London, 1993), pp. 269–352.

30. Hubbard, *Rideau Hall*, pp. 195–208; N. Frankland, *Prince Henry, Duke of Gloucester* (London, 1980), pp. 176–83.

31. P. de Serville, *Pounds and Pedigrees: The Upper Class in Victoria, 1850–1880* (Melbourne, 1991), pp. 63–7; P. Magnus, *King Edward the Seventh* (Harmondsworth, 1967), pp. 172–83, p. 177; B. S. Cohn, *Colonialism and Its Forms of Knowledge: The British in India* (Princeton, NJ, 1996), pp. 125–7.

32. Frankland, *Witness of a Century*, pp. 222–7, 262–5, 369–72.

33. H. Nicolson, *King George V: His Life and Reign* (London, 1967), pp. 104–14, 125–33, 228–37; K. Rose, *King George V* (London, 1983), pp. 43–7, 61–7, 131–6; S. Alomes, 'Ceremonial Visions of Australia', *Journal of Australian Studies*, xx (1987), pp. 50–52.

34. I. Butler (ed.), *The Viceroy's Wife: Letters of Alice, Countess of Reading, from India, 1921–1925* (London, 1969), pp. 73–8; F. Donaldson, *Edward VIII* (London, 1978), pp. 62–98; P. Ziegler, *King Edward VIII: The Official Biography* (London, 1990), pp. 115–63; K. Fewster, 'Politics, Pageantry and Purpose: The 1920 Tour of Australia by the Prince of Wales', *Labour History*, xxxviii (1980), pp. 59–66; J. W. Wheeler-Bennett, *King George VI: His Life and Reign* (London, 1958), pp. 198–206, 215–32, 371–94, 685–92; S. Bradford, *The Reluctant King: The Life and Reign of George VI, 1895–1952* (New York, 1990), pp. 120–25, 281–300, 389–93.

35. Geertz, 'Centers, Kings and Charisma', pp. 16, 22.

36. Ranger, 'Invention of Tradition in Colonial Africa', pp. 230–34; Morris, *Farewell the Trumpets*, p. 499; Sir J. Colville, *The Fringes of Power: Downing Street Diaries, 1939–1955* (London, 1985), p. 620.

37. *The Times, Crown and Empire* (London, 1937), p. 184.

38. Chapman, *Arthur Hamilton Gordon*, p. 283; W. D. McIntyre, 'Australia, New Zealand and the Pacific Islands', in *OHBE* iv, p. 670; P. Spearritt, 'Royal Progress: The Queen and Her Australian Subjects', in S. L. Goldberg and F. B. Smith (eds.), *Australian Cultural History* (Melbourne, 1988), pp. 138–52; J. Connors, 'The 1954 Royal Tour of Australia', *AHS*, c (1993), pp. 371–82; B. Pimlott, *The Queen: A Biography of Elizabeth II* (London, 1996), pp. 111–19, 222–9.

9. Perspectives

1. P. Burroughs, 'Imperial Institutions and the Government of Empire', in *OHBE* iii, p. 184; A. G. Hopkins, *The Future of the Imperial Past* (Cambridge, 1997), p. 23; D. A. Washbrook, 'Orients and Occidents: Colonial Discourse Theory and the Historiography of the British Empire', in *OHBE* v, p. 604; P. J. Marshall, 'Empire and Authority in the Later Eighteenth Century', *JICH*, xv (1987), p. 105.

2. D. Cannadine, *Class in Britain* (London, 1998).

3. J. Morris, *The Spectacle of Empire* (London, 1982), p. 11.

4. T. O. Ranger, 'Making Northern Rhodesia Imperial: Variations on a Royal Theme, 1924–1938', *African Affairs*, lxxix (1980), p. 373. But it had not always been thus. Between the mid-seventeenth and mid-eighteenth centuries, the imperial ideology (it has recently been persuasively argued) may be best described as having been 'Protestant, commercial, maritime and free' (D. Armitage, *The Ideological Origins of the British Empire*) (Cambridge, 2000, pp. 170–98). Its subsequent late-eighteenth-century evolution into something rather different still awaits its historian.

5. Lord Crew, *Rosebery* (2 vols., London, 1931), vol. ii, p. 623.

6. *Hansard*, House of Commons, 13 June 1910, cols. 1134–6, 1139–46. Most of Balfour's speech is reprinted in A. P. Thornton, *The Imperial Idea and Its Enemies: A Study in British Power* (London, 1959), pp. 357–60.

7. E. W. Said, *Orientalism: Western Conceptions of the Orient* (Harmondsworth, 1995 edn.), pp. 31–6, 333, 336.

8. Quoted as the epigraph to A. Ross, *Ranji* (London, 1988 edn.).

9. K. O. Kupperman, *Settling with the Indians: The Meeting of English and Indian Cultures in America, 1580–1640* (Totowa, NJ, 1980), pp. 2, 4; P. Hockings, 'British Society in the Company, Crown and Congress Eras', in P. Hockings (ed.), *Blue Mountains: The Ethnography and Biogeography of a South Indian Region* (New Delhi, 1989), pp. 345–6; D. A. Low, 'Laissez-Faire and Traditional Rulership in Princely India', in R. Jeffrey (ed.), *People, Princes and Paramount Power: Society and Politics in the Indian Princely States* (New Delhi, 1978), p. 377.

10. R. E. Robinson, 'Non-European Foundations: Sketch for a Theory of Collaboration', in R. Owen and B. Sutcliffe (eds.), *Studies in the Theory of Imperialism* (London, 1972), pp. 117–42. The distinction between *saying* and *doing* in an imperial context has been well drawn in the case of Winston Churchill in R. Hyam, 'Churchill and the British Empire', in R. Blake and W. R. Louis (eds.), *Churchill* (Oxford, 1993), pp. 183–4.

11. C. Bolt, *Victorian Attitudes to Race* (London, 1971), p. 186; D. Omissi, ' "Martial Races": Ethnicity and Security in Colonial India, 1858–1939', *War & Society*, ix (1991), p. 1; A. G. Hopkins, 'Back to the Future: From Natural History to Imperial History', *P & P*, no. 164 (1999), pp. 223–4.

12. P. Lawson and J. Phillips, ' "Our Execrable Banditti": Perceptions of Nabobs in Mid-Eighteenth Century Britain', *Albion*, xvi (1984), pp. 225–41.

13. J. Morris, *Pax Britannica: The Climax of an Empire* (London, 1968), pp. 227–8; G. W. Martin, *Britain and the Origins of Canadian Confederation, 1837–1867* (London, 1995), pp. 139–42, 240, 258–61, 264–5.

14. A. L. Stoler, *Race and the Education of Desire: Foucault's History of Sexuality and the Colonial Order of Things* (London, 1995), p. 102.

15. K. Malik, *The Meaning of Race: Race, History and Culture in Western Society* (London, 1996), pp. 223–33; C. A. Bayly, *Empire and Information: Intelligence Gathering and Social Communication in India, 1780–1870* (Cambridge, 1996), pp. 365–70; D. A. Washbrook, 'Orients and Occidents: Colonial Discourse Theory and the Historiography of the British Empire', in *OHBE* v, pp. 596–611.

16. H. Liebersohn, 'Discovering Indigenous Nobility: Tocqueville, Chamisso and Romantic Travel Writing', *AHR*, xci (1994), p. 766. For one example of such 'cultivation of affinities', see J. Fingard, 'Race and Respectability in Victorian Halifax', *JICH*, xx (1992), pp. 169–95.

17. In which regard see P. Gilroy, *Between Camps: Race, Identity and Nationalism at the End of the Colour Line* (London, 2000), on the need to get beyond the oppositional identities of contemporary racial collectivities.

18. D. Cannadine, 'Introduction: Divine Rites of Kings', in D. Cannadine and S. Price (eds.), *Rituals of Royalty: Power and Ceremonial in Traditional Societies* (Cambridge, 1987), pp. 1–19.

19. D. Cannadine, *The Decline and Fall of the British Aristocracy* (London, 1990), pp. 602–5; J. Schumpeter, *Imperialism and Social Classes* (New York, 1951), pp. 83–4, 128, 195–7, 203; B. Anderson, *Imagined Communities: Reflections on the Origin and Spread of Nationalism* (London, 1983), pp. 136–7; Liebersohn, 'Discovering Indigenous Nobility', p. 757.

20. V. I. Lenin, *Imperialism: The Highest Stage of Capitalism* (Moscow, 1947); D. K. Fieldhouse (ed.), *The Theory of Capitalist Imperialism* (London, 1967); E. T. Stokes, 'Late Nineteenth-Century Colonial Expansion and the Attack on the Theory of Economic Imperialism: A Case of Mistaken Identity?', *HJ*, xii (1969), pp. 285–301. For a recent attempt to write history in this mode, see E. J. Hobsbawm, *The Age of Empire, 1875–1914* (London, 1987). The phrase 'gentlemanly capitalism' was coined and popularized by P. J. Cain and A. G. Hopkins, *British Imperialism*, vol. i, *Innovation and Expansion, 1688–1914*;

vol. ii, *Crisis and Deconstruction, 1914–1990* (London, 1993). For discussion and criticism of the term, see A. N. Porter, 'Gentlemanly Capitalism and Empire: The British Experience since 1750?', *JICH*, xviii (1990), pp. 265–95; D. K. Fieldhouse, 'Gentlemen, Capitalists and the British Empire', *JICH*, xxii (1994), pp. 531–41; D. Cannadine, 'The Empire Strikes Back', *P & P*, no. 147 (1995), pp. 180–94.

21. S. Howe, *Anti-Colonialism in British Politics: The Left and the End of Empire, 1918–1964* (Oxford, 1993), p. 34.

22. A. N. Porter, 'Religion and Empire: British Expansion in the Long Nineteenth Century, 1780–1914', *JICH*, xx (1992), pp. 375–6; B. Porter, 'An Awfully Big Colonial Adventure', *TLS*, 14 January 2000, pp. 4–5.

23. As the *Church Missionary Intelligencer* put it in 1857: 'Christianity strengthens lawful authority, concurs with it in action, makes the man more loyal, more submissive to his superiors, more attentive to their commands.' Quoted in Bolt, *Victorian Attitudes to Race*, p. 159.

24. D. McCaughey, N. Perkins and A. Trumble, *Victoria's Colonial Governors, 1839–1900* (Melbourne, 1993), p. 316; E. A. Buettner, 'Families, Children and Memories; Britons in India, 1857–1947' (University of Michigan Ph.D., 1998), pp. 12–13, 278–339; E. M. Forster, *A Passage to India* (Harmondsworth, 1986 edn.), pp. 49–50.

25. F. G. Hutchings, *The Illusion of Permanence: British Imperialism in India* (Princeton, NJ, 1967), pp. 24, 107–8; Hockings, 'British Society in the Company, Crown and Congress Eras', p. 345; E. Richards, 'South Australia Observed, 1836–1986', in *idem* (ed.), *The Flinders History of South Australia: Social History* (Adelaide, 1992), p. 12.

26. D. Cannadine, 'The Context, Performance and Meaning of Ritual: The British Monarchy and the "Invention of Tradition", *c.* 1820–1977', in E. J. Hobsbawm and T. O. Ranger (eds.), *The Invention of Tradition* (Cambridge, 1983), pp. 145–9.

27. Cannadine, *Class in Britain*, pp. 123–4, 144–5; G. Orwell, *The Lion and the Unicorn: Socialism and the English Genius* (Harmondsworth, 1982 edn.), p. 52; D. A. Washbrook, 'Orients and Occidents: Colonial Discourse Theory and the Historiography of the British Empire', in *OHBE* v, p. 604.

28. P. J. Marshall, 'Empire and Authority in the Later Eighteenth Century', *JICH*, xv (1987), p. 106; B. Anderson, *Imagined Communities: Reflections on the Origin and Spread of Nationalism* (London, 1983), pp. 136–7.

29. T. R. Metcalf, *An Imperial Vision: Victorian Architecture and Britain's Raj* (London, 1989), p. 234; Hopkins, 'Back to the Future', p. 220; J. Darwin, 'Imperialism in Decline? Tendencies in British Imperial Policy Between the Wars', *HJ*, xxiii (1980), pp. 663–4; G. Studdert-Kennedy, 'The Christian

Imperialism of the Die-Hard Defenders of the Raj, 1926–1935', *JICH*, xviii (1990), pp. 342–61.

30. D. Clarke, 'The Conservative Faith in a Modern Age', in R. A. Butler (ed.), *Conservatism, 1945–1950* (London, 1950), pp. 15, 19, 41; A. J. Davies, *We, the Nation: The Conservative Party and the Pursuit of Power* (London, 1995), p. 348; A. Gamble, *The Conservative Nation* (London, 1974), pp. 166–7, 203.

31. L. S. Amery, *The Framework of the Future* (Oxford, 1944), pp. 4–18, 136–59.

32. F. R. Dulles and G. E. Ridinger, 'The Anti-Colonial Policies of Franklin D. Roosevelt', *Political Science Quarterly*, lxx (1955), pp. 1–18; W. R. Louis, *Imperialism at Bay, 1941–1945: The United States and the Decolonization of the British Empire* (Oxford, 1977), pp. 19–21; D. Reynolds, *The Creation of the Anglo-American Alliance, 1937–1941: A Study in Competitive Co-operation* (London, 1981), pp. 23–5.

33. W. F. Moneypenny and G. F. Buckle, *The Life of Benjamin Disraeli, Earl of Beaconsfield* (rev. edn., 2 vols., London, 1929), vol. ii, *1860–1881*, p. 805.

34. Lord Ronaldshay, *The Life of Lord Curzon* (3 vols., London, 1928), vol. iii, pp. 373–5; D. Cannadine, *Aspects of Aristocracy: Grandeur and Decline in Modern Britain* (London, 1994), pp. 77–90; Sir E. Gigg, *The Faith of an Englishman* (London, 1937), p. 385; P. Ziegler, 'Churchill and the Monarchy', in Blake and Louis, *Churchill*, pp. 187–8; W. S. Churchill, *My Early Life* (London, 1930), p. 118; R. Rhodes James (ed.), *Winston S. Churchill: His Complete Speeches, 1897–1963* (8 vols., London, 1974), vol. vi, *1935–1942*, p. 6,295.

35. K. Perkins, *Menzies: Last of the Queen's Men* (London, 1968), pp. 220–26; P. Joske, *Sir Robert Menzies, 1894–1978 – A New, Informal Memoir* (London, 1978), pp. 347–53.

36. M. Malia, *Russia Under Western Eyes: From the Bronze Horseman to the Lenin Mausoleum* (Cambridge, Mass., 1999), p. 9; J. H. Elliott, *The Old World and the New, 1492–1650* (Cambridge, 1996), pp. 17–21.

10. Limitations

1. A. J. Stockwell, 'Power, Authority and Freedom', in P. J. Marshall (ed.), *The Cambridge Illustrated History of the British Empire* (Cambridge, 1996), p. 147; M. Lynn, 'British Policy, Trade, and Informal Empire in the Mid-Nineteenth Century', in *OHBE* iii, p. 120.

2. A. J. P. Taylor, *The Trouble Makers: Dissent over Foreign Policy, 1792–1939* (London, 1957); A. P. Thornton, *The Imperial Idea and Its Enemies: A*

Study in British Power (London, 1959); B. Porter, *Critics of Empire: British Radical Attitudes to Colonialism in Africa, 1895–1914* (London, 1968); P. Rich, *Race and Empire in British Politics* (2nd edn., Cambridge, 1990), pp. 70–91. For non-British critics of empire, see J. Schneer, *London 1900: The Imperial Metropolis* (London, 1999), pp. 184–226.

3. J. K. Chapman, *The Career of Arthur Hamilton Gordon, First Lord Stanmore, 1829–1912* (Toronto, 1964), p. 6; W. D. Rubinstein, 'Men of Wealth', in S. L. Goldberg and F. B. Smith (eds.), *Australian Cultural History* (Melbourne, 1988), pp. 109–22; G. Martin, 'Canada from 1815', in *OHBE* iii, p. 528; *idem, Bunyip Aristocracy: The New South Wales Constitution Debate of 1853 and Hereditary Institutions in the British Colonies* (Beckenham, 1986), p. 181; D. McCaughey, N. Perkins and A. Trumble, *Victoria's Colonial Governors, 1839–1900* (Melbourne, 1993), pp. 198–9.

4. D. Denoon with M. Wyndham, 'Australia and the Western Pacific', in *OHBE* iii, p. 565; E. Richards, 'South Australia Observed, 1836–1986', in *idem* (ed.), *The Flinders History of South Australia: Social History* (Adelaide, 1992), pp. 22–3. See also M. Fairburn, *The Ideal Society and Its Enemies: The Foundations of Modern New Zealand Society, 1850–1900* (Auckland, 1989), pp. 81–116, where he explicitly inquires whether New Zealand was a 'hierarchical society', and concludes that it was not. In her obituary of Professor Robert Scribner (*Guardian*, 2 February 1998), Lyndal Roper defined his 'Australian-ness' as encompassing 'hatred of hierarchy'.

5. J. Darwin, 'A Third British Empire? The Dominion Idea in Imperial Politics', in *OHBE* iv, p. 72; D. Fitzpatrick, 'Ireland and the Empire', in *OHBE* iii, pp. 518–19. See also J. B. Condliffe, B. Braatoy and T. H. Marshall, 'Class in New Zealand and Scandinavia', *Listener*, 8 December 1938, pp. 1,233–5.

6. A. B. Keith, *Responsible Government in the Dominions* (2nd edn., 2 vols., Oxford, 1928), vol. ii, pp. 1,027–8; C. Cunneen, *King's Men: Australia's Governors-General from Hopetoun to Isaacs* (Sydney, 1983), pp. 19, 75, 149; D. Cannadine, *The Decline and Fall of the British Aristocracy* (London, 1990), pp. 433–5.

7. Chapman, *Arthur Hamilton Gordon*, pp. 236–8; Cannadine, *Decline and Fall*, pp. 590–93; Cunneen, *King's Men*, pp. 4–5, 89, 103, 109, 151, 182.

8. This is the argument generally advanced in C. A. Bayly, *Empire and Information: Intelligence Gathering and Social Communication in India, 1780–1870* (Cambridge, 1996), esp. pp. 7, 48–9, 167–71, 365.

9. The king–emperor was personally opposed to the Morley–Minto reforms, because he believed the princes would resent an Indian 'who would be very inferior in caste to themselves' sitting with them on the viceroy's council. But Indian princes belonged to various castes, and Brahmans were of purer caste

than most princes: A. B. Keith, *The King and the Imperial Crown: The Powers and Duties of His Majesty* (London, 1936), p. 416; T. R. Metcalf, *Ideologies of the Raj* (Cambridge, 1995), pp. 117–21; S. Bayly, *Caste, Society and Politics in India from the Eighteenth Century to the Modern Age* (Cambridge, 1999), pp. 97–143; S. Khilnani, *The Idea of India* (London, 1997), pp. 18–19.

10. D. Gilmour, *Curzon* (London, 1994), pp. 185–90; R. Jeffrey, 'Introduction' to R. Jeffrey (ed.), *People, Princes and Paramount Power: Society and Politics in the Indian Princely States* (New Delhi, 1978), p. 18; I. Copland, 'The Other Guardians: Ideology and Performance in the Indian Political Service', in Jeffrey, *People, Princes and Paramount Power*, pp. 275–305; P. Woodruff, *The Men Who Ruled India*, vol. ii, *The Guardians* (London, 1963), p. 307.

11. Woodruff, *The Guardians*, p. 203; R. J. Moore, 'Imperial India, 1858–1914', in *OHBE* iii, pp. 432, 437. Kipling, predictably, disliked the 'educated Bengali': Metcalf, *Ideologies of the Raj*, pp. 165–6.

12. Jeffrey, 'Introduction', p. 2; J. W. Cell, *Hailey: A Study in British Imperialism, 1872–1969* (Cambridge, 1992), p. 55; F. G. Hutchins, *The Illusion of Permanence: British Imperialism in India* (Princeton, NJ, 1967), pp. 156–7, 192.

13. J. W. Cell, 'Colonial Rule', in *OHBE* iv, p. 313; idem, *Hailey*, p. 200; T. R. Metcalf, *An Imperial Vision: Victorian Architecture and Britain's Raj* (London, 1989), p. 241; Hutchins, *Illusion of Permanence*, p. 187; Keith, *King and the Imperial Crown*, p. 422; I. Copland, *The British Raj and the Indian Princes: Paramountcy in Western India 1857–1930* (New Delhi, 1982), pp. 155, 231, 313.

14. A. N. Porter, 'Introduction', in *OHBE* iii, p. 18; J. Tosh, *Clan Leaders and Colonial Chiefs in Lango: The Political History of an East African Stateless Society, c. 1800–1939* (Oxford, 1978), p. 246.

15. T. C. McCaskie, 'Cultural Encounters: Britain and Africa in the Nineteenth Century', in *OHBE* iii, pp. 682, 685; T. Falola and A. D. Roberts, 'West Africa', in *OHBE* iv, pp. 518–19; I. F. Nicolson, *The Administration of Nigeria, 1900–1960: Men, Methods and Myths* (Oxford, 1969); A. E. Afigbo, *The Warrant Chiefs: Indirect Rule in South Eastern Nigeria, 1891–1929* (London, 1972); J. A. Atanda, *The New Oyo Empire: Indirect Rule and Change in Western Nigeria, 1894–1934* (London, 1973).

16. F. Robinson, 'The British Empire and the Muslim World', in *OHBE* iv, p. 407; M. W. Daly, *Empire on the Nile: The Anglo-Egyptian Sudan, 1898–1934* (Cambridge, 1986), pp. 360–79; idem, *Imperial Sudan: The Anglo-Egyptian Condominium, 1934–1956* (Cambridge, 1991), pp. 27–45.

17. J. W. Cell, 'Colonial Rule', in *OHBE* iv, pp. 250–51; J. Lonsdale, 'East Africa', in *OHBE* iv, p. 532; T. O. Ranger, 'European Attitudes and African

Realities: The Rise and Fall of the Matola Chiefs of South-East Tanzania', *Journal of African History*, xx (1979), pp. 63–82; J. Iliffe, *A Modern History of Tanganyika* (Cambridge, 1979), pp. 318, 323–4, 328–30; H. A. Gailey, *Sir Donald Cameron: Colonial Governor* (Stanford, CA, 1974), pp. 70, 76–80. For similar mistakes and misperceptions elsewhere in British Africa, see: H. Kuklick, *The Imperial Bureaucrat: The Colonial Administrative Service in the Gold Coast, 1920–1939* (Stanford, CA, 1979), pp. 43–59; Tosh, *Clan Leaders and Colonial Chiefs*, pp. 219–50.

18. P. Burroughs, 'Imperial Institutions and the Government of Empire', in *OHBE* iii, p. 182; Daly, *Empire on the Nile*, pp. 377–8; S. C. Smith, 'The Rise, Decline and Survival of the Malay Rulers during the Colonial Period, 1874–1957', *JICH*, xxii (1994), p. 88.

19. P. Hethrington, *British Paternalism and Africa, 1920–1940* (London, 1978), pp. 131–49; S. J. S. Cookey, 'Sir Hugh Clifford as Governor of Nigeria: An Evaluation', *African Affairs*, lxxix (1980), pp. 534–8.

20. W. R. Louis, *The British Empire in the Middle East, 1945–1951: Arab Nationalism, the United States, and Post-War Imperialism* (Oxford, 1984), pp. 337–9.

21. E. Kedourie, 'The Kingdom of Iraq: A Retrospect', in *idem, The Chatham House Version and Other Middle Eastern Studies* (London, 1970), p. 278.

22. A. H. Hourani, *Great Britain and the Arab World* (London, 1946), pp. 25–7; A. S. Kleiman, *Foundations of British Policy in the Arab World: The Cairo Conference of 1921* (London, 1970), pp. 246–7; F. Robinson, 'The British Empire and the Muslim World', in *OHBE* iv, pp. 407–8.

23. E. Monroe, *Britain's Moment in the Middle East, 1914–1971* (London, 1981), pp. 82, 116–30; J. Morris, *Farewell the Trumpets: An Imperial Retreat* (Harmondsworth, 1979), p. 266.

24. Louis, *British Empire in the Middle East*, p. 345; N. Owen, 'Britain and Decolonization: The Labour Governments and the Middle East, 1945–1951', in M. J. Cohen and M. Kolinsky (eds.), *Demise of the British Empire in the Middle East: Britain's Response to Nationalist Movements, 1943–1955* (London, 1998), p. 10.

25. Monroe, *Britain's Moment in the Middle East*, pp. 128–9; N. Daniel, 'Contemporary Perceptions of the Revolution in Iraq on 14 July 1958', in R. A. Fernea and W. R. Louis (eds.), *The Iraqi Revolution of 1958: The Old Social Classes Revisited* (London, 1991), p. 6.

26. C. Barnett, *The Collapse of British Power* (London, 1972), pp. 176, 207; D. Harkness, *The Restless Dominion: The Irish Free State and the British Commonwealth of Nations, 1921–1931* (London, 1969).

27. R. G. Menzies, *Afternoon Light* (London, 1967), pp. 259–81; *idem, The*

Measure of the Years (London, 1970), pp. 44–60; R. Lewin, *Slim the Stan-dardbearer* (London, 1976), pp. 289–91; D. Day, *Menzies and Churchill at War* (London, 1986); D. A. Low, *Eclipse of Empire* (Cambridge, 1991), pp. 356–7; W. D. McIntyre, 'Australia, New Zealand, and the Pacific Islands', *OHBE* iv, pp. 676–9; D. Lee, 'Australia, the British Commonwealth, and the United States, 1950–1953', *JICH*, xx (1992), pp. 445–69.

28. Metcalf, *Imperial Vision*, pp. 128–40; C. W. Nuckolls, 'The Durbar Incident', *MAS*, xxiv (1990), pp. 529–59; J. F. Codell, 'Resistance and Performance: Native Informant Discourse in the Biographies of Maharaja Sayaji Rao III of Baroda (1863–1939)', in J. F. Codell and D. S. Macleod (eds.), *Orientalism Transposed: The Impact of the Colonies on British Culture* (Aldershot, 1998), pp. 13–45; C. S. Sundram, '"Martial" Indian Aristocrats and the Military System of the Raj: The Imperial Cadet Corps, 1900–1914', *JICH*, xxv (1997), pp. 415–39.

29. E. S. Haynes, 'Rajput Ceremonial Interactions as a Mirror of a Dying Indian State System, 1820–1947', *MAS*, xxiv (1990), p. 489; Morris, *Farewell the Trumpets*, p. 62, n. 1; I. Copland, *The Princes of India in the Endgame of Empire, 1917–1947* (Cambridge, 1997), pp. 113–82; G. Mehta, *Raj* (New Delhi, 1993).

30. T. O. Ranger, 'The Invention of Tradition in Colonial Africa', in E. J. Hobsbawm and T. O. Ranger (eds.), *The Invention of Tradition* (Cambridge, 1983), p. 242; P. K. Tibenderana, 'The Role of the British Administration in the Appointment of the Emirs of Northern Nigeria, 1903–1931: The Case of Sokoto Province', *Journal of African History*, xxviii (1987), pp. 231–57.

31. Smith, 'Rise, Decline and Survival of the Malay Rulers', pp. 86–92; T. O. Ranger, 'Making Northern Rhodesia Imperial: Variations on a Royal Theme, 1924–1938', *African Affairs*, lxxix (1980), pp. 349–73.

32. Louis, *British Empire in the Middle East*, pp. 310–11; Kedourie, 'The Kingdom of Iraq: A Retrospect', pp. 239–43; Monroe, *Britain's Moment in the Middle East*, p. 122.

33. Louis, *British Empire in the Middle East*, pp. 226–8, 252–64, 311–13, 331–44; M. Kolinsky, 'Lampson and the Wartime Control of Egypt', in Cohen and Kolinsky, *Demise of the British Empire in the Middle East*, pp. 96–111.

34. Keith, *Responsible Government*, vol. ii, pp. 1,018–24.

35. B. Knox, 'Democracy, Aristocracy and Empire: The Provision of Colonial Honours, 1818–1870', *AHS*, xxv (1992–3), pp. 249, 253; N. Frankland, *Witness of a Century: The Life and Times of Prince Arthur, Duke of Connaught, 1850–1942* (London, 1993), pp. 344–7.

36. Martin, *Bunyip Aristocracy*, pp. 186–7; D. W. Thomson, 'The Fate of Titles in Canada', *Canadian Historical Review*, x (1929), pp. 236–46; C. Bissell,

The Imperial Canadian: Vincent Massey in Office (Toronto, 1986), pp. 263–8, 293.

37. Ranger, 'Making Northern Rhodesia Imperial', p. 373.

38. M. French, 'The Ambiguity of Empire Day in New South Wales, 1901–1921: Imperial Consensus or National Division?', *Australian Journal of Politics and History*, xxiv (1978), pp. 61–74; S. Firth and J. Hoorn, 'From Empire Day to Cracker Night' in P. Spearritt and D. Walker (eds.), *Australian Popular Culture* (Sydney, 1979), pp. 17–38; K. S. Inglis, 'The Anzac Tradition', *Meanjin*, xxiv (1965), pp. 25–44; E. Kwan, 'The Australian Flag: Ambiguous Symbol of Nationality in Melbourne and Sydney, 1920–1921', *AHS*, xvi (1995), pp. 280–303; D. Adair, ' "On Parade": Spectacles, Crowds and Collective Loyalties in Australia, 1901–1938' (Flinders University Ph.D., 1994), pp. 126–93.

39. N. Frankland, *Prince Henry, Duke of Gloucester* (London, 1980), pp. 209–16; *idem*, *Witness of a Century*, p. 268; H. Bolitho, *Edward VIII* (Philadelphia, PA, 1938), p. 190.

40. P. M. Cowburn, 'The Attempted Assassination of the Duke of Edinburgh, 1868', *Royal Australian Historical Society Journal*, lv (1969), pp. 19–42.

41. Cunneen, *King's Men*, p. 19; S. Alomes, 'Ceremonial Visions of Australia', *Journal of Australian Studies*, xx (1987), p. 52; Frankland, *Witness of Century*, p. 370; F. Donaldson, *Edward VIII* (London, 1978), p. 92; P. Ziegler, *King Edward VIII: The Official Biography* (London, 1990), pp. 138–40; S. Bradford, *The Reluctant King: The Life and Reign of George VI, 1895–1952* (New York, 1990), pp. 219–23; A. Trevithick, 'Some Structural and Sequential Aspects of the British Imperial Assemblages at Delhi, 1877–1911', *MAS*, xxiv (1990), pp. 575–6.

42. Bradford, *Reluctant King*, p. 390; B. Pimlott, *The Queen: A Biography of Elizabeth II* (London, 1996), p. 119; E. Morris, 'Forty Years On: Australia and the Queen, 1954', *Journal of Australian Studies*, no. 40 (1994), pp. 1–13.

43. J. Darwin, 'A Third British Empire?', in *OHBE* iv, pp. 69, 77.

44. Keith, *King and the Imperial Crown*, p. 12; H. Nicolson, *King George V: His Life and Reign* (London, 1967), pp. 620–24; W. R. Louis, 'Introduction', in *OHBE* iv, p. 32; S. Marks, 'Southern Africa', in *OHBE* iv, p. 555; D. McMahon, 'Ireland the Empire-Commonwealth, 1900–1948', in *OHBE* iv, p. 157.

45. Keith, *King and the Imperial Crown*, p. vii; Nicolson, *George V*, pp. 602–17.

46. E. Hammerton and D. Cannadine, 'Conflict and Consensus on a Ceremonial Occasion: The Diamond Jubilee in Cambridge in 1897', *HJ*, xxiv (1981), pp. 111–46; S. Lukes, 'Political Ritual and Social Integration', in *idem*, *Essays in Social Theory* (London, 1977), pp. 62–73.

47. D. Haynes, 'Imperial Ritual in a Local Setting: The Ceremonial Order in Seurat, 1890–1939', *MAS*, xxiv (1990), p. 516.

48. Nuckolls, 'The Durbar Incident', pp. 545–6.

49. Q. Bell, *Virginia Woolf: A Biography*, vol. i, *Virginia Stephen, 1882–1912* (London, 1973), pp. 157–61.

50. P. de Serville, *Pounds and Pedigrees: The Upper Class in Victoria,1850–1880* (Melbourne, 1991), pp. 197–206; Sir B. Burke, *A Genealogical and Heraldic History of the Colonial Gentry* (2 vols., London, 1891–5), vol. ii, pp. xvii–xxiii, prints extensive corrigenda to vol. i. A promised third volume never appeared.

51. Copland, *The Princes of India*, pp. 24–5. Disraeli's claim, during debates on the Royal Titles Bill, that the Indian princes 'occupy thrones which were filled by their ancestors when England was a Roman province' was pure – and predictable – hyperbole: Metcalf, *Ideologies of the Raj*, p. 61.

52. Metcalf, *Imperial Vision*, pp. 105, 139–40; Hutchins, *Illusion of Permanence*, p. 172.

53. J. Morris, *Pax Britannica: The Climax of an Empire* (London, 1968), pp. 359–78; *idem, Farewell the Trumpets*, pp. 338–62.

54. Copland, *British Raj and the Indian Princes*, p. 123; Metcalf, *Imperial Vision*, p. 245.

PART FOUR: ENDINGS

11. Dissolution

1. V. Woolf, *A Moment's Liberty: The Shorter Diary* (ed. A. O. Bell, London, 1997), p. 400.

2. W. D. McIntyre, *British Decolonization, 1946–1997* (London, 1998), pp. 1–6; A. G. Hopkins, 'Back to the Future: From National History to Imperial History', *P & P*, no. 164 (1999), pp. 219–20; J. Darwin, 'British Decolonization since 1945: A Pattern or a Puzzle?', *JICH*, xii (1984), pp. 187–209.

3. A. P. Thornton, *The Imperial Idea and Its Enemies: A Study in British Power* (London, 1959), chs. v–vii, sketched out an early interpretation to this effect.

4. D. Cannadine, *The Decline and Fall of the British Aristocracy* (London, 1990), pp. 103–6, 177–80, 472–87.

5. Anon., 'Last Days of Dublin Castle', *Blackwood's Magazine*, ccxii (1922), pp. 138–9, 156–7, 181, 189–90; R. B. McDowell, *The Irish Administration,*

1801–1914 (London, 1963), pp. 292–4; E. Brynn, *Crown & Castle: British Rule in Ireland, 1800–1830* (Dublin, 1978), pp. 153–60; E. Goldstein, ' "Quis Separabit?": The Order of St Patrick and Anglo-Irish Relations, 1922–1934', *Historical Research*, lxii (1989), pp. 70–80.

6. D. A. Low, *Eclipse of Empire* (Cambridge, 1991), p. 327; McIntyre, *British Decolonization*, pp. 19–20; D. McMahon, *Republicans and Imperialists: Anglo-Irish Relations in the 1930s* (London, 1984), pp. 63–5, 94–100, 200–201, 214–15.

7. J. Morris, *Farewell the Trumpets: An Imperial Retreat* (Harmondsworth, 1979), p. 221.

8. P. Ziegler, *Mountbatten: The Official Biography* (London, 1985), pp. 404–15.

9. J. Morris, *Stones of Empire: The Buildings of the Raj* (Oxford, 1983), p. 185.

10. P. Woodruff, *The Men Who Ruled India*, vol. ii, *The Guardians* (London, 1963), p. 342; Sir C. Corfield, 'Some Thoughts on British Policy and the Indian States, 1935–1947', in C. H. Philips and M. D. Wainwright (eds.), *The Partition of India: Policies and Perspectives, 1935–1947* (London, 1970), pp. 527–34; P. Mason, *A Shaft of Sunlight: Memories of a Varied Life* (London, 1978), p. 214; Lord Birkenhead, *Walter Monckton: The Life of Viscount Monckton of Brenchley* (London, 1969), pp. 217–54; I. Copland, *The British Raj and the Indian Princes: Paramountcy in Western India, 1857–1930* (New Delhi, 1982), p. 313; *idem, The Princes of India in the Endgame of Empire, 1917–1947* (Cambridge, 1997), pp. 185–7, 219–20; J. Brown, 'India', in *OHBE* iv, p. 437.

11. Copland, *Princes of India*, pp. 1, 239, 253; Mason, *Shaft of Sunlight*, p. 203.

12. W. D. McIntyre, 'Commonwealth Legacy', in *OHBE* iv, pp. 696–7; *idem, British Decolonization*, pp. 110–18; P. N. S. Mansergh, *The Commonwealth Experience* (London, 1969), p. 405; R. J. Moore, *Making the New Commonwealth* (Oxford, 1987), pp. 120–204, esp. pp. 183–6.

13. M. Kennedy, *Portrait of Walton* (Oxford, 1990), pp. 93, 167; B. Pimlott, *The Queen: A Biography of Elizabeth II* (London, 1996), pp. 181–3.

14. P. C. Gordon Walker, 'Crown Divisible', *The Twentieth Century*, cliii (1953), pp. 425–9; J. W. Wheeler-Bennett, *King George VI: His Life and Reign* (London, 1958), pp. 725–9; Pimlott, *The Queen*, p. 203.

15. S. Heffer, *Like the Roman: The Life of Enoch Powell* (London, 1998), pp. 182–5; W. D. McIntyre, 'Commonwealth Legacy', in *OHBE* iv, p. 696; *idem, British Decolonization*, pp. 107–8; Hopkins, 'Back to the Future', p. 220, sees the 'decisive break' with the old dominions occurring in the 1950s.

16. Cannadine, *Decline and Fall*, p. 686; R. Hubbard, *Rideau Hall* (London, 1977), p. 219.

17. D. McCaughey, N. Perkins and A. Trumble, *Victoria's Colonial Governors, 1839–1900* (Melbourne, 1993), pp. 325–6; P. Simpson, 'The Recognition of Difference', in G. W. Rice (ed.), *The Oxford History of New Zealand* (2nd edn., Auckland, 1992), pp. 571–2. This trend was also encouraged by the separate Canadian flag (1965) and the repatriation of the Canadian constitution (1982). And in 1986 the Australian and New Zealand parliaments both passed Constitution Acts ending the last vestiges of imperial subordination by repealing the Statute of Westminster and confirming their own sovereign independence. See D. MacKenzie, 'Canada, the North Atlantic Triangle and the Empire', in *OHBE* iv, p. 594; S. McIntyre, 'Australia, New Zealand and the Pacific Islands', in *OHBE* iv, p. 689.

18. J. Flint, 'Planned Decolonization and Its Failure in British Africa', *African Affairs*, lxxxii (1983), p. 395; S. C. Smith, 'The Rise, Decline and Survival of the Malay Rulers during the Colonial Period, 1874–1957', *JICH*, xxii (1994), pp. 91–2.

19. J. W. Cell, 'Colonial Rule', in *OHBE* iv, p. 249; *idem, Hailey: A Study in British Imperialism, 1872–1969* (Cambridge, 1992), pp. 254–65.

20. McIntyre, *British Decolonization*, p. 104; R. E. Robinson, 'Imperial Theory and the Question of Imperialism after Empire', *JICH*, xii (1984), pp. 47–9.

21. J. Darwin, *Britain and Decolonization: The Retreat from Empire in the Post-War World* (London, 1988), pp. 175–9; B. Lapping, *End of Empire* (London, 1985), pp. 366–89.

22. R. E. Robinson, 'Why "Indirect Rule" has been Replaced by "Local Government" in the Nomenclature of British Native Administration', *Journal of African Administration*, iii, 3 (July 1950), pp. 12–15; D. A. Low, *Eclipse of Empire*, p. 228; T. Falola and A. D. Roberts, 'West Africa', in *OHBE* iv, p. 524; Darwin, *Britain and Decolonization*, pp. 179–83, 191–3, 259–61; A. M. Yakubu, 'The Demise of Indirect Rule in the Emirates of Northern Nigeria', in T. O. Ranger and O. Vaughan (eds.), *Legitimacy and the State in Twentieth-Century Africa* (London, 1999), pp. 162–90. For one account of the vexed post-war, pre-independence relations between the British, the traditional rulers and the nationalists in an African colony, see R. Rathbone, *Nkrumah and the Chiefs: The Politics of Chieftaincy in Southern Ghana, 1951–1960* (Oxford, 1999). I am most grateful to Professor Rathbone for allowing me to see chapters of this book before publication.

23. N. Owen, ' "More than a Transfer of Power": Independence Day Ceremonies in India, 15 August 1947', *Contemporary Record*, vi (1992), pp. 443–4.

24. Low, *Eclipse of Empire*, pp. 19, 316; McIntyre, *British Decolonization*, p. 56.

25. D. Cannadine, *Aspects of Aristocracy: Grandeur and Decline in Modern England* (London, 1994), pp. 127–9.

26. Except in Saudi Arabia. But this was of no comfort to the British. Between 1945 and 1948, King Ibn Sa'ud shifted his loyalty from the British to the Americans, in large part because of their massive investments, during and since the Second World War, in Arabian oil: W. R. Louis, *The British Empire in the Middle East, 1945–1951: Arab Nationalism, the United States, and Post-War Imperialism* (Oxford, 1984), pp. 197–204.

27. Louis, *British Empire in the Middle East*, pp. 1–15, 19, 240, 604; N. Owen, 'Britain and Decolonization: The Labour Governments and the Middle East, 1945–1951', in M. J. Cohen and M. Kolinsky (eds.), *Demise of the British Empire in the Middle East: Britain's Response to Nationalist Movements, 1943–1955* (London, 1998), pp. 3–22.

28. Darwin, *Britain and Decolonization*, pp. 206–14; E. Monroe, *Britain's Moment in the Middle East, 1914–1971* (London, 1981), pp. 170–71; C. Tripp, 'Egypt, 1945–52: The Uses of Disorder', in Cohen and Kolinsky, *Demise of the British Empire in the Middle East*, pp. 135–6.

29. Monroe, *Britain's Moment in the Middle East*, pp. 189–90, 211; Low, *Eclipse of Empire*, pp. 291, 297; W. R. Louis, 'The British and the Origins of the Iraqi Revolution', in R. A. Fernea and W. R. Louis (eds.), *The Iraqi Revolution of 1958: The Old Social Classes Revisited* (London, 1991), pp. 31–61; W. R. Louis and R. E. Robinson, 'The Imperialism of Decolonization', *JICH*, xxii (1994), p. 482; M. Eppel, 'The Decline of British Influence and the Ruling Elite in Iraq', in Cohen and Kolinsky, *Demise of the British Empire in the Middle East*, pp. 185–97; I. Pope, 'British Rule in Jordan, 1943–1955', in ibid., pp. 198–219.

30. Monroe, *Britain's Moment in the Middle East*, pp. 213–15; G. Balfour-Paul, *The End of Empire in the Middle East* (Cambridge, 1991), pp. 80–95; Lapping, *End of Empire*, pp. 290–310.

31. McIntyre, *British Decolonization*, pp. 64–5; G. Balfour-Paul, 'Britain's Informal Empire in the Middle East', in *OHBE* iv, pp. 508–11; *idem, End of Empire in the Middle East*, pp. 122–36; F. Robinson, 'The British Empire and the Muslim World', in *OHBE* iv, p. 409.

32. D. Gilmour, *Curzon* (London, 1994), p. 240.

33. Darwin, *Britain and Decolonization*, pp. 298–307; McIntyre, *British Decolonization*, pp. 9, 122; J. O. Springhall, 'Lord Meath, Youth and Empire', *Journal of Contemporary History*, v, 4 (1970), p. 106.

34. Mountbatten was KG, OM, GCB, GCSI, GCIE and GCVO; Alexander was KG, OM, GCB, GCMG and CSI; and Slim was KG, GCB, GCMG,

GCVO and GBE. See Sir I. de la Bere, *The Queen's Orders of Chivalry* (London, 1964), pp. 19, 178–9; P. Ziegler, *Mountbatten: The Official Biography* (London, 1985), pp. 310–11, 638; N. Nicolson, *Alex: The Life of Field Marshal Earl Alexander of Tunis* (London, 1973), p. 318; R. Lewin, *Slim the Standardbearer* (London, 1976), p. 299.

35. Cannadine, *Aspects of Aristocracy*, p. 129. The last authentic British proconsul, Lord Maclehose of Beoch, who was governor of Hong Kong from 1971 to 1982, was a life peer, KT, GBE, KCMG and KCVO, and died on 27 May 2000.

36. P. Chapman, 'New Zealand to Abolish Knight and Dame Titles', *Daily Telegraph*, 11 April 2000; B. Gould, 'Lessons from Down Under', *Observer*, 17 Sept. 2000.

37. Cannadine, *Aspects of Aristocracy*, p. 129; Hubbard, *Rideau Hall*, pp. 225, 239; W. D. McIntyre, 'Australia, New Zealand and the Pacific Islands', in *OHBE* iv, p. 690; C. Bissell, *The Imperial Canadian: Vincent Massey in Office* (Toronto, 1986), pp. 264–5, 310.

38. P. Spearritt, 'Royal Progress: The Queen and Her Australian Subjects', in S. L. Goldberg and F. B. Smith (eds.), *Australian Cultural History* (Melbourne, 1988), pp. 152–4.

39. Pimlott, *The Queen*, pp. 318–19, 338–9; J. Dimbleby, *The Prince of Wales: A Biography* (London, 1994), pp. 545–9. See also the discussion in Sir G. Palmer and M. Palmer, *Bridled Power: New Zealand Government under MMP* (3rd edn., Oxford, 1997), pp. 40–51.

40. W. R. Louis, 'Introduction', in *OHBE* iv, p. 14; S. Constantine, 'Migrants and Settlers', in *OHBE* iv, p. 184; W. D. McIntyre, 'Australia, New Zealand and the Pacific Islands', in *OHBE* iv, pp. 690–91; R. J. Walker, 'Maori People since 1950', in G. W. Rice (ed.), *The Oxford History of New Zealand* (2nd edn., Auckland, 1992), pp. 498–519; J. M. Brown, 'Epilogue', in *OHBE* iv, p. 708.

41. J. Freedland, 'The Future is Kiwi', *Guardian*, 3 May 2000.

42. Moore, *Making the New Commonwealth*, pp. 103–20.

43. Louis and Robinson, 'The Imperialism of Decolonization', p. 489.

44. Morris, *Farewell the Trumpets*, pp. 511, 543; Darwin, *Britain and Decolonization*, p. 278.

45. Darwin, *Britain and Decolonization*, pp. 324, 327–8.

46. D. Cannadine, *Class in Britain* (London, 1998), pp. 158–9; Pimlott, *The Queen*, pp. 275–87, 369; P. Worsthorne, 'Class and Conflict in British Foreign Policy', *Foreign Affairs*, xxxvii (1959), pp. 419–31; A. P. Thornton, *The Habit of Authority: Paternalism in British History* (London, 1966), pp. 367, 377;

H. Pelling, *Popular Politics and Society in Late Victorian Britain* (London, 1968), pp. 176–7; J. Darwin, 'The Fear of Falling: British Politics and Imperial Decline since 1900', *TRHS*, 5th ser., xxxvi (1986), pp. 27–43.
47. D. Cannadine, *History in Our Time* (London, 1998), pp. 3–18.
48. Cannadine, *Decline and Fall*, pp. 661–90.

12. Epilogue

1. J. H. Elliott, 'Final Reflections', in K. O. Kupperman (ed.), *America in European Consciousness* (Chapel Hill, NC, 1995), p. 404; P. D. Morgan, 'Encounters between British and "Indigenous" Peoples, *c.* 1500–*c.* 1800', in M. J. Daunton and R. Halpern (eds.), *Empire and Others: British Encounters with Indigenous Peoples, 1600–1850* (London, 1999), p. 68.
2. C. A. Bayly, 'Held on the Cheap', *TLS*, 21 January 2000, p. 29.
3. J. Darwin, *Britain and Decolonization: The Retreat from Empire in the Post-War World* (London, 1988), p. 327.
4. W. L. Richter, 'Traditional Rulers in Post-Traditional Societies: The Princes of India and Pakistan', in R. Jeffrey (ed.), *People, Princes and Paramount Power: Society and Politics in the Indian Princely States* (New Delhi, 1978), pp. 329–54; R. G. Irving, *Indian Summer: Lutyens, Baker and Imperial Delhi* (London, 1981), pp. 344–5; N. Dirks, 'Castes of Mind', *Representations*, no. 37 (1992), p. 56; S. Bayly, *Caste, Society and Politics in India from the Eighteenth Century to the Modern Age* (Cambridge, 1999), pp. 380–81; I. Copland, *The Princes of India in the Endgame of Empire, 1917–1947* (Cambridge, 1997), p. 13.
5. J. Darwin, *Britain and Decolonization*, pp. 106–10.
6. S. C. Smith, 'The Rise, Decline and Survival of the Malay Rulers during the Colonial Period, 1874–1957', *JICH*, xxii (1994), pp. 92–104; *idem*, *British Relations with the Malay Rulers from Decentralization to Malayan Independence, 1930–1957* (Kuala Lumpur, 1995).
7. W. D. McIntyre, *British Decolonization, 1946–1997* (London, 1998), pp. 60, 63, 71; D. A. Low, *Eclipse of Empire* (Cambridge, 1991), p. 300; J. D. Hargreaves, *The End of Colonial Rule in West Africa* (London, 1979), pp. 77–80; For one debate over the disappearance or survival or revival of native chiefs, see T. O. Ranger, 'Tradition and Travesty: Chiefs and the Administration in the Makoni District, Zimbabwe, 1960–1980', *Africa*, lii (1982), pp. 20–41; D. Maxwell, *Christians and Chiefs in Zimbabwe: A Social History of the Hwesa People, c. 1870s–1990s* (Edinburgh, 1999), pp. 149–86.
8. A. Sampson, *Mandela: The Authorized Biography* (London, 1999),

pp. 3–13; R. J. Walker, 'Maori People since 1950', in G. W. Rice (ed.), *The Oxford History of New Zealand* (2nd edn., Auckland, 1992), p. 519.

9. A. Adonis, 'New Order of Merit Open to Honour All', *Observer*, 8 June 1997.

10. G. Robertson, 'Dumping Our Queen', *Guardian*, 6 November 1999; M. Parris, 'The Queen in a State', *The Times*, 6 November 1999.

11. B. Pimlott, *The Queen: A Biography of Elizabeth II* (London, 1996), pp. 241–4, 369, 462–9, 580.

12. J. Dimbleby, *The Prince of Wales: A Biography* (London, 1994), p. 523; D. Cannadine, *History in Our Time* (London, 1998), pp. 68–75; P. Goldberger, 'A Royal Defeat', *New Yorker*, 13 July 1998, pp. 52–9.

13. Dimbleby, *Prince of Wales*, pp. 226–7, 409–10, 544–9; the prince of Wales, 'Foreword' to J. Brooke, *King George III* (St Albans, 1994), pp. 10–11; *Daily Telegraph*, 6 July 1999; *The Times*, 6 July 1999. This notion of the Bedouin as 'true aristocrats, with a nobility of tradition' has often appealed to those who have felt themselves alienated from their contemporary world, and who prefer what they believe to be a more sure and ordered past: S. J. Nasir, *The Arabs and the English* (London, 1979), pp. 118, 161. The same may possibly be said of those who continue to believe in the idea of the English gentleman.

APPENDIX: *An Imperial Childhood?*

1. Sir H. Johnston and L. H. Guest (eds.), *The Outline of the World Today*, vol. ii, *The British Empire* (London, 1926), pp. 1, 4.

2. S. Reed Brett, *A History of the British Empire and Commonwealth* (rev. edn., London, 1959).

3. P. N. S. Mansergh, *The Commonwealth Experience* (London, 1969); J. A. Gallagher and R. E. Robinson, 'The Imperialism of Free Trade', *Economic History Review*, 2nd ser., vi (1953), pp. 1–15; R. E. Robinson and J. A. Gallagher, with A. Denny, *Africa and the Victorians: The Official Mind of Imperialism* (London, 1961); E. T. Stokes, *The English Utilitarians and India* (London, 1959).

4. R. E. Robinson, 'Non-European Foundations of European Imperialism: Sketch for a Theory of Collaboration', in R. Owen and B. Sutcliffe (eds.), *Studies in the Theory of Imperialism* (London, 1978), p. 117–42; *idem*, 'The Ex-centric Idea of Imperialism, with or without Empire', in W. J. Mommsen and J. Osterhammel (eds.), *Imperialism and After: Continuities and Disconti-nuities* (London, 1986), pp. 267–89; E. T. Stokes, *The Peasant and the*

Raj: Studies in Agrarian Society and Peasant Rebellion in Colonial India (Cambridge, 1978); *idem, The Peasant Armed: The Indian Revolt of 1857* (Oxford, 1986).

5. J. Morris, *Farewell the Trumpets: An Imperial Retreat* (Harmondsworth, 1978), p. 558.

Illustration Acknowledgements

La Belle Aurore/Steve Davey 25; by permission of the British Library, Oriental & India Office Collections *frontispiece*, 8, 9, 10, 20; Camera Press 32, 36; Castle Howard Collection 3; Foreign & Commonwealth Office Library Collection 7, 13, 14, 15, 21, 22, 24; Hulton Getty Picture Collection 1, 2, 5, 11, 16, 17, 18, 19, 26, 27, 28, 30, 31, 34, 35; Mary Evans Picture Library 23; National Archives of Canada 6; Popperfoto 29; © Tate Gallery, 2000, 4; Topham Picturepoint 33.

Index